STUDIES IN GERMAN LITERATURE,
LINGUISTICS, AND CULTURE
Vol. 54

STUDIES IN GERMAN LITERATURE, LINGUISTICS,
AND CULTURE

Editorial Board

Frank Banta, Donald Daviau, Ingeborg Glier, Michael Hamburger,
Gerhart Hoffmeister, Herbert Knust, Egbert Krispyn, Victor Lange,
James Lyon, Michael Metzger, Hans-Gert Roloff, John Spalek,
Frank Trommler, Heinz Wetzel, A. Leslie Willson

**Managing Editors**
James Hardin and Gunther Holst

*(South Carolina)*

CAMDEN HOUSE
Columbia, South Carolina

PETER MORGAN

# The Critical Idyll

TRADITIONAL VALUES AND
THE FRENCH REVOLUTION
IN GOETHE'S
*HERMANN UND DOROTHEA*

CAMDEN HOUSE

Copyright © 1990
CAMDEN HOUSE, INC.
Drawer 2025
Columbia, SC 29202 USA

All Rights Reserved
Printed in the United States of America
First Edition

ISBN: 0-938100-85-8

Library of Congress Cataloging-in-Publication Data

Morgan, Peter, 1954-
  The critical idyll : traditional values and the French Revolution in Goethe's Hermann und Dorothea. -- 1st ed.
    p.  cm. -- (Studies in German literature, linguistics, and culture ; vol. 54)
  "Bibliography to Hermann und Dorothea": p.
  Includes bibliographical references (p.   ) and index.
  ISBN 0-938100-85-8
  1. Goethe, Johann Wolfgang von, 1749-1832. Hermann und Dorothea.
  2. France--History--Revolution, 1789-1799--Influence on literature. I. Title. II. Series: Studies in German literature, linguistics, and culture ; v. 54.
  PT1911.H7M67  1990                                              90-1939
  831'.6--dc20                                                       CIP

# Acknowledgments

THIS BOOK WAS WRITTEN with the encouragement and support of Prof. Leslie Bodi (Monash University, Melbourne). From the beginning, Leslie has offered detailed and painstaking criticisms and imaginative suggestions. I take this opportunity to thank him for his friendship and wise advice over many years.

My thanks also go to Dimitry Moraitis and my mother, Jean, for assistance with proof-reading and typing of drafts, and to my family for their support.

The book was written at Monash University and the University of Western Australia. Thanks to my colleagues in the German Departments of both institutions for their interest.

I would also like to thank Prof. James Hardin (University of South Carolina) and Dr. Pavel Petr (Monash University) for editorial advice and encouragement.

The financial support of the Monash University Publications Committee, the Deutscher Akademischer Austauschdienst (Federal Republic of Germany), and the University of Western Australia is gratefully acknowledged.

Early versions of parts of Chapters 2 and 8 were published in the *German Quarterly* (1984) and *Comic Relations: Studies in the Comic, Satire and Parody*, ed. P. Petr et al. (Frankfurt am Main: Lang, 1985).

For Dimitry

# Contents

Introduction ... 1

## 1. The Idyll and German Identity ... 14

The Middle-Class Idyll: Goethe and Voss
From the Tragic to the Ironic Idyll
Epic, Parody and a German Classical Literature

## 2. Prosperity and Progress in the Home Town ... 23

Idyllic Perspectives: The Innkeeper and the Apothecary
Internal Crisis and Social Change
Social Relationships and Individual Self-Perception

**Excursus:** Parody of Voss's *Luise* ... 36

## 3. The Revival of Traditional Values ... 41

Disruption and Provocation
Alienation in the Home Town
Hermann's Transfigured Fatherland
The Inadequacy of *Gemeinschaft*: The Mother

**Excursus:** Language and the Nation in Eighteenth-Century Germany ... 63

## 4. The Crisis of Enlightenment ... 69

The Failure of Freedom: The Judge
The Critique of Dogmatic Enlightenment: The Vicar

## 5. The Critical Idyll ... 81

Perception and Reality in the Idyll
History and Literary Form: The Function of the "Idyllic" in *Hermann und Dorothea*

## 6. The Paradigm of Individual Identity ... 90

> Dorothea and Ruth
> Dorothea and Iphigenie
> Dorothea in the Home Town

## 7. The Story of the Salzburg Protestants ... 100

> Göcking's Source Story
> The Transposition from 1731 to 1796

## 8. The Restitution of Idyll? ... 106

> Life and Death in the Idyll
> The Final Retarding Moment
> The Tragedy of Revolutionary Enlightenment
> The Nation as *Gemeinschaft*

**Excursus:** Revolutionary Enlightenment, the German Jacobins, and Dorothea's First Fiancé ... 121

**Conclusion: Paradox in the Idyll** ... 136

**Appendix:** "Das erste Volksgedicht ..." The Critical Reception of *Hermann und Dorothea* ... 140

> *Ordnung, Sittlichkeit* and the Beginnings
> of a German Classical Canon (1798-1814)
> National Identity and Political Liberty (1814-1848)
> The *Bildung* of the Nation (1848-1918)
> Europe and the *Volk* (The Nazi Period)
> In the Shadow of Nazism (1949-1968)
> "A Sleeping Hercules" — Re-Evaluations of
> German Identity (1970-1989)

**Bibliography to *Hermann und Dorothea*** ... 163

**General Bibliography** ... 168

**Index** ... 178

# Introduction

DURING THE NINETEENTH CENTURY Goethe's verse-idyll, *Hermann und Dorothea*, was considered the most popular of his works, the classic repository of traditional German characters and values. The writer and critic, August Wilhelm Schlegel referred to it as "accessible, warm, patriotic and popular: a book full of golden advice of wisdom and virtue."[1] As traditional values became increasingly discredited by the historical developments of the twentieth century, however, *Hermann und Dorothea* became a problem — or an embarrassment — for literary and cultural criticism.

The Hungarian Marxist thinker, Georg Lukács, judged *Hermann und Dorothea*, along with the novel, *Wilhelm Meisters Lehrjahre* (*Wilhelm Meister's Apprenticeship*), to be a seminal work in the development of modern German literature: "Despite its ancient form, *Hermann and Dorothea* is just as 'sentimental' and problematical as *Wilhelm Meister*, only in a different way."[2] Lukács identified the contradiction between form and content in this work in terms of the effects of the French Revolution in Germany, thereby rejecting all 'naive' readings of the work, whether nationalist or classical.[3]

Goethe realized that enlightened absolutism, and enlightenment as an ideology, was entering a critical phase well before the French Revolution broke out. The "necklace affair" of 1785, in which members of Marie Antoinette's court were implicated in a plot to steal a priceless piece of jewelry, was symptomatic for

---

All textual references to *Hermann und Dorothea* are to vol. 2 of the "Hamburg" edition of Johann Wolfgang von Goethe, *Werke*, ed. Erich Trunz, 8th rev. ed. 14 vols. (Munich: Beck, 1974-1978), with canto number (Roman) and line-number (Arabic). Translations of *Hermann and Dorothea* are from Johann Wolfgang von Goethe, *Verse Plays and Epic*, ed. Cyrus Hamlin and Frank Ryder, trans. Michael Hamburger, Hunter Hannum, and David Luke, vol. 8 of *Goethe's Collected Works* (New York: Suhrkamp, 1987). Other works by Goethe are cited from the "Hamburg" edition (H.A.) or, if not included in that edition, from the "Weimar" edition (W.A.): Johann Wolfgang von Goethe, *Werke*, (Weimar: Hermann Böhlaus Nachfolger, 1887-1912), by section (Roman) volume (Arabic) and page (Arabic) number. Translations are my own unless otherwise stated.

[1] August Wilhelm Schlegel, "Goethes Hermann und Dorothea," *Über Literatur, Kunst und Geist des Zeitalters: Eine Auswahl aus den kritischen Schriften*, ed. Franz Finke (Stuttgart: Reclam, 1964), 147.

[2] Georg Lukács, *Goethe and his Age*, trans. Robert Anchor, (London: Merlin Press, 1968), 86.

[3] Lukács, *Goethe*, 88.

Goethe of the moral crisis of the *ancien régime*.⁴ His decision to travel to Italy in 1786, too, was a response to the frustration of his hopes for social and political improvement and personal self-fulfillment in petty absolutist Weimar. By the early 1790s he had begun to accept that the *ancien régime* was over and that a new era had begun. The French Revolution added a socio-political and historical dimension to his personal sense of crisis. However he was by no means sure of the future. Shortly after the Cannonade of Valmy, the first major victory of the Revolutionary troops over a foreign opponent (19/20 September 1792), Goethe wrote to his Weimar colleague, Voigt:

> Ich habe mit Betrübniß gesehen, daß das Geheime Conseil unbewunden diesen Krieg für einen Reichskrieg erklärt hat. Wir werden also auch mit der Heerde ins Verderben rennen — Europa braucht einen Dreißigjährigen Krieg um einzusehen, was 1792 vernünftig gewesen wäre.⁵

His fears for the political stability of Europe in 1792 were justified, and his choice of the Thirty Years' War is significant. This war ended in 1648, but it had determined German development for the following century and a half.⁶ At Valmy in 1792 Goethe saw symbolized the end of the culture of the European Enlightenment and the beginnings of a new era of French national predominance over Germany and Europe.

Goethe's works from the early to mid 1790s are generally considered uneven in quality. Along with the second-rate dramas of the early 1790s, he wrote the *Unterhaltungen deutscher Ausgewanderten* (*Conversations of German Emigrés*) including the "Märchen" ("Fairy-Tale"), the satiric epic, *Reineke Fuchs* (*Reynard the Fox*), parts of *Faust*, essays on the theory of science, optics, botany, geology and comparative anatomy, the "Xenien" or "Distichs," lyric poems, *Wilhelm Meisters Lehrjahre* (*Wilhelm Meister's Apprenticeship*), and *Hermann und Dorothea*.⁷ The unevenness of the works of this period was the result of the major re-orientation of creative perspectives needed to come to terms with the Revolution and its significance for Germany.⁸ While the French Revolution dominated Goethe's thinking during the

---

⁴ Goethe, W.A. I, 35, 11; *Campagne in Frankreich*, H.A. 10:356. Cf. Hans Mayer, *Goethe: Ein Versuch über den Erfolg* (Frankfurt am Main: Suhrkamp, 1973), 16-24.

⁵ "I viewed with sadness the decision of the Privy Council to declare this war an Imperial war. We shall run with the herd headlong into destruction — Europe needs a Thirty Years' War in order to see what would have been sensible in 1792." Goethe to C.G. Voigt, Luxemburg, 15 October 1792, W.A. IV, 10, 34-35.

⁶ Gerhard Schulz, *Die deutsche Literatur zwischen Französischer Revolution und Restauration, 1789-1806*, vol. 7/1 of *Geschichte der deutschen Literatur von den Anfängen bis zur Gegenwart*, ed. Helmut de Boor and Richard Newald, (Munich: Beck, 1983), 22.

⁷ The so-called "Revolutionsstücke" are: *Der Groß-Cophta* (1791), *Der Bürgergeneral* (1793) and *Die Aufgeregten* (1793).

⁸ Mayer, *Goethe*, 41-57.

1790s, however, the epic subject of the Revolution is avoided in the novel, *Wilhelm Meisters Lehrjahre*, and it provides merely a backdrop for the frame-narrative of the *Unterhaltungen deutscher Ausgewanderten* and the provincial idyll of *Hermann und Dorothea*.

In the fairy-tale which ends the *Unterhaltungen deutscher Ausgewanderten*, Goethe found a way of representing the creative impasse which the Revolution and the end of French Enlightenment had signified. "Das Märchen" is the literary culmination, in form as well as theme, of the European Enlightenment. In the fairy-tale, the end of enlightened absolutism and the *ancien régime* is resolved into a utopia through a humane and democratic "revolution" occurring at once from above and below.[9] The fairy-tale becomes a means of self-liberation from the limitations imposed by the epoch. It is not a rejection of the Enlightenment worldview, but a release which creates the conditions for a fresh perspective, in which the old can be incorporated with the new. "Das Märchen" uses the language and symbols of Enlightenment, of enlightened absolutism and the *ancien régime*. But everything in the story — even the old society — ultimately contributes to and is subsumed into the new. The brutality, violence and injustice, which were a part of the process of revolutionary liberation from the oppressive structures of the *ancien régime*, are transmuted into beauty, order and progress.

Among the works of the 1790s, "Das Märchen" and *Hermann und Dorothea* stand on either side of a creative turning-point. Where "Das Märchen" is the utopia of the failed hopes of the Enlightenment and enlightened absolutism, *Hermann und Dorothea* represents the first mapping out of post-revolutionary identities — tentatively through irony, parody and ambivalence rather than through mimetic representation.[10]

After the coming to terms with the "crisis of enlightenment" in "Das Märchen," Goethe was able in *Hermann und Dorothea* to introduce into literature the new theme of the problematic cultural and national identity of post-revolutionary Germany. This theme arises from the change in perception, from the eighteenth-century Enlightenment view of the Revolution as self-liberation from absolutist tyranny, to the nineteenth-century nationalist view of it as the traumatic birth of the modern French nation-state. *Hermann und Dorothea* brings the French Revolution into the fictive "horizon" and thereby begins to comprehend its significance for Germany. In the archetypal German character, Hermann, confronted with the social upheaval of the emigration of German refugees from the left-bank territories in late summer 1796, the problem-complex of German identity, traditional values and response to social change is introduced into post-revolutionary literature.

---

[9] Cf. Hans Mayer, "Vergebliche Renaissance: Das 'Märchen' bei Goethe und Gerhart Hauptmann," *Von Lessing bis Thomas Mann* (Pfullingen: Neske, 1959), 356-82; *Goethe*, 56; and Peter Morgan, "The Fairy-Tale as Radical Perspective: Enlightenment as Barrier and Bridge to Civic Values in Goethe's 'Das Märchen,'" *Orbis Litterarum* 40 (1985): 222-43.

[10] Hans Mayer refers to the "Ironie und verhüllende Symbolik" of Goethe's works after *Tasso*: Mayer, *Goethe*, 51.

In this study *Hermann und Dorothea* is analyzed in the light of the apparent contradictions between ancient form and modern problems, revolutionary upheaval and idyllic German identity. The end of Enlightenment and the development of a post-revolutionary German identity are of central importance to this work of the mid 1790s.

These questions have not been analyzed in detail in relation to Goethe's works from this formative period for German cultural and national identity. While themes of national identity occur earlier in the works of Klopstock and the *Sturm und Drang* writers, Goethe focuses on the development of "national" feelings in the character of Hermann on an emotional, rather than an intellectual, critical or self-reflexive level. The "national" feelings expressed by Hermann are closer to Herder's concepts of a cultural unity based on language-community than to earlier territorial or dynastic concepts of the German "nation."

Modern studies have avoided these socio-literary issues. Ever since the publication of *Hermann und Dorothea*, the idyllic environment of the small town and the character of Hermann have been used in support of arguments for a German national identity. The association with nationalist ideology brought many non-literary influences to bear on interpretation of the work, especially in the main periods of German nationalism, during the Wars of Liberation, after 1848, and during the Nazi period. After the discrediting of the German nationalist tradition by Nazism and the war, critics avoided these issues. The relationships of irony, parody and ambivalence to questions of enlightenment, revolution and modern German identity have remained unexplored. For this reason, much of the criticism and interpretation of *Hermann und Dorothea* is relevant from the point of view of what is omitted, rather than what is included. While several important passages have often been excerpted and used in support of various causes, few modern studies have been based on a close reading of the whole text. A critical and analytic history of the reception of *Hermann und Dorothea* has been included in the Appendix.

Some short definitions of terms used throughout the analysis are included below. They will be further defined as they occur in the text.

## Enlightenment, Enlightened Absolutism, the German Intelligentsia and the "Crisis of Enlightenment"

Enlightenment is a broad term of European intellectual history after the Renaissance, focusing on the use of reason, the re-appraisal of the "natural" and the belief in the possibility of human progress. In both France and England the Enlightenment was linked with the development of capitalism, capitalist ideologies and the growth of the "bourgeoisie" and the "middle class." In Germany this was only partly so. The semantic similarity between *Bürger* and *bourgeois* conceals important differences in regional and historical development. In Germany a non-aristocratic intelligentsia developed under petty absolutism, and achieved at least partial integration with the gentry. The German *Aufklärung* is linked to the development of this social group, rather than to an economically and politically independent middle class, as for example, in England.[11]

The German Enlightenment includes the "functional" or "practical" enlightenment of the court bureaucracies and the education systems which were set up in order to rationalize and legitimize absolutist despotisms. From within enlightened absolutism, critical, humanistic, rationalist attitudes were developed by an intelligentsia which was both dependent on, and, to a limited extent, critical of petty absolutism. The terms "instrumental" or "practical," and "critical" enlightenment are used to identify these dual aspects.[12] "Critical" enlightenment can be seen especially in developments in the second half of the eighteenth century, in, for example, the *Sturm und Drang* writers of the 1770s and early 1780s, and the "Enlightenment debate" of the mid 1780s, which was continued into the revolutionary period by critical intellectuals such as Lichtenberg and Forster.[13] The idealist philosopher Kant summarized and influenced the development of this type of enlightenment in 1784 with his definition of enlightenment as "the emergence of man from his self-incurred minority."[14]

The critical thinking that developed from within absolutism, which was expressed in the intellectual and political ferment in France (especially after the American Revolution), and in the literary and cultural revival in Germany in the

---

[11] On the German middle classes of the eighteenth century, see Karl Biedermann, *Deutschland im 18. Jahrhundert*, 4 vols., 1854 (2nd ed. Leipzig, 1880; repr., Aalen: Scientia, 1969), Helmuth Kiesel and Paul Münch, *Gesellschaft und Literatur im 18. Jahrhundert: Voraussetzungen und Entstehung des literarischen Marktes in Deutschland* (Munich: Beck, 1977), Franklin Kopitsch, ed., *Aufklärung, Absolutismus und Bürgertum in Deutschland* (Munich: Nymphenburg, 1976), Hans Gerth, *Bürgerliche Intelligenz um 1800: Zur Soziologie des deutschen Frühliberalismus* (Göttingen: Vandenhoeck & Ruprecht, 1976).

[12] On the German Enlightenment, see: Lukács, *Goethe*; Max Horkheimer and Theodor W. Adorno, *Dialektik der Aufklärung* (Amsterdam: de Munter, 1968); Fritz Valjavec, *Geschichte der abendländischen Aufklärung* (Vienna: Herold, 1961); Reinhard Koselleck, *Kritik und Krise: Eine Studie zur Pathogenese der bürgerlichen Welt* (Frankfurt am Main: Suhrkamp, 1976), 49-80; Peter Pütz, *Die deutsche Aufklärung* (Darmstadt: Wissenschaftliche Buchgesellschaft, 1978). The terminology of "practical" and "theoretical" enlightenment originates in a pamphlet of 1784 by Johann Friedel, justifying the reformist policies of Joseph II, Leslie Bodi, *Tauwetter in Wien: Zur Prosa der österreichischen Aufklärung 1781-1795* (Frankfurt am Main: Fischer, 1977), 170-76. The term "critical" enlightenment originates from Kant's "critical philosophy" of the 1780s, cf. S. Körner, *Kant* (Harmondsworth: Penguin, 1974), 13-32.

[13] Wolfgang Rödel, *Forster und Lichtenberg: Ein Beitrag zum Problem deutsche Intelligenz und Französische Revolution* (Berlin: Rütten und Loening, 1960), 125-81 and passim.

[14] Immanuel Kant, "Beantwortung der Frage: Was ist Aufklärung," in *Was ist Aufklärung? Beiträge aus der Berlinischen Monatsschrift 1783-1786*, ed. Norbert Hinske, (Darmstadt: Wissenschaftliche Buchgesellschaft, 1981), 452.

1770s, had begun to worry absolutist governments by the mid 1780s.[15] The "Enlightenment debate" in the *Berlinische Monatsschrift* (in which the leading thinkers of the German Enlightenment participated), the discussion of the function of the secret societies throughout Germany, and the controversies in Vienna in the mid 1780s were all symptomatic of the divergence between "practical" and "critical" enlightenment, and of the politically subversive potential of this divergence.

In the Habsburg lands a period of instability had begun with the reforms of Joseph II, especially in the late 1780s. With the beginning of the Revolution in 1789 and the deaths of Joseph II and Leopold II in the early 1790s, a period of reaction set in, culminating with the Jacobin trials. In Bavaria the "Illuminati" scandal in the 1780s marked the end of the Bavarian Enlightenment.[16] The "Illuminati" affair and the Jacobin trials in the Habsburg Empire were used as a means of increasing control over the radical fringes of enlightenment, while simultaneously reasserting enlightened absolutism (i.e. "practical" or "instrumental" enlightenment) as the means to and the legitimation of absolutist despotism.

Before the Revolution, the absolutist bureaucrat and the critical freethinker were often one and the same person. In the "secrecy" of the Freemasons' lodges he mixed with colleagues, superiors and even with the gentry and aristocracy. This duality of roles was the "open secret" of which Lessing speaks in his *Masonic Dialogues*.[17] Because critical thinking and enlightenment were so closely linked, it is not possible to regard the "crisis of enlightenment" of the early 1790s in dualistic terms, of a ruling class and radical, subversive groups. The crisis occurred when the intellectuals realized that "practical" and "critical" enlightenment could no longer be considered complementary aspects of the one world-view.

Many political commentators in Germany considered the unrest in France to be the result of a timely, if dramatic, last-bid attempt to force "practical" enlightened reforms onto the French monarchy. A.L. v. Schlözer, editor of the

---

[15] Hans Kohn, *The Idea of Nationalism: A Study in its Origins and Background* (New York: Macmillan, 1944), 324-25; R.R. Palmer, *The Age of the Democratic Revolution: A Political History of Europe and America, 1760-1800*, 2 vols. (Princeton: Princeton University Press, 1959), 1:265-66; and Horst Dippel, *Germany and the American Revolution 1770-1800: A Sociohistorical Investigation of late Eighteenth Century Political Thinking*, trans. B.A. Uhlendorf (Wiesbaden: Steiner, 1978), 329-44.

[16] Ernst Wangermann, *From Joseph II to the Jacobin Trials: Government Policy and Public Opinion in the Habsburg Dominions in the Period of the French Revolution* (London: Oxford University Press, 1959); Bodi, *Tauwetter*, 227-79, 395-431; Hans Graßl, *Aufbruch zur Romantik: Bayerns Beitrag zur deutschen Geistesgeschichte, 1765-85* (Munich: Beck, 1968), passim; and Richard van Dülmen, *Der Geheimbund der Illuminaten: Darstellung, Analyse, Dokumentation* (Stuttgart/Bad Cannstatt: Frommann-Holzboog, 1975), passim; Klaus Epstein, *The Genesis of German Conservatism* (Princeton: Princeton University Press, 1966), 84-111.

[17] Gotthold Ephraim Lessing, "Ernst und Falk: Gespräche für Freimaurer," *Werke*, ed. Kurt Wölfel, 3 vols. (Frankfurt am Main: Insel, 1967), 3:509-43; cf. Koselleck, 68-74.

# Introduction

*Staats-Anzeigen*, for example, considered the French monarchy to be lagging behind the Habsburgs and the more progressive German princes, who had gradually adopted enlightenment as a political ideology, and who thereby had prevented a revolutionary situation arising.[18] Consequently many intellectuals responded enthusiastically to the Revolution between 1789 and 1791. They expected enlightened reforms such as the moderation of absolutism by constitutional monarchy, the end of aristocratic privilege, and the "curtailment of Catholic privilege and superstition in the name of rational religion and ... religious toleration," although by no means all shared Schlözer's extreme opinion that enlightenment had already penetrated the courts of Germany and Austria.[19] Of the major intellectual figures, only Möser and Goethe rejected the Revolution from the beginning. Klopstock, Wieland, Voss,[20] Schiller, Kant, Herder, Fichte, Rehberg, Gentz and many other writers and intellectuals supported the early stages.[21]

Few realized before late 1792 that the Revolution was developing in an entirely different direction. Still living under petty absolutism, the German intelligentsia could not follow the transformation of revolutionary enlightenment into the bourgeois nation-state after 1793.

The realization that fifty years of French Enlightenment had led to an incomprehensible and aggressive new state, rather than to a democracy founded on reason, induced a sense of crisis among enlightened intellectuals. The turning point, the "crisis of enlightenment," occurred between mid 1792 and mid 1794. Three events in particular brought about the change in attitudes: the escalation of the Revolution into a European war in mid 1792, the execution of the king in January 1793, and the consolidation of power in France under the dictatorship of the Committee of Public Safety after July 1793. The behavior of the revolutionary armies in some areas forced many intellectuals to reconsider the theoretical distinction between revolutionary liberation and oppression; the execution of the king was an act against the sovereign monarch, whose position was still central to German enlightened political theory; and the political tactics of the Jacobins were an affront to the ideals of enlightened humanity and democracy.[22]

---

[18] Rudolf Vierhaus, "Politisches Bewußtsein in Deutschland vor 1789," *Der Staat* 6 (1967): 184.

[19] Epstein, 435-36; see also Fritz Valjavec, *Die Entstehung der politischen Strömungen in Deutschland 1770-1815* (1951; Kronberg/Ts.: Athenäum; Düsseldorf: Droste, 1978), 146-254.

[20] Throughout I have used the spelling "Voss" rather than "Voß" for the sake of uniformity since contemporary orthography varied between both spellings.

[21] Epstein, 485.

[22] The writer and political commentator, Chr. M. Wieland makes these points in his article, "Ueber teutschen Patriotismus," in *Der Neue Teutsche Merkur*, (May 1793): 16-17. On the question of liberation versus occupation, see Walter Grab, *Eroberung oder Befreiung? Deutsche Jakobiner und die Franzosenherrschaft im Rheinland 1792-1799*, Schriften aus dem Karl Marx Haus Trier 4 (Trier: n.p., 1971), rev. ed., *Studien zu Jakobinismus und Sozialismus*, ed. H. Pelger (Berlin: Dietz, 1974), 1-102; T.C.W. Blanning, *Reform and Revolution in Mainz*

The educated classes which had read and more or less openly sympathized with the problems of Werther, Karl Moor and Minna von Barnhelm were in a difficult position by 1793. The execution of the king could not be looked upon as "practical" enlightenment in the sense that the reforms of 1788 to 1791 had been. At the level of philosophical theory, on such questions as religious tolerance and aesthetic theory, German thinkers could adopt the language of enlightenment from the capitalist, middle-class cultures in the West. However in the areas of political theory and social consciousness the gaps between eastern and western enlightenment became clear. The latent split between the (relatively open) ideological commitment to "critical" enlightenment and the actual dependency on enlightened absolutism became manifest.[23] The middle-class intelligentsia was socially and politically intimidated in the new situation. Moreover the policies of occupation of the Rhine territories turned the common people against the Revolution.

Although some historians have attempted to prove otherwise, relatively few German intellectuals maintained their revolutionary attitudes after the reoccupation of Mainz in July 1793 by the Coalition forces.[24] The intelligentsia polarized over the years from 1792 until 1798, with a minority supporting the Revolution, and the majority turning away from political engagement. Those intellectuals who supported the Revolution (such as Georg Forster) were considered subversives, traitors and/or criminals. The experience for most was that political awareness had been an illusion, ending in division, failure and loss of confidence.

A new intellectual provincialism set in, characterized by splinter groups, cliques and circles of like-minded thinkers and writers (or as in Prussia, sycophantic, ritualistic and mystical cliques associated with court factions). Lacking the sense of community of the pre-revolutionary Enlightenment, and shown to have been naive in their political optimism, the intellectuals after 1792 lost their critical confidence.[25] In the "Materialien zur Farbenlehre" Goethe wrote:

---

*1743-1803* (London: Cambridge University Press, 1974), 241-302, and *The French Revolution in Germany: Occupation and Resistance in the Rhineland 1792-1802* (Oxford: Clarendon Press, 1983), 59-134.

[23] Only the most perceptive commentators before 1792 recognized that the Revolution could culminate in the execution of the king. The execution of Charles I, and the restoration of the monarchy in England is rarely mentioned. Cf. Chr. M. Wieland, "Ueber Krieg und Frieden," *Der Neue Teutsche Merkur* (June 1794): 194.

[24] Heinrich Scheel, *Süddeutsche Jakobiner: Klassenkämpfe und republikanische Bestrebungen im deutschen Süden am Ende des 18. Jahrhunderts* (Berlin: Akademie, 1962); Walter Grab, *Leben und Werke norddeutscher Jakobiner* (Stuttgart: Metzler, 1973); Axel Kuhn, *Linksrheinische deutsche Jakobiner* (Stuttgart: Metzler, 1978), and Gerhard Kaiser, "Über den Umgang mit Republikanern, Jakobinern und Zitaten," *DVjs* 49, Sonderheft (1975): 226-42.

[25] Wolfgang von Groote, *Die Entstehung des Nationalbewußtseins in Nordwestdeutschland 1790-1830* (Göttingen: Musterschmidt, 1955), 9.

Niemals haben sich die Individuen vielleicht mehr vereinzelt und voneinander abgesondert als gegenwärtig. Jeder möchte das Universum vorstellen und aus sich selbst darstellen.[26]

And in the "Tag- und Jahreshefte" he described the malaise of the intellectuals:

Das allgemeine Interesse, sittlich, moralisch, war doch ein vages, unbestimmtes, und es fehlte im ganzen wie im einzelnen an Richtung zu besondern Tätigkeiten. Daher zerfiel der große unsichtbare Kreis in kleinere, meist lokale, die manches Löbliche erschufen und hervorbrachten; aber eigentlich isolierten sich die Bedeutenden immer mehr und mehr.[27]

## *Gemeinschaft / Gesellschaft* and *Wunschbild Land / Schreckbild Stadt*

Ferdinand Tönnies's terms, *Gemeinschaft* (community) and *Gesellschaft* (society or association) are used to describe contrasting images of society in *Hermann und Dorothea*. This juxtaposition can be seen in the German village community, and the modern city, Paris, with its huge population, stratified society and alienated social relations. Tönnies writes:

The theory of the *Gesellschaft* deals with the artificial construction of an aggregate of human beings which superficially resembles the *Gemeinschaft* in so far as the individuals peacefully live and dwell together. However, in the *Gemeinschaft* they remain essentially united in spite of all separating factors, whereas in the *Gesellschaft* they are essentially separated in spite of all uniting factors.[28]

Neither of these ideal types actually appears in the work. *Gemeinschaft* appears rather as a *Wunschbild* (ideal) for Hermann, in the image of the fountain where he used to play as a child, and in the memory of his father in the cotton dressing-gown which figures so largely in the work. These images can be compared to the idyllic provincial setting of "Wahlheim" in Goethe's early novel, *Die Leiden des jungen Werthers* (*The Sorrows of Young Werther*). Likewise the *Gesellschaft* of Paris

---

[26] "Never, perhaps, have we as individuals been more isolated and detached from each other than now. Each wishes to represent the universe and create it from within himself." W.A. II, 3, 122.

[27] "The general feeling ... was indeed vague and undefined, and on a general as well as individual level there was a lack of direction towards particular activities. As a result, the whole invisible circle fell apart into smaller, mostly local (circles), which created and produced some praiseworthy things; but in fact the significant individuals became more and more isolated." W.A. I, 35, 38.

[28] Ferdinand Tönnies, *Community and Association (Gemeinschaft und Gesellschaft)*, trans. Charles P. Loomis (London: Routledge & Kegan Paul, 1955), 74.

never appears in *Hermann und Dorothea*. It is mentioned as the place of origin of the Revolution, where Dorothea's first fiancé, the "German Jacobin" was executed. The French Revolution and the *Gesellschaft* of Paris are represented as a *Schreckbild* (image of horror). This juxtaposition underlies a formulation by Friedrich Sengle, *Wunschbild Land / Schreckbild Stadt*, which is seen as a *topic* of eighteenth-century German literature.[29]

## Home Town

Mack Walker's sociological term, "home town," is used to describe the town in *Hermann und Dorothea*. Walker identifies the home town as having developed from the particular socio-political relations that were the legacy of the Holy Roman Empire:

> The frame of the German towns' external relations was quite different from the pattern discerned in most of Europe, because of the division of juridical and political power between the constitutional sovereignty of the Empire and the territorial sovereignty — 'Landeshoheit' — of the territorial rulers, the 'Landesherren,' large and small: a vague and flexible division of authority that reflected the vague and flexible political balance.[30]

Most European towns had supported strong monarchs against the local landed nobility, which led to their becoming incorporated into monarchic states as the price of local security. This did not occur in the Holy Roman Empire of the early modern period. While 'sovereign' imperial authority defended the towns against the territorial princes, it was unable to dominate them.[31] The imperial rights of the communities, were protected in fact not by the Empire, but by neighboring states, as part of the stalemate in German relations from the sixteenth century.

Walker defines the towns as autonomous, (having "almost no penetration into their internal affairs from the outside"), uneven in terms of structure and "subject to no common rhythm of economics or politics." They had little to do with the "'fremde Güter oder Angelegenheiten'" ("'foreign goods or matters'") that "would invite the attention of administrators, tax collectors, and Roman lawyers."[32] The freedom from economic interchange with the outside world was "as important for

---

[29] Friedrich Sengle, "Wunschbild Land und Schreckbild Stadt: Zu einem zentralen Thema der neueren deutschen Literatur," *Europäische Bukolik und Georgik*, ed. Klaus Garber, Wege der Forschung, 355 (Darmstadt: Wissenschaftliche Buchgesellschaft, 1976), 432-60. Goethe's use of *topoi* is discussed in chapter five.

[30] Mack Walker, *German Home Towns: Community, State and General Estate 1648-1871* (Ithaca: Cornell University Press, 1971), 19.

[31] Walker, 19.

[32] Walker, 18, citing the "Abriss der Staats-Verfassung, Staats-Verhältnis, und Bedürfniss des Römischen Reichs deutscher Nation, Mainz 1761."

the preservation of the home town's autonomy and integrity as freedom from political penetration."[33] The economic organization of the home town was quite elaborate because although it produced no surplus for export, its very autonomy demanded internal diversification and sophistication:

> it was ... a high development of small-scale commerce and manufacture in a time and place where great commerce and manufacture were all but impossible, or at least were economically inappropriate.[34]

In terms of size and population, the home town corresponds to Tönnies's definition of a town as "an organism with collective life," as opposed to a city, where "free persons ... stand in contact with each other, exchange with each other and co-operate without any *Gemeinschaft* or will thereto developing among them."[35] Walker defines the home town as being small enough for the citizens to be familiar with each other. Above a certain size, familiarity is lost and "a more formal and anonymous pattern of law and politics is necessary." In towns above that size a patriciate, or ruling caste, and a class of "non-citizens" begin to form.[36] Walker concludes:

> The hometownsman lived by exchange among people he intimately knew and whose polity he fully shared. ... The hometownsman both needed his neighbors and he knew them, and his politics incorporated what he needed and what he knew into a stable and circumscribed world.[37]

The home town too lacked the type of public sphere which was associated with the development of the city or metropolis. Jürgen Habermas has analyzed the different types of "public spheres" in England, France and Germany since the beginning of the eighteenth century, and Leslie Bodi has pointed out the differences in this respect between the metropolis of Vienna in the later eighteenth century and non-Habsburg petty absolutist Germany.[38]

The home town in *Hermann und Dorothea* is beginning to develop beyond the above boundaries, with an incipient patriciate, a "class" of laborers (who are unknown to the innkeeper) and the beginnings of commercial expansion and wider trade links.

---

[33] Walker, 24.

[34] Walker, 25.

[35] Tönnies, 70, 267.

[36] Walker, 27.

[37] Walker, 33; cf. also Blanning, *Mainz*, 70-95.

[38] Jürgen Habermas, *Strukturwandel der Öffentlichkeit: Untersuchungen zu einer Kategorie der bürgerlichen Gesellschaft* (Neuwied: Luchterhand, 1962), 50f., and Bodi, *Tauwetter*, 45f.

## Nationalism, National Identity

Thinkers of the French Enlightenment, such as Rousseau, had emphasized issues of ethnic and national identity as well as political freedom and republicanism. However the impact of the revolutionary armies on Germany discredited these Enlightenment ideals as the liberators increasingly were perceived to be oppressors. The Revolution represents both the culmination of French political enlightenment and the beginnings of modern nationalism. Dorothea's first fiancé, the *Weltbürger* ("cosmopolitan"), who hopes that the Revolution will lead to the transcendence of political fragmentation and social divisions, ignores aspects of ethnic and cultural identity, which Goethe represents in Hermann, as deep-lying, confused and unarticulated. As a result of social change both within and beyond the town, Hermann becomes a spokesman for a "pre-national" identity on an unreflexive level, combining earlier feelings of patriotism with an incipient nationalism built on a sense of linguistic, cultural and ethnic unity, against a foreign enemy.[39] The changes in the home town, the internal and external forces behind these changes, and the results of social change are analyzed in this study.

## "Modes of Ambivalence": Irony, Parody and Paradox

Irony is defined by Norman D. Knox as:

> the conflict of two meanings which has a dramatic structure peculiar to itself: initially, one meaning, the *appearance*, presents itself as the obvious truth, but when the context of this meaning unfolds, in depth or in time, it surprisingly discloses a conflicting meaning, the *reality*, measured against which the first meaning now seems false or limited and, in its self-assurance, blind to its own situation.[40]

D. C. Muecke regards irony in terms of "contradictory meanings" rather than "appearance" and "reality." It occurs in the form of "those contradictions, apparently fundamental and irremediable, that confront men when they speculate upon such topics as the origin and purpose of the universe, free will and determinism, reason and instinct."[41] The growing awareness of irony is seen by

---

[39] Concepts of nationalism, national consciousness and ethnic identity are based on Kohn, *The Idea of Nationalism*, 263-454; Joshua Fishman, *Language and Nationalism: Two Integrative Essays* (Rowley, Mass.: Newbury House, 1973), 3-29; Nathan Glazer, and Daniel P. Moynihan, eds., *Ethnicity: Theory and Experience* (Cambridge, Mass.: Harvard University Press, 1975), 1-26.

[40] Norman D. Knox, "Irony," *Dictionary of the History of Ideas: Studies of Selected Pivotal Ideas*, ed. P. Wiener, 4 vols. and index (New York: Scribner, 1973), 2:626-34.

[41] D C. Muecke, *The Compass of Irony* (London: Methuen, 1969), 121.

Muecke in relation to secularization and the change from closed (religious) to open (secular) ideologies.[42]

For the artist "the very ability of the mind to recognize the inescapable predicament" was a way of escape, and provided a sense of freedom.[43] Friedrich Schlegel formulated the theory of "Romantic Irony" as the expression of "an ironical attitude adopted as a means of recognizing and transcending, but still preserving" the contradictions of life and art. Schlegel sees the paradox as the "conditio sine qua non" of the modern, ironic artist's world-view, for it signifies "recognition of the fact that the world in its essence is paradoxical, and that an ambivalent attitude alone can grasp its contradictory totality."[44] For Schlegel the function of art is, in presenting chaos, to transcend it. The modern work of art is open, self-reflexive and contradictory.

Parody is related to irony as a "mode of ambivalence." However parody specifically uses an existing text (or work of art), in order to present paradoxes or contradictions.[45] For Margaret Rose, parody confuses the normal processes of communication "by offering more than one message to be decoded by the reader," a process which may also serve to "conceal the author's intended meaning from immediate interpretation." It quotes parts or the whole of another text, thereby attacking or criticizing the pre-existent text, but also establishing an ambivalent attitude to its object, on which it is "dependent for a part of its own material and structure." This dependence may also conceal an ironic relationship to the "multiplicity of messages which the embedding of another text in its structure may create." Ironic parody is described in Schlegel's term as *Potenzierung*, and in Hegelian terms as supersession or sublation (*Aufhebung*) of a text "through the refunctioning of it as part of another work."[46]

---

[42] Muecke, 124-33.

[43] Muecke, 122.

[44] Muecke, 159.

[45] The term "modes of ambivalence" was coined by Leslie Bodi, and is used in his "Comic Ambivalence as an Identity Marker: The Austrian Model," *Comic Relations: Studies in the Comic, Satire and Parody*, ed. Pavel Petr, David Roberts, and Philip Thomson, (New York: Herbert Lang, 1985), 74.

[46] Margaret Rose, *Parody/Metafiction: An Analysis of Parody as a Critical Mirror to the Writing and Reception of Fiction* (London: Croom Helm, 1979), 51. *Potenzierung*, while having the general meaning of heightening or charging, is also a mathematical term meaning radicalization or "raising to a power."

# 1: The Idyll and German Identity

### The Middle-Class Idyll: Goethe and Voss

IN THE SECOND HALF of the eighteenth century changes had occurred in the intellectual, cultural and social self-definition of the German middle classes, especially in the Protestant north, but also in Bavaria and the Rhineland.[1] German writers could look back over the period since the mid 1770s and see clear lines of development of a middle-class consciousness in literature. Despite the lack of political and economic power, a pre-national consciousness of shared German identity had begun to develop on a wider level as a result of factors such as the relative stability in German internal relations since the Seven Years' War, economic progress, population increases, the growth of literacy and scientific and intellectual progress in the second half of the eighteenth century.

Where the blueprint for a bourgeois future had been sketched by the French Enlightenment thinkers, and was laid out in revolutionary documents such as the American "Declaration of Independence" and Thomas Paine's *Rights of Man*, literature and philosophy had not performed these functions in petty absolutist Germany. The German middle-class writers had censured the morality of the courts rather than the political structure of petty absolutism. W. Krauss uses the term "die nationale Pädagogik" for the tendency of the German middle classes to see themselves as the bearers of German national culture while courtly society dissipated its patrimony by imitating French absolutism.[2]

Pietism united religion and language for the middle classes into a culture which was pregnant with themes and images of national unity. Religious and class identity markers, such as *Bürgertugend* (middle-class virtue), became linked with patriotic concepts in the opposition to the worldliness and corruption of the courts, which were seen to be emulating French models. This tendency was veiled early in the century but became clearer in Klopstock, for example, who no longer

---

[1] See T.C.W. Blanning, "The Enlightenment in Catholic Germany," in *The Enlightenment in National Context*, ed. Roy Porter and Mikulas Teich (Cambridge: Cambridge University Press, 1981), 118-26; and Graßl, passim.

[2] Werner Krauss, *Perspektiven und Probleme: Zur französischen und deutschen Aufklärung und andere Aufsätze* (Neuwied: Luchterhand, 1965), 254, 260.

expressed himself in strictly religious (pietist) terms, but who made use of an amalgam of religious, linguistic, historical and social identity-markers.[3]

The middle classes found an idealized self-reflection especially in the works of Voss from the 1770s onward. Voss had modified the classical, Renaissance and courtly models of the idyll for a German middle-class audience. Building on the works of Geßner, and influenced by the language of Klopstock, he created the *bürgerliche Idylle* (middle-class idyll) in which moral goodness was identified with the middle classes and located in an idyllic German countryside. In place of the contrived settings of courtly-rococo idyll, he presented a middle-class image of nature as local environment, and provided an alternative to the earlier idyll by using everyday language and even dialect. By making use of classical forms and metres he built on earlier attempts to rescue classical forms for German literature.

Rejection of courtly society and European politics lies at the core of Voss's works.[4] Bitter polemic against the courts is combined with the idyllic vision of the middle-class families of *Luise* (1784/1795) and "Der siebzigste Geburtstag" ("The Seventieth Birthday," 1781). This polemic strengthens the sense of moral and traditional autonomy of his idyllic families. His middle-class characters and provincial environments are unaffected by the movements of European politics. The criticism in *Luise* is aimed at a world which is outside and around the idyll, but which cannot penetrate the core of middle-class values, religious faith and cultural purity. Voss's idylls present an uncritical and unmediated vision of the middle-class family. They lack even the gentle irony and humor of his model, Goldsmith.

The crucial difference between Goethe's early novel, *Die Leiden des jungen Werthers* (1774) and Voss's *Luise* is that the former does not present idyll as an ideal or as a blueprint for future society. In *Luise* in 1784 Voss transfigured earlier patriarchal-feudal structures, where in *Werther* Goethe had depicted the process of self-destruction to which petty absolutism condemned his generation. In this sense *Luise* marks a retrograde step from *Werther*. In *Werther* the idyll is problematic and tragic, where in *Luise* it is transfigured and idealized.

After *Werther*, Goethe was critical of the type of "phantastische Idyllenwelt" created by Voss.[5] He continued the critique of idyll in *Torquato Tasso*, *Iphigenie auf Tauris*, the "Gretchen tragedy" of *Faust I* and finally in the "Philemon und Baucis" episode of *Faust II*. These works focus on the impossibility of idyll in the modern world. In 1794 this theme was formulated in the image of the peasant couple in

---

[3] Gerhard Kaiser, *Klopstock: Religion und Dichtung* (Gütersloh: Gerd Mohn, 1963), 123-203, 327-48.

[4] Voss's family was impoverished by the Seven Years' War, which established Prussia as a military power. Wilhelm Herbst, *Johann Heinrich Voss*, 3 vols. (Leipzig: Teubner, 1872; repr. Bern: Herbert Lang, 1970), 1:29-31.

[5] Böttiger uses this expression in reporting a discussion with Goethe of *Hermann und Dorothea*, Hans Gerhard Gräf, *Goethe über seine Dichtungen: Versuch einer Sammlung aller Äusserungen des Dichters über seine poetischen Werke*, 3 pts. in 9 vols. (Frankfurt am Main, 1901; repr. Darmstadt: Wissenschaftliche Buchgesellschaft, 1968), 1/1:96.

"Das Märchen," whose idyll is both destroyed and recreated in the fairy tale ending.

Works such as *Luise* had offered a comforting image of provincial middle-class life. The problem for Goethe after the Revolution lay in finding a way of maintaining the humanistic functions of the Vossian idyll in the new political and social environment. After the Revolution the Vossian idyll was no longer an appropriate form for the depiction of German middle-class life. To evoke the reality of everyday life in Germany in the aftermath of the French Revolution meant redefining the traditional literary form of the middle classes. Voss's idyll, refunctioned into a critical and ironic form, became the means of representing the problematic constellation of class, literary, cultural and national identity in the immediate post-revolutionary situation in Germany.

### From the Tragic to the Ironic Idyll

Both *Werther* in 1774, and *Hermann und Dorothea* in 1797 introduced important paradigm changes into German narrative literature. Goethe used scientific analogies to describe the genesis of both works. He wrote of *Hermann und Dorothea*: "Ich habe das reine Menschliche der Existenz einer kleinen deutschen Stadt in dem epischen Tiegel von seinen Schlacken abzuscheiden gesucht ..."[6]

A comparable metaphor was used in retrospect for *Werther*. The moment of creation of the work is likened to the instant in which freezing water turns to ice:

> In diesem Augenblick war der Plan zu 'Werthern' gefunden, das Ganze schoß von allen Seiten zusammen und ward eine solide Masse, wie das Wasser im Gefäß, das eben auf dem Punkte des Gefrierens steht, durch die geringste Erschütterung sogleich in ein festes Eis verwandelt wird.[7]

The scientific metaphor in each case expresses the interplay of forces beyond the immediate conscious control of the author: historical and social forces and archetypal human themes of love and identity. In each case a familiar material changes state in reaction to external forces. The freezing water and the breakdown of metals in a crucible are both metaphors expressing change in paradigm. The water-metaphor of *Werther* suggests the formation of a structure from a loose and

---

[6] "In the epic crucible I have tried to separate the purely human aspects of the existence of a small German town from the dross ..." Goethe to Heinrich Meyer, 5 December 1796, W.A. IV, 11, 273.

[7] "At this moment I found the plan for *Werther*. From all sides the whole thing crystallized into a solid mass, just as water in a bucket, when at freezing point, can be immediately changed to firm ice by the slightest shock." H.A. 9:585. Johann Wolfgang von Goethe, *From my Life: Poetry and Truth, Parts One to Three*, ed. Thomas P. Saine and Jeffrey L. Sammons, trans. Robert R. Heitner, vol. 4 of *Goethe's Collected Works* (New York: Suhrkamp, 1987), 430.

formless mass, where the metal-metaphor of *Hermann und Dorothea* indicates the breaking down of received forms.[8]

The irony of *Werther* has been thoroughly documented.[9] While the character Werther falls victim to the narrowness of petty absolutist society, the novel, *Werther*, created a socio-literary profile for German middle-class youth in the 1770s. The achievement of literary form stands in ironic relation to the protagonist's loss of identity.

Georg Lukács pointed out the implicit social critique in *Werther*.[10] However this interpretation should not obscure the idyllic and subjective nature of the work. *Werther* is not a social novel. Class identity and social conflict are implicit in *Werther*, not explicit, and there is no sense of, or even hope for, social change. Goethe himself, looking back at the mid 1770s in *Dichtung und Wahrheit* (*Poetry and Truth*) wrote:

> In dieser Zeit war meine Stellung gegen die oberen Stände sehr günstig. Wenn auch im 'Werther' die Unannehmlichkeiten an der Grenze zweier bestimmter Verhältnisse mit Ungeduld ausgesprochen sind, so ließ man das in Betracht der übrigen Leidenschaftlichkeiten des Buches gelten, indem jedermann wohl fühlte, daß es hier auf keine unmittelbare Wirkung abgesehen sei.[11]

The paradigm change from the tragic idyll of *Werther* to the critical-ironic idyll of *Hermann und Dorothea* can be illustrated through a comparison of Goethe's Rousseauian primitivism of 1772 with the use of idyllic motives in *Werther*. In 1771,

---

[8] In the essay "Der Versuch als Vermittler von Objekt und Subjekt" (1792), H.A. 13:10-20, Goethe discussed questions of objectivity in science, and worked out a dialectical theory of scientific perception. See George A. Wells, *Goethe and the Development of Science 1750-1900* (Alphen aan den Rijn: Sijthoff & Noordhoff, 1978), 130-36; H.B. Nisbet, *Goethe and the Scientific Tradition* (London: Institute of Germanic Studies, University of London, 1972), 23-34; and Erich Heller, "Goethe and the Idea of Scientific Truth," *The Disinherited Mind: Essays in Modern German Literature and Thought* (Harmondsworth: Penguin, 1961), 3-32.

[9] Fritz Brüggemann, *Die Ironie als entwicklungsgeschichtliches Moment: Ein Beitrag zur Vorgeschichte der deutschen Romantik* (Jena, 1909; repr. Darmstadt: Wissenschaftliche Buchgesellschaft, 1976), 39-56; Victor Lange, "Die Sprache als Erzählform in Goethes Werther," in *Formenwandel: Festschrift zum 65. Geburtstag von Paul Böckmann*, ed. Walter Müller-Seidel, and Wolfgang Preisendanz, (Hamburg: Hoffmann und Campe, 1964), 261-72; Anthony Thorlby, "From What Did Goethe Save Himself in *Werther*?" in *Versuche zu Goethe: Festschrift für E. Heller*, ed. Volker Dürr and Geza Molnar (Heidelberg: Lothar Stiehm, 1976), 150-66.

[10] Lukács, *Goethe*, 35-49.

[11] "My position with regard to the upper classes at this time was very favorable. Even though impatience is expressed in *Werther* with the troubles which arise at the boundaries between two distinct classes, this was overlooked in view of the book's generally passionate character, since everyone sensed that no direct attack was intended here." H.A. 10:116.

Joseph von Sonnenfels, a Viennese nobleman and bureaucrat in the service of Maria Theresia, published a pamphlet, *Über die Liebe des Vaterlandes* (*On Love of the Fatherland*), in which he argued that the reforms carried out by the enlightened absolutist Habsburg monarchy should encourage a form of dynastic patriotism.[12] In 1772 Goethe reviewed this pamphlet for the *Göttinger Gelehrte Anzeigen*:

> Wenn wir einen Platz in der Welt finden, da mit unseren Besitztümern zu ruhen, ein Feld, uns zu nähren, ein Haus, uns zu decken, haben wir da nicht ein Vaterland? und haben das nicht tausend und tausende in jedem Staat? und leben sie nicht in dieser Beschränkung glücklich? Wozu nun das vergebene Aufstreben nach einer Empfindung, die wir weder haben können noch mögen, die bei gewissen Völkern, nur zu gewissen Zeitpunkten, das Resultat vieler glücklich zusammentreffender Umstände war und ist? — Römerpatriotismus? Davor bewahre uns Gott wie vor einer Riesengestalt![13]

The idyll is used here as a counter-image to the multi-national Habsburg state with its social, linguistic and ethnic complexities, and implicitly also to the absolutism of Prussia under Friedrich II. However the Promethean primitivism and rebellious contempt for state patriotism could not constitute a long-term answer to the social insecurity of the German middle classes. *Die Leiden des jungen Werthers* revealed the inadequacy of idyll as a solution to the political and class problems of the young intelligentsia in the mid 1770s. Werther's increasingly unbalanced experience of the natural environment in his idyllic "Wahlheim" as "ein ewig verschlingendes, ewig wiederkäuendes Ungeheuer" manifests his frustration at the failure of his idyll to resolve the conflicts he feels in both middle-class and courtly society.[14] His euphoria in "Wahlheim" alternates with suicidal depression. Finally, Werther's idyll is resolved through tragedy.

The milieu of the courts and the "Werther generation" is absent from the idyllic home town of *Hermann und Dorothea*.[15] Yet the themes of individual,

---

[12] Joseph von Sonnenfels, *Über die Liebe des Vaterlandes*, ed. Jörn Garber (Vienna, 1771; Repr. Königstein/Ts.: Scriptor, 1979).

[13] "When we find a place in the world, to rest with our possessions, a field to nourish us, a house to cover our heads, is this not a fatherland? And do not thousands and thousands in every state have this? And do they not live happily in this small world? Why then the vain aspirations to a feeling which we can neither have nor would want, which is the result of many coincidences of fortune for certain peoples at certain times? — Roman patriotism? God protect us from this as from an ogre!" "Joseph von Sonnenfels, Über die Liebe des Vaterlandes," W.A. I, 37, 20.

[14] "am 18. August, 177_," H.A. 6:53. "An all-consuming, devouring monster," Johann Wolfgang von Goethe, *The Sorrows of Young Werther, Elective Affinities, Novella*, trans. Victor Lange and Judith Ryan, ed. David E. Wellbery, vol. 11 of *Goethe's Collected Works* (New York, Suhrkamp, 1988), 37.

[15] Except for the vicar, who had been a tutor (VI, 306-10).

society and national identity are comparable. Hermann, like Werther, opts for idyll as an answer to individual and social problems. *Werther* ended tragically, with the protagonist unable to reconcile the demands of personality with the outside world, and retreating to a self-destructive idyll. In the free home town of *Hermann und Dorothea*, however, the problematic themes are resolved into an apparently idyllic image of Germany. *Hermann und Dorothea* marks the paradigm-change from the tragic to the ironic or critical idyll. The inwardly turned aggression of Werther is turned outward in *Hermann und Dorothea* against the national enemy, the French, and becomes the main motive force in the self-definition of the young German, Hermann.

## Epic, Parody and a German Classical Literature

The town in *Hermann und Dorothea* is a quite different environment to Werther's idealized village of "Wahlheim" or the family enclaves of Voss's idylls. In his article "Wunschbild Land, Schreckbild Stadt," Friedrich Sengle writes that *Hermann und Dorothea* is important because Goethe brings classical, Homeric proportions to the simple, uncomplicated "small world" of the German town.[16] However the problem for Goethe was not to show that epic themes and middle-class life were not incompatible. Voss and other middle-class writers had made this progressive, humanistic step in the 1770s. Rather it was to distance the image of everyday reality in a small German town in such a way as to both avoid the Vossian oversimplification of complex relationships, and to achieve a comprehensiveness in depiction of the social spectrum of a developing German town on the edge of the revolutionary arena.

In 1795 Goethe wrote the essay, "Literarischer Sanskulottismus," in response to the article, "Über Prose und Beredsamkeit der Deutschen," by Daniel Jenisch (1762-1804), the critic and author of the national epic, *Borussias* (1794). Jenisch had criticized German writers for not having produced a German classical literature. Goethe responded:

> Aber auch der deutschen Nation darf es nicht zum Vorwurfe gereichen, daß ihre geographische Lage sie eng zusammenhält, indem ihre politische sie zerstückelt. Wir wollen die Umwälzungen nicht wünschen, die in Deutschland klassische Werke vorbereiten könnten.[17]

---

[16] Sengle, "Wunschbild Land," 441.

[17] "We cannot criticize the German nation because it is politically splintered despite its representing a geographic unit. We do not wish for the political turmoil that would pave the way for classical works in Germany." H.A. 12:241. Johann Wolfgang von Goethe, "Thoughts of a Literary Rabble-Rouser," *Essays on Art and Literature*, ed. John Gearey, trans. Ellen von Nardroff and Ernst von Nardroff, vol. 3 of *Goethe's Collected Works* (New York: Suhrkamp, 1986), 190.

In "Literarischer Sanskulottismus," written less than two years before *Hermann und Dorothea*, Goethe identified the foundations for national literatures such as those of France and England in terms of cohesive geographical, historical, political, sociocultural and linguistic identities. In Germany these factors were either missing, or undermined one another. Goethe explicitly rejected the possibility or the desirability of the type of national, classical literature for Germany in the mid 1790s, that Sengle finds in the epic form of *Hermann und Dorothea*.

Goethe wrote the first version of *Hermann und Dorothea* quickly between October and December of 1796 as a long idyll. In December 1796 he wrote to Heinrich Meyer:

> ich habe die Kühnheit meines Unternehmens nicht eher wahrgenommen, als bis das Schwerste schon überstanden war. In Absicht auf die poetische sowohl als prosodische Organisation des Ganzen habe ich beständig vor Augen gehabt, was in diesen letzten Zeiten bei Gelegenheit der Vossischen Arbeiten mehrmals zur Sprache gekommen ist ...[18]

During the second phase of composition in the first half of 1797, Goethe's conception of the work changed significantly. At this stage he added Dorothea's remembrance of her first fiancé (IX, 256-290) and Hermann's final speech, recast the original six cantos into nine, and gave each a thematic heading as well as the name of one of the nine Muses of classical literature and mythology.[19] During this period as well, Goethe studied Voss's revised *Luise* of 1795, and discussed with Schiller questions of idyllic and epic form in *Hermann und Dorothea* and *Wilhelm Meisters Lehrjahre*.

One of the main interpretative problems of *Hermann und Dorothea* has been to explain the relevance of the classical canto headings to the work as a whole. There is no clear thematic relationship. Generically, however, these headings establish a relationship with a literary form which had been popular earlier in the century, the mock-epic. Goethe's comments regarding the "Episierung der Idylle," and his inconsistent use of generic terms for *Hermann und Dorothea* suggest the relevance of this form.[20] In England the mock-epic had been used by middle-class writers such as Samuel Butler and Alexander Pope as a satirical political weapon. From the 1740s until the 1780s in Germany, the works of Thümmel, Zachariä and

---

[18] "I did not realize the audacity of my undertaking until after the hardest part was completed. As regards the poetic as well as the prosodic organization of the whole, I continually was aware of that which has several times recently become a topic of discussion in the context of Voss's works ..." Goethe to Heinrich Meyer, 5 December 1796, W.A. IV, 11, 273.

[19] Hermann Schreyer, "Goethes Arbeit an 'Hermann und Dorothea,'" *Goethe-Jahrbuch* 10 (1889): 205; Heinz Helmerking, *"Hermann und Dorothea": Entstehung, Ruhm und Wesen*, (Zurich: Artemis, 1948), 10-25.

[20] He used terms such as "bürgerliche Idylle," "Idylle," "idyllisches Epos," and "das epische Gedicht," see ch. 5, fn. 22.

Wieland had focused on the disparities between social, literary and intellectual life. In Germany the mock-epic was less openly political, and functioned primarily as a means of self-irony of the intelligentsia (Zachariä, Wieland) and/or the nobility (Thümmel). The mock-epic culminated with Wieland's *Oberon* (1780) in verse, and was reformed into the prose idyll by Jean Paul in the 1790s.

*Hermann und Dorothea* is a richer and more complex text than works such as Thümmel's *Wilhelmine* or Wieland's *Oberon*. But the mock-epic conventions of the canto headings and the ironically playful, rococo interpolations are closer in style to Wieland than to Homer, and owe their origin to the German mock-epic of the early to mid eighteenth century. Using the parodic conventions of mock-epic, Goethe refunctions his idyllic-epic model, Voss's *Luise*.[21] The resulting work is certainly serious in intention, but is not the German national epic that Jenisch had demanded. Through his parody of Voss, Goethe registers his indebtedness to the Vossian idyll which locates human values with the middle classes in *Luise*, and the peasantry in poems such as "Die Freigelassenen" ("The Freedmen"). At the same time however, he rejects aspects of the Vossian idyll, in particular its artificial closure to the larger world of society, politics and national change.

Margaret Rose describes literary parody as a form of irony, in which multiple meanings are implied through the use of verbal markers undercutting the apparent meaning of any given text.[22] The quotation of an established form or characteristic in a new context can be used as a verbal marker to create parodic ambivalence. By quoting a "pre-formed" text, an author refunctions or re-creates it at a new level in a new relationship for the reader. Parody in *Hermann und Dorothea* is a "mode of ambivalence," a means of diversifying perspectives. Through parody Goethe brings into the literary work complexities of social and national development in the light of the French Revolution. In a period of social instability and upheaval, when the relationships between states, nations and regions, and ethnic and cultural identities were changing in unforeseeable ways, parody functioned as a modern, multi-facetted and open form of literary discourse. Parody in this case both "criticizes" and sublates a pre-existing form, reworking the "traditional" into the "new."

*Werther* was written at a time when the concept of a German national identity hearkened back to an idealized feudal past (the Holy Roman Empire) with few surviving bases in contemporary geographical, social or political structures. Twenty-three years after *Werther*, a new German identity was beginning to be formulated in response to external political events, but still in politically and culturally vague terms. *Hermann und Dorothea* represents the changes for two generations in a small German town which is outgrowing its village origins, on the economically prosperous right bank of the Rhine. While the intelligentsia who had

---

[21] Cf. Frank G. Ryder and Benjamin Bennett, "The Irony of Goethe's *Hermann und Dorothea*: Its Form and Function," *PMLA* 90 (1975): 433-46.

[22] Rose, 51.

dominated thinking about German nationality and identity since the mid century are not central to this work, questions of national identity are.

The home town, the idyllic environment of the German middle classes, is seen in the context of the internal changes in German society, and the external changes in European politics at the time of the Coalition Wars. The conflicts which in *Werther* are expressed in terms of a tragic subjectivity are seen in a social perspective in *Hermann und Dorothea*. The questions of homeland and social and national identity, which are implicit in *Werther* as particularly the problems of a young middle-class intellectual, appear in *Hermann und Dorothea* in broader terms, provoked by the revolutionary wars and the redefinition of national identity in France.

In "Literarischer Sanskulottismus" Goethe rejected the possibility of a classical national literature comparable to that of England or France. The use of mock-epic conventions in *Hermann und Dorothea* suggests that the German home town is not the setting for the first classical epic in German literature. Where the absolutist-rococo poets and Wieland had incorporated playful, erotic themes into the idyll, and Voss had created an idealized middle-class fiction, Goethe ironically and parodically refunctions the conventions and themes of the European idyll: the *locus amoenus* and the *locus terribilis*, the sense of belonging to and identification with a familiar environment against expatriation and alienation in a foreign world, categories of innocence and experience, of the small world and the large world, of stasis and change. Daniel Jenisch had demanded from his contemporary writers a blueprint of "Germanness" in a classical epic of the German nation. Against this expectation that German writers should be affirmative and authoritative rather than critical and ambivalent, Goethe wrote the ironic "idyllic epic" or "epic idyll" of German identity at a crucial turning-point in modern German intellectual history.

# 2: Prosperity and Progress in the Home Town

### Idyllic Perspectives: The Innkeeper and the Apothecary

INTERPRETERS HAVE ASSUMED THAT the home town is presented as a German idyll against the image of revolutionary upheaval in Paris and the occupied territories.[1] However this interpretation ignores ironic, parodic and structural aspects throughout the text. The juxtaposition of differing points of view on characters and events, for example, is a central structural feature. Hermann is discussed at length by his father and the neighbors before he appears. Likewise the judge speaks about Dorothea before she speaks for herself. The history of the town and the story of the fire too are described from multiple perspectives.

*Hermann und Dorothea* opens with Hermann's father and mother sitting in front of their inn, as the townspeople return home from watching the refugees passing by the outskirts of the town. Located in south-western Germany, probably near the triangle marked by Frankfurt, Strasbourg and Mannheim, the town is characterized as independent, middle-class and prosperous. Close to the Rhine, with a mild climate and the promise of good harvests (I, 50), it enjoys the blessings of nature and geographical position. Its prosperity (I, 53-58) springs from the network of commerce and trade with other German towns and beyond the Rhine (I, 190-95). Self government is understood as town planning and administration — the building of roads, canals, drainage systems and the town hall — not battles over revolutionary ideology and socio-economic and political policies as in France (III, 3-39).

Against the refugees' experiences of flight, lack of food and shelter, illness and social turmoil (fleeing the revolutionary armies in August 1796), the German home town is built up as a counter-image of peace, order and social harmony. It is seen predominantly through the eyes of Hermann's father, the innkeeper:

'Möcht' ich mich doch nicht rühren vom Platz, um zu sehen das Elend
Guter fliehender Menschen, die nun, mit geretteter Habe,
Leider das überrheinische Land, das schöne, verlassend,

---

[1] H.A. Korff, "Ordnung und Umsturz: Hermann und Dorothea," *Geist der Goethezeit*, 4 vols. (1923-1955; repr. Leipzig: Koehler & Amelang, 1979), 2:341-52; Emil Staiger, *Goethe*, 3 vols. (Zurich: Atlantis, 1956), 2:253; Dieter Borchmeyer, "Weimar im Zeitalter der Revolution und der Napoleonischen Kriege: Aspekte bürgerlicher Klassik," *Geschichte der deutschen Literatur vom 18. Jahrhundert bis zur Gegenwart*, ed. Viktor Zmegac, 3 vols. (Königstein/Ts.: Athenäum, 1979), 1/2:10; and Schulz, 327.

Zu uns herüberkommen und durch den glücklichen Winkel
Dieses fruchtbaren Tals und seiner Krümmungen wandern.
Trefflich hast du gehandelt, O Frau, daß du milde den Sohn fort
Schicktest mit altem Linnen und etwas Essen und Trinken,
Um es den Armen zu spenden; denn Geben ist Sache des Reichen.'

(I, 8-15)[2]

However while the town is described as an idyllic spot, the opening image is strangely negative, with its association of death and cleanliness:

'Hab' ich den Markt und die Straßen doch nie so einsam gesehen!
Ist doch die Stadt wie gekehrt! wie ausgestorben!'

(I, 1-2)[3]

The refugees outside the town boundaries provoke a feeling of unease in the innkeeper which drives him repeatedly to seek comfort in the material safety and the quality of life of the town, to which he has contributed so greatly:

Und es sagte darauf gerührt der menschliche Hauswirt:
'Möge doch Hermann sie treffen und sie erquicken und kleiden!
Ungern würd' ich sie sehn; mich schmerzt der Anblick des Jammers.
Schon von dem ersten Bericht so großer Leiden gerühret,
Schickten wir eilend ein Scherflein von unserm Überfluß, daß nur
Einige würden gestärkt, und schienen uns selber beruhigt.
Aber laßt uns nicht mehr die traurigen Bilder erneuern!
Denn es beschleichet die Furcht gar bald die Herzen der Menschen
Und die Sorge, die mehr als selbst mir das Übel verhaßt ist.'

(I, 151-59)[4]

---

[2] "'I'd not make such a trip myself, just to gaze at the hardships / of those fugitive people from west of the Rhine. What a fine land / They had to leave! and now, with the goods and chattels they salvaged, / They've come over to us and are finding a fortunate refuge, / Trekking slowly along through our fertile meandering valley. / You did a generous deed, my good wife, in sending our son out / With those piles of old linen and food and drink to relieve them, / Poor good souls, in their plight; it's up to rich people to give things.'"

[3] "'Look how empty the marketplace is, and the streets! It's the first time / I've seen this. The whole town's swept clear! Have our fellow townsfolk / All dropped dead?'"

[4] "And the kindly landlord was touched, and spoke thus in answer: / 'Let us hope Hermann will find them and give them some clothes and refreshment. / I shouldn't care to see them, the sight of such misery upsets me. / We were already so touched by the first reports of their suffering / That from our own abundance we quickly sent off a small trifle, / Hoping that it would at least help some, and that comforted our minds. / But let us not now dwell any more on these sad recollections! / Fear and anxiety only too easily creep into men's hearts; / And to be anxious, that's something I hate more than actual trouble.'"

The innkeeper allays the sense of unease aroused by the refugees by retreating from the summer heat and the reminders of personal misery and political strife to the coolness of his parlor, where he can share a glass of wine with his friends:

'Tretet herein in den hinteren Raum, das kühlere Sälchen!
Nie scheint Sonne dahin, nie dringet wärmere Luft dort
Durch die stärkeren Mauern; und Mütterchen bringt uns ein Gläschen
Dreiundachtziger her, damit wir die Grillen vertreiben.
Hier ist nicht freundlich zu trinken; die Fliegen umsummen die Gläser.'
Und sie gingen dahin und freuten sich alle der Kühlung.
Sorgsam brachte die Mutter des klaren, herrlichen Weines
In geschliffener Flasche auf blankem, zinnernem Runde,
Mit den grünlichen Römern, den echten Bechern des Rheinweins.
Und so sitzend, umgaben die drei den glänzend gebohnten,
Runden, braunen Tisch, er stand auf mächtigen Füßen.

(I, 160-70)[5]

The innkeeper's preoccupations are underscored by the elevated and artificial language of the narrative commentary (I, 165-70). Everything is solid, tangible and comforting. Each noun is loaded with homely adjectives. The wine, the decanter, the tray, even the goblets — in a line which has become one of the more famous pieces of German literary kitsch — are overloaded with local detail. Likewise the table becomes an argument for unadorned simplicity with no ornamentation to undermine its solid values. The use of adjectives in the comparative form ("das kühlere Sälchen," "die wärmere Luft," etc.) suggests the innkeeper's need for confirmation of values and sense of order. The diminutives ("Mütterchen," "Gläschen"), the reference back to pre-revolutionary times ("ein Gläschen / Dreiundachtziger") and the repetition of images of motherly protection ("Mütterchen," "Sorgsam brachte die Mutter...") are psychological barriers against the misery, political upheaval and civil disturbance, which the apothecary has made all too real in his long description of the refugees (I, 102-50).

The apothecary's outlook is the very opposite of the innkeeper's. Having just returned from the refugee camp, he dwells on the details of misery and chaos to the same extreme as the innkeeper avoided them. Where the innkeeper submerges his anxieties in the comforts of home- and town-life, the apothecary tells of the

---

[5] "'Let's go through to the back! We'll be cooler in our little parlor, / It's quite out of the sun, and the warm air never gets through those / Thick strong walls; and my dear little wife will bring us a glass now / Of that '83 vintage, to put us back into a good mood. / It's disagreeable drinking out here, the flies buzz round the glasses.' / So they went into the house, and they all were glad of the coolness. / Now with care his good wife brought the clear, magnificent wine out, / In a decanter of fine cut glass, on a round tray of gleaming / Pewter, and with it the rummers, the true green goblets for Rhine wine. / So the three of them sat, at the polished glistening table: / Round and brown it was, and its legs were powerful and solid."

refugees' predicament as if it were his own, and compares their situation to that of the townspeople twenty years before, when the town was destroyed by fire.

The innkeeper in the time of crisis had encouraged self-help in the community in order to rebuild the town. The apothecary can see nothing beyond the hopelessness of the individual. Where others see acts of goodness, altruism or community feeling, he sees only selfishness and opportunism:

'Und so lag zerbrochen der Wagen und hülflos die Menschen;
Denn die übrigen gingen und zogen eilig vorüber,
Nur sich selber bedenkend und hingerissen vom Strome.'

(I, 144-46)[6]

Where the innkeeper represses his fear that the revolutionary upheavals may affect him and his home town, the apothecary's anxiety drives him to pre-empt the crisis:

da nahm der gesprächige Nachbar
Gleich das Wort und rief: 'O glücklich, wer in den Tagen
Dieser Flucht und Verwirrung in seinem Haus nur allein lebt,
Wem nicht Frau und Kinder zur Seite bange sich schmiegen!
Glücklich fühl' ich mich jetzt; ich möcht' um vieles nicht heute
Vater heißen und nicht für Frau und Kinder besorgt sein.
Öfters dacht' ich mir auch schon die Flucht und habe die besten
Sachen zusammengepackt, das alte Geld und die Ketten
Meiner seligen Mutter, das alles noch heilig verwahrt liegt.'

(II, 82-90)[7]

Fear of change has killed all incentive and desire. He cannot contemplate marriage, having a family, or even maintaining his shop for fear of having to cope with change, upheaval or misfortune:

'Und doch waren die unsern gleich nach dem Brande die schönsten,
Die Apotheke zum Engel so wie der Goldene Löwe.
So war mein Garten auch in der ganzen Gegend berühmt, und
Jeder Reisende stand und sah durch die roten Staketen

---

[6] "'There they lay, then, the cart all smashed and the passengers helpless; / For the others went by and hurried past without stopping, / Only considering themselves, and swept along by the mainstream.'"

[7] "their talkative neighbor / Spoke at once and exclaimed: 'Oh happy the man who in these days / Of confusion and exile lives quite by himself in his own house / With no wife and no children to cling in alarm to his coat-tails! / I feel now that I'm lucky; it would be quite hard to persuade me / To be a father and have the worry of wife and of children. / I've often thought myself I might pack up and leave, and already / I've put together the things I value — my savings, the gold chains / That used to be my late mother's, all safely preserved as old relics.'"

Nach den Bettlern von Stein und nach den farbigen Zwergen.
...
Neulich kam mir's in Sinn, den Engel Michael wieder,
Der mir die Offizin bezeichnet, vergolden zu lassen,
Und den greulichen Drachen, der ihm zu Füßen sich windet;
Aber ich ließ ihn verbräunt, wie er ist; mich schreckte die Fordrung.'
(III, 85-89, 107-10)[8]

This is in stark contrast to the innkeeper who repeatedly stresses the need for maintenance and aesthetic improvement of the town. The apothecary's experience widens the picture of the town presented otherwise predominantly through the eyes of the innkeeper. The latter's idealization of the town as a *Gemeinschaft* is shown to be personal and selective, the response to a traumatic past.

### Internal Crisis and Social Change

The fire which destroyed the town twenty years earlier is central to the theme of crisis and social change in this work. It is mentioned six times — each time in relation to the refugees.[9] The story of the fire is first told by Hermann's mother. It had begun on a warm Sunday in summer, a similar day to that of the action, when most of the town's inhabitants were out in the countryside. It broke out on the edge of the town (II, 117) and destroyed almost everything. The aftermath of the fire was terrible, with houses and animals incinerated. However amid the misery, the mother also remembers the joy of her engagement to the innkeeper, and later, the birth of Hermann:

'Denn mir gab der Tag den Gemahl, es haben die ersten

---

[8] "'All the same, our two houses, the Angel Pharmacy and the / Golden Lion, just after the fire, our two were the finest; / And what's more, my garden was famous all over the district; / Every traveller who came here would stand outside the red railings / Peering in at my colored dwarfs and my little stone beggars ... It did occur to me lately I might have the archangel Michael, / Since he's the trade-sign over my shop, regilded, and that fierce / Dragon that writhes around at his feet; but I left him all brown with / Age as he is, the bill for the work would have been so enormous.'"

[9] I, 121, 176ff.; II, 109ff.; III 32, 85; V, 107. On the symbolism of the fire, see Robert Leroux, "La Révolution française dans *Hermann et Dorothée*," *Etudes Germaniques* 4 (1949): 180; Oskar Seidlin, "Über *Hermann und Dorothea*: Ein Vortrag," *Lebendige Form: Interpretationen zur deutschen Literatur, Festschrift Heinrich E. K. Henel*, ed. Jeffrey Sammons and Ernst Schürer (Munich: Fink, 1970), 102; and Dieter Borchmeyer, *Höfische Gesellschaft und französische Revolution bei Goethe: Adliges und bürgerliches Wertsystem im Urteil der Weimarer Klassik* (Kronberg/Ts.: Athenäum, 1977), 336.

Zeiten der wilden Zerstörung den Sohn mir der Jugend gegeben.'

(II, 153-54)[10]

Even Hermann echoes his mother's thoughts later, when, justifying his intention to bring home a refugee girl as his bride, he says to his father:

'Sollte nicht auch ein Glück aus diesem Unglück hervorgehn
Und ich, im Arme der Braut, der zuverlässigen Gattin,
Mich nicht erfreuen des Kriegs, so wie Ihr des Brandes Euch freutet?'

(V, 105-7)[11]

The parson quickly incorporates the bad memories into his enlightened belief in Providence:

Heiter sagte darauf der treffliche Pfarrer und milde:
'Haltet am Glauben fest und fest an dieser Gesinnung;
Denn sie macht im Glücke verständig und sicher, im Unglück
Reicht sie den schönsten Trost und belebt die herrlichste Hoffnung.'

(I, 185-88)[12]

That some good came of the crisis is clear in hindsight to all of the characters, except of course the apothecary who remembers nothing but the panic and loss:

'Ach! und es nimmt die Gefahr, wie wir beim Brande vor zwanzig
Jahren auch wohl gesehn, dem Menschen alle Besinnung,
Daß er das Unbedeutende faßt und das Teure zurückläßt.'

(I, 121-123)[13]

But the dialectic of destruction and progress is clearest in the words of the innkeeper:

---

[10] "'For it was that day gave me my husband, and those early times of / Wild desolation that brought me the son of my youth to rejoice in.'"

[11] "'May not some happiness too, some good fortune be born of misfortune, / And why should I, in the arms of a bride, of a good faithful wife, not / Come to feel glad of this war, just as you were glad of that fire once?'"

[12] "And with a smile the excellent parson kindly made answer: / 'Hold on fast to that faith, and hold fast to that way of thinking! / For in good fortune it makes us wise and secure, and in bad times / Gives to our hearts the revival of hope and a sweet consolation.'"

[13] "'And, dear me, the same thing is true as we saw in the great fire / Twenty years back: that in panic one loses all sense of proportion, / Snatching at worthless things, leaving objects of value behind one.'"

'Sollt' er [i.e. God] die blühende Stadt, die er erst durch fleißige Bürger
Neu aus der Asche gebaut und dann sie reichlich gesegnet,
Jetzo wieder zerstören und alle Bemühung vernichten?'

(I, 182-84)[14]

The fire brought with it the opportunity to lead the town to a greater prosperity than ever, and to achieve influence and social status.

'Rühmt nicht jeder das Pflaster, die wasserreichen, verdeckten,
Wohlverteilten Kanäle, die Nutzen und Sicherheit bringen,
Daß dem Feuer sogleich beim ersten Ausbruch gewehrt sei?
Ist das nicht alles geschehn seit jenem schrecklichen Brande?
Bauherr war ich sechsmal im Rat und habe mir Beifall,
Habe mir herzlichen Dank von guten Bürgern verdienet,'

(III, 29-34)[15]

H.A. Korff identified a liberal, moderately progressive trend in the innkeeper.[16] However his use of these terms must be put into context. The innkeeper's outlook cannot be seen in terms of English bourgeois liberalism, or the moderate liberalism of the German middle classes after 1848. The home town in *Hermann und Dorothea* is still pre-industrial, despite its many workshops ("Fabriken," I, 58) and its trading and commercial links with the surrounding countries (III, 23-24).[17]

Korff bases his interpretation on the innkeeper's angry rebuke to Hermann for refusing to take an interest in community affairs:

'Einmal für allemal gilt das wahre Sprüchlein der Alten:

---

[14] "'Why, having only just raised this town from its ashes, rebuilt it / By its good citizens' labours and then abundantly blessed it, / Should he [God] destroy it again and bring all our efforts to nothing?'"

[15] "'Are not our cobblestones widely admired, and our paved-over conduits, / Well laid out for safety and use and full of good water / Ready at once if ever another fire should break out? / Hasn't all this been done since that terrible fire that we had here? / I've six times been in charge of the works when I sat on the council, / And been applauded and heartily thanked by our good fellow-townsfolk;'"

[16] "Ein leicht-liberaler, gemäßigt-fortschrittlicher Zug, der merkwürdigerweise dem Vater eigen ist." Korff, 2:372.

[17] On the theme of economic change in the town, cf. Maria Lypp, "Bürger und Weltbürger in Goethes *Hermann und Dorothea*," *Goethe: Neue Folge des Jahrbuchs der Goethe-Gesellschaft* 31 (1969): 131, and T. M. Holmes, "Goethe's *Hermann und Dorothea*: The Dissolution of the Embattled Idyll," *Modern Language Review* 82 (1987): 113f.

Wer nicht vorwärts geht, der kommt zurücke! So bleibt es.'

(III, 65-66)[18]

The reference to the ancestors puts a different cast on Korff's recognition of liberal and progressive qualities in the innkeeper. In the proverb is preserved the collective memory of a community attitude to the civic environment, which is far removed from (English) liberal capitalism. The innkeeper's civic consciousness is reminiscent of one of Wickram's sixteenth-century merchants in *Von guten und boesen Nachbaurn*, rather than of a citizen of eighteenth-century London or Paris. He embodies a typically Protestant outlook, he trusts Providence to help those who help themselves (I, 196-97), and he expresses local patriotism (i.e. love of his home town, the Rhineland countryside, and local culture) rather than any incipient "nationalism." In his devotion to the betterment of the town he combines entrepreneurial skill with community spirit. In his envy of his rich neighbor, and in the apothecary's reference to the splendor of the houses "am Markt," there is even an indication that his enthusiasm for rebuilding and bettering the town has not always been simply to his own advantage.

The fire certainly made a type of progress possible which could not have been achieved otherwise. But at the same time it had a traumatic effect, and it symbolizes a force of destruction which can strike at any time. In his rebuilding program, the innkeeper has erected a protective barrier of safety, order and cleanliness against the outside world of hazard, chance and fate. The canals, the safety precautions, the clean roads and the functional layout of the town are also protection against the fear of recurrence of destruction and chaos. The fear of renewed destruction and the experience of hardship and starting over are part of the history of the new town. What Korff calls the liberal, moderately progressive trend in the innkeeper's personality is the product of a history in which *Ordnung* (order), self-help and community support have been necessary for survival.

Goethe's title for the first canto, "Schicksal und Anteil" indicates the dynamic nature of the town as a social structure. The dialectic of "Schicksal" ("fate") and "Anteil" ("contribution," "inheritance") is the dialectic of individual personality and the communal institutions of the town as a political, social and cultural system. Communal institutions here include language, culture (i.e. local culture as against the Viennese "high-culture" of Mozart's *Magic Flute*, II, 220ff.), social structure and administrative organization, the physical infrastructure and the collectively remembered history of the town. Individuals are represented in terms of socio-economic relationships in the community — to the extent that of all the characters in the work, only Hermann and Dorothea are given names rather than descriptive titles. (The mother's name "Lieschen," is used once by the father, II, 140.)

The ambiguity of "Schicksal" and "Anteil" is manifested in the different reactions which the presence of the refugees and the memory of the fire produce

---

[18] "'That was a true word, once and for all, that our ancestors taught me: / 'He who does not press forward, falls back!' That's the fact of the matter.'"

Prosperity and Progress in the Home Town                                    31

in the three members of the older generation. The fire stimulates the innkeeper to rebuild the town along improved and modernized lines as a safeguard against future crisis. For the apothecary it reinforces a traumatic link between activity, progress and death, sown early in life by a dour, pious father (IX, 15-45). And for Hermann's mother its memory is mitigated by the events which it indirectly brought about, marriage and the birth of her son.

The date of the action of *Hermann und Dorothea* was identified by Goethe as late August 1796.[19] However the location has a symbolic importance for all of the German territories.[20] In the final decade of the eighteenth century, the German territories were beginning to surpass the levels of population of the period immediately before the Thirty Years' War.[21] This relative growth of population and prosperity is mirrored in the history of the town in *Hermann und Dorothea*. Neither a bourgeoisie nor a laboring class has formed, although the beginnings of class-formations are implied in the innkeeper's comments about workshops and workers (I, 57-58). On the periphery of European affairs, with little political or strategic significance, and with good conditions for agriculture to maintain a level of provincial wealth and demographic stability, it has remained a home town. The relationship with the hinterland, the pre-industrial social relationships, and the semi-autonomous nature of town life reveal its roots in the village community.

When the French adopted policies of revolutionary liberation of neighboring lands, the western border of Germany, along with the Netherlands, became strategically vital again for the first time since the Reformation. From 1792 onward this area was the fault-line between western and eastern Europe, between the newly formed modern nation-state and the remnants of European petty absolutism, between capitalism and feudalism, and between concepts of enlightenment as revolutionary democracy and as absolutist despotism.

The innkeeper is mistaken in thinking that he can rebuild and restore the town within a political vacuum. The town's moderate prosperity and measured progressiveness are the result of its geography, its climate and its peripheral location in terms of European development since the fifteenth century. With the change in the political relations of Europe after the French Revolution, the town

---

[19] Goethe to Heinrich Meyer, 5 December 1796, Gräf, 1/1:91.

[20] Pressed by Eckermann to reveal the precise location and date of the story, Goethe answered: "Da wollen Sie wissen, welche Stadt am Rhein bei meinem 'Hermann und Dorothea' gemeint sei. Als ob es nicht besser wäre, sich jede beliebige zu denken! Man will Wahrheit, man will Wirklichkeit und verdirbt dadurch die Poesie." Gräf, 1/1:194-95.

[21] Kiesel and Münch, 13-42; Hermann Aubin and Wolfgang Zorn, eds., *Handbuch der deutschen Wirtschafts- und Sozialgeschichte* (Stuttgart: Union Verlag, 1971), 507-14, 531-36; Carlo M. Cipolla, ed., *The Industrial Revolution 1700-1914*, vol. 3 of *Fontana Economic History of Europe* (Brighton: Harvester, 1976), 33-34; G.R. Potter, ed., *The American and French Revolutions 1763-1793*, vol. 8 of *The New Cambridge Modern History* (Cambridge: Cambridge University Press, 1976), 563.

has suddenly been shifted from the periphery towards the center, with the Rhine becoming the line of demarcation for the French nation-state.[22]

Furthermore, urban growth and provincial prosperity have enlarged the town beyond the limits of a village community. There is a new rich elite with their ostentatious houses, who have developed commercial and cultural links with France (I, 56) and Vienna (II, 221ff). The innkeeper wants Hermann to marry into this new rich class. And even the innkeeper's own plans for civic improvement are beginning to reach out beyond the semi-autonomous unity of town and hinterland. With prosperity has come the financial means for more wide ranging enterprises:

'Alle bestreben sich jetzt, und schon ist der neue Chausseebau
Fest beschlossen, der uns mit der großen Straße verbindet.
Aber ich fürchte nur sehr, so wird die Jugend nicht handeln!'

(III, 38-40)[23]

A main road linking the smaller roads leading out of the town to the highway will generate expansion beyond the "idyllic" boundaries of the town, creating an economic network which must ultimately accelerate internal urban development. Ironically, it is on the new highway that Hermann meets Dorothea after his mother had taken so long to pack food and clothing for the refugees (II, 21-22). The innkeeper sees the positive aspect of this development, the expansion of trade, commerce and wealth. He is only vaguely aware of a negative aspect, the loss of the traditional community.

The rebuilding of the town was a response to an internal crisis. Following the old plans, rebuilding what had survived, with a modernized infrastructure, the restoration of the town was an expression of reform conservatism, of modernization within traditional community structures. The crisis which strikes the next generation, Hermann's generation, whose early lives were formed before the Revolution, but whose adult lives will be lived out after it, is external in origin. It cannot be prevented by the internal precautions of which Hermann's father is so proud. Indeed traditional forms may not even be able to comprehend the coming crisis.

---

[22] The question of the Rhine as the "natural" German border became important after 1792. The Mainz revolutionaries envisaged the creation of a "links-rheinische Republik" ("left-bank" Rhine Republic). For left-bank territories such as Alsace, which had a history of interchange between French and German rulers, the boundaries where "French" ended and "German" began were not clear-cut in the eighteenth century (cf. Dorothea, VIII, 40f.). The refugees from the left-bank fled the Revolution, not necessarily the French, as both the judge and Dorothea state (VI, 4ff. and VIII, 40ff.). The French advance through the left-bank territories did not stir opinion in Germany in the way that the crossing of the Rhine, the symbolic boundary, did.

[23] "'Now they're all working on them, and already there's formal approval / For the construction of our new road between here and the highway. / But I'm afraid our example is lost on the young generation!'"

The innkeeper's roles as businessman, community leader and paterfamilias overlap but do not conflict. For his son, Hermann, however, self-definition and social change in the home town have become problematic. This internal conflict is brought into the open by the crisis of the Revolution, sending waves of German refugees out of their homelands. In the wake of this, Hermann's home town consciousness is disrupted, and a new consciousness begins to form in its place.

## Social Relationships and Individual Self-Perception

The innkeeper's cotton dressing-gown, which is given away to the refugees, becomes a symbol of changing social relationships. Mentioned eight times in the work, it is a *Leitmotif* of themes of social change, presentation of self and personal integrity.[24] Passing from Hermann's father to the mother of the newborn child, and becoming the warm wrapper which preserves the life of the child, (VII, 155, 166), it symbolizes human needs and priorities. In canto one the mother reveals that she has given away the dressing-gown without telling her husband. He regrets the loss of a favorite article of clothing, and the change in social mores associated with it. But he is not upset, and he dismisses his fondness for past patterns of personal and social interaction as nostalgia:

Aber es lächelte drauf der treffliche Hauswirt und sagte:
'Ungern vermiss' ich ihn doch, den alten kattunenen Schlafrock
Echt ostindischen Stoffs; so etwas kriegt man nicht wieder.
Wohl! ich trug ihn nicht mehr. Man will jetzt freilich, der Mann soll
Immer gehn im Surtout und in der Pekesche sich zeigen,
Immer gestiefelt sein; verbannt ist Pantoffel und Mütze.'

(I, 32-37)[25]

Changes in fashion reflect changing social relationships. The undifferentiated presentation of the private and the public self in the *Gemeinschaft* (slippers and nightcap) is displaced by formal fashions, appropriate for interpersonal interaction within the more developed social structure (*Gesellschaft*), the vest and topcoat of the prosperous *Bürger* and town-councillor. The old *Gemeinschaft* forms of self-presentation have been banned by mutual consent from the public to the private sphere. The father's nostalgia is compensated by the advantages of the modernized town. To him changes in fashion signify social change and progress, but not disruption. He can present both a "town" and a "home" self. He makes the best of the fact that his dressing-gown has already been given away, and can justify to

---

[24] I, 29ff.; II, 48, 55; IV, 67; VI, 133, 175; VII, 157, 166.

[25] "But the excellent landlord smiled at her words, and he answered: / 'It was a fine old gown all the same, and I'm sorry to lose it. / Best East Indian cotton! You can't get that sort of thing now. / Well I had given up using it. After all, men are expected / These days always to wear a top-coat, and a fur-braided tunic, / And a good pair of boots; no slippers and nightcap allowed now.'"

himself that he has helped the refugee woman and her newborn child. At the same time he recognizes that the gown was no longer of any use since town life now demands forms of clothing which will differentiate social roles and status in the more complex society.

Hermann, not his father, bears the full force of these changes. The two episodes which Hermann retells from his past focus on this theme: his early fights with the children of the neighborhood over his father's old fashioned attitude to clothing and public appearance (his old habit of appearing in public in his dressing-gown, IV, 162-72), and his later objection to the false values and snobbery of the rich neighbor (II, 210-37). In both episodes clothing represents forms of, and changes in, personal behavior, presentation of self, and social relationships.

Change is thus not merely seen to originate from "outside," from the Revolution. Conflicts arise as a result of the internal development of the home town community beyond its traditional limits. The home town is not presented as a static, idyllic German community and it is not simply threatened from outside by a problematic and changing world. The motive forces of socio-economic change and human nature are simultaneously changing it from within. History operates both in the greater and the smaller worlds.

So far the town has figured as the sphere of the father, of the prosperous innkeeper and landowner. However there is a tension between the innkeeper's home town consciousness and the economic and social growth of the town, to which he has contributed. The new highway will be both the means for economic development and the road by which future refugees — and armies — may make their way towards the town. The innkeeper protects himself from the unwanted aspects of this progress with the material and psychological comforts of his house, his cellar, the solid furniture and the reassurance that he has done his best to make the town safe and politically stable. However his conviction that civic stability is the product of good administration, trade and traditional values has been shaken by the refugees, Germans like himself, who have been forced from their homes by the Revolution.

For the innkeeper, warfare and small town commercialism are contingent but unrelated. Wars are fought by press-ganged or mercenary armies, not by civilians. The aggressive new nationalism of the French is not a part of his world-view. Unlike Hermann later on, he does not experience the war at an emotional level as a threat to his "fatherland." The concept of the Rhine as a national boundary is alien to him: the river is primarily an avenue of communication, characterized by the natural south-north motion, which nurtured commerce and interchange among cities, states and towns. The image of the Rhine as an east-west barrier, the border of a "national" Germany, signifies a change in the previously unproblematic symbolic relations of the local landscape:

'Wie begrüßt' ich so oft mit Staunen die Fluten des Rheinstroms,
Wenn ich, reisend nach meinem Geschäft, ihm wieder mich nahte!
Immer schien er mir groß und erhob mir Sinn und Gemüte;
Aber ich konnte nicht denken, daß bald sein liebliches Ufer

Sollte werden ein Wall, um abzuwehren den Franken,
Und sein verbreitetes Bett ein allverhindernder Graben.'

(I, 190-95)[26]

The innkeeper sees the war in "national" terms, but his emphasis is on the geographical and the religious. For him Germany is home, expressed in the emotive image of the Rhine, "die wackeren Deutschen," ("the valiant Germans," I, 196) and the religious belief that God is on his side. The war came as a surprise, and means for him little more than a hindrance to commerce with regions which are closer than most of the other German territories. His home town consciousness knows nothing of the new nationalism of the French, nor of the political upheavals which had begun in Mainz in 1792, and which in a decade would put an end to the Holy Roman Empire of the German Nation. He does not allow his son to become one of the "valiant Germans" who will protect the fatherland, but insists that he remain to manage affairs at home (IV, 91-92).

Such expressions as "die wackeren Deutschen" were used in propaganda pamphlets, newsletters and poems to coerce young men to enlist for the Coalition Wars.[27] However as an identity marker in the 1790s, "Deutsch" was vague in comparison to "French" or "English." It signified a certain linguistic unity, geographical ties, and to some extent a shared history, determined more often than not by foreign intervention in German affairs. It did not evoke a common national bond in the way that the term "French" did by this period.[28] The *levée en masse*, the manifestation of the new national identity in France, did not occur in Germany.

As Goethe pointed out in "Literarischer Sansculottismus" in 1795, and again in the "Xenien" of 1797, Germany was not a nation in the political sense.[29] Given the innkeeper's close identification with the town and the local culture and economy, his appeal to "die wackeren Deutschen" has a local-patriotic and traditional, but hardly a modern, nationalistic, significance.

The French Revolution brought large-scale political and social change to the German territories for the first time since the Thirty Years' War. Hermann

---

[26] "'Many's the time I've greeted the Rhine's great waters with wonder, / When I have happened to see it again while travelling on business: / Always its grandeur impressed my mind and lifted my spirits. / But I would never have thought that its beautiful banks would so soon be / Used as a rampart against the French and a fortification, / And its wide bed as a moat, a defence against foreign invaders.'"

[27] E.g. F.L.J., "Treue Geschichte der Drangsale die das deutsche Dorf J. ... bei Mainz im ersten Revolutionskriege durch die Franzosen erlitten: Dem deutschen Volke nach eigenen Erlebnissen berichtet" (repr. Leipzig 1859); see also Epstein, 451-58; and Blanning, *Mainz*, 294ff.

[28] Norbert Elias, *Über den Prozeß der Zivilisation: Soziogenese und psychogenetische Untersuchungen*, 2 vols. (Frankfurt am Main: Suhrkamp, 1978), 2:129-42.

[29] H.A. 12:239-44; "Deutscher Nationalcharakter" and "Das deutsche Reich," W.A. I, 5, 218. See ch. 3, fn. 60.

represents the generation which was coming to maturity during the mid 1790s, when questions of "occupation" or "liberation" of Europe by the French revolutionary armies were urgent political issues. It is no accident that the ideologues of German nationalism in the early years of the nineteenth century were contemporaries of Hermann, born in the decade between 1769 and 1779: Kleist, Jahn and Arndt.[30] For Hermann the conflict between *Gemeinschaft* and *Gesellschaft* becomes crucial to the decisions which he makes on the day of the action, and which will influence the rest of his life. He is the spokesman for a younger generation, for whom the Revolution and the Coalition Wars will mark the beginnings of development of a new consciousness of being "German."

The disruption of the "small world" of the idyll through the intrusion of the "great world" of European politics (i.e. the refugees and the Revolution) is not the central critical problem in this work. The presence of the refugees outside the town is a sign to the townspeople that their lives too may eventually be disrupted by the Revolution. However the refugees do not enter the town itself. The innkeeper states at the beginning of canto one that they have passed by in the distance, and that their camp is an hour's walk away (I, 5ff.). Any suggestion that the Revolution or the refugees have directly affected the town is avoided from the beginning. The work focuses on the way in which the crisis affects the self-understanding of the inhabitants, in particular the young German, Hermann. Unresolved conflicts already present in the history of the town and the lives of its inhabitants, are exacerbated by the new situation, and they begin to manifest themselves more dramatically, disrupting established attitudes and self-definitions.

Hence the problematic aspect of *Hermann und Dorothea* is not that Germans such as Hermann were willing to defend themselves against an invading enemy. Rather the work focuses on the changes in Hermann's consciousness and self-perception, brought about by revolutionary politics after 1792, which lead to the realization of what the Revolution has actually done to Germans like himself (V, 96-100). *Hermann und Dorothea* questions the extent to which traditional categories of German identity could come to terms with the changes in Germany after 1792, the period of which Goethe later wrote: "Von hier und heute geht eine neue Epoche der Weltgeschichte aus ..."[31]

### Excursus: Parody of Voss's *Luise*

In *Hermann und Dorothea* Goethe parodies two literary models in particular: Homer's *Iliad* and Voss's *Luise*. The parody of Homer has been documented and

---

[30] *Hermann und Dorothea* is set in August 1796; Hermann was born approximately a year after the fire which destroyed the town twenty years earlier, and is hence about nineteen at the time of the action, having been "born" c. 1777. Kleist was born in 1777, Jahn in 1778, and Arndt in 1769.

[31] "From this place and time a new epoch of world history is beginning ..." *Campagne in Frankreich*, H.A. 10:235.

described by Frank Ryder and Benjamin Bennett.[32] Goethe's parody of Voss in this and other sections of the work (e.g. the mother's search for Hermann through the garden) has not been so closely analyzed.

Parts of *Luise: Ein ländliches Gedicht in drei Idyllen* were published in the periodicals, the *Hamburger Musenalmanach* and the *Teutscher Merkur* in 1783-1784, and the work was revised and republished in book form in 1795. Goethe valued Voss's works, and stressed his indebtedness to the idyllic form of *Luise* for the conception of *Hermann und Dorothea*.[33] When revising it for a later edition, he even sent it to Voss's son, an expert like his father on the technicalities of versification, for suggestions on metrical improvement. (Goethe carefully collated these, but did not include them in his published revision.)[34]

Most readers of *Hermann und Dorothea* saw the similarities with *Luise*, which had also been very popular. However more perceptive readers such as Schiller and Humboldt saw the differences as well as the similarities between the two works:

> Es ist eine Art bürgerlicher Idylle, durch die Luise von Voss in ihm zwar nicht veranlaßt, aber doch neuerdings dadurch geweckt; übrigens in seiner ganzen Manier, mithin Vossen völlig entgegengesetzt.[35]

---

[32] Ryder and Bennett analyze the "calculated discrepancies between form and content" (434) in *Hermann und Dorothea*. Through metrical analysis and comparison of the "heroic" or "mock-epic" sections of the work with the *Iliad* of Homer, they put forward an argument that Goethe's "opinion" of the "bourgeoisie in general" is "composed of entirely unreconciled opposites" (433): "what Goethe is concerned with here is not the purely human but the specifically bourgeois ..." (434). Mock-conventions are used to make Hermann look ridiculous, by implicitly comparing him with the hero Hector of the *Iliad*. Goethe's use of diminutives to belittle Hermann (e.g. "Kütschchen") is contrasted with Homer's heroic exaggeration of Hector as the "tamer of horses." Ryder and Bennett interpret this irony and parody only in very general terms as a send-up of the "bourgeoisie." Cf. Seidlin, 107-8.

[33] Gräf, 1/1:96.

[34] See Josef Schmidt, ed., *Johann Wolfgang Goethe: Hermann und Dorothea, Erläuterungen und Dokumente* (Stuttgart: Reclam, 1970). 85-87; and Goethe, W.A. I, 50, 375-83.

[35] "It is a type of middle-class idyll, which was not exactly inspired in him [Goethe] by Voss's *Luise*, although that work certainly awakened his interest. Incidentally in its whole manner it is completely opposed to Voss." Schiller to Körner, 28 October 1796, *Briefwechsel zwischen Schiller und Körner*, ed. Klaus L. Berghahn (Munich: Winkler, 1973), 249; see also: Wilhelm von Humboldt to Schiller, 20 January 1798, *Goethe in vertraulichen Briefen seiner Zeitgenossen*, ed. Wilhelm Bode, rev. ed., ed. Regine Otto and Paul-Gerhard Wenzlaff, 3 vols. (Berlin: Aufbau, 1979), 2:123; Friedrich Schlegel to August Wilhelm Schlegel, 26 August 1797, Bode, 2:111; and Athenäum-Fragment 254, *Kritische Friedrich Schlegel Ausgabe*, ed. Ernst Behler (Munich: Ferdinand Schöningh, 1967), 2:258.

Voss himself was critical of *Hermann und Dorothea* and its relationship to *Luise*.[36] Goethe had not only shown a much finer eye than Voss for the detail of provincial Germany, but he had represented it with such perfection and distance, as to draw attention to the artificiality and pathos of the middle-class idyll itself, especially in sections such as the wine drinking episode in canto one. Hegel first referred to this episode in *Hermann und Dorothea* as an improvement on the coffee scene in *Luise*.[37] In the first idyll of *Luise*, "Das Fest im Walde," the family prepares coffee in the wood, after the midday meal:

Aber das Mütterchen goß in die bräunliche Kanne den Kaffee
Aus der papierenen Tute, [sic] gemengt mit klärendem Hirschhorn,
Strömte die Quelle darauf und stellt' auf Kohlen die Kanne,
Hingekniet, bis steigend die farbige Blase geplatzt war.
'Schleunig an jetzt' rief jene, das Haupt um die Achsel gewendet:
'Setze die Tassen zurecht, mein Töchterchen; gleich ist der Kaffee
Gar. Die Gesellschaft nimmt mit unserem täglichen Steinzeug
Wohl im Grünen vorlieb und ungetrichtertem Kaffee.
Vater verbot Umständ; und dem Weibe geziemt der Gehorsam.'
Sprach's; und die Tochter enthüllt' aus dem Deckelkorbe die Tassen,
Auch die Flasche mit Rahm und die blecherne Dose voll Zucker,
Ordnend umher auf dem Rasen;[38]

The elements of Goethe's parody are immediately identifiable: the Homeric epithets, the diminutives, the affected use of the adjective "bräunlich" (cf. Goethe's "grünlichen Römern"), the exaggerated attention to local detail, the coy platitudes, elevated poetic syntax, and idealized tone.

By the later eighteenth century coffee was a standard beverage for even the poorer provincial middle classes. However in the literary fiction of the idyll it is an exoticism, with wide-ranging associations, which break the idyllic unity. Goethe's replacement of coffee and coffee cups with "Rheinwein" and "Römer"

---

[36] To Gleim, 24 September 1797: "Dorothea may please whomever she will — Luise she is not!" Bode, 2:113.

[37] Georg Wilhelm Friedrich Hegel, *Vorlesungen über die Ästhetik*, *Werke*, ed. Eva Moldenhauer and Karl Markus Michel, 20 vols. (Frankfurt am Main: Suhrkamp, 1970), 13:339-41.

[38] "But mother poured the coffee into the stained brown pot / From a paper bag, mixed with clarifying horn, / Poured spring water on it and placed the pot on the coals, / Kneeling there, until the colored bubble burst as it rose. / Hastily then she called, turning her head on her shoulders: / 'Put the cups out, my daughter; the coffee will be ready / In a moment. Our guests will surely enjoy their coffee unfiltered / In our everyday stoneware, outside on the grass. / Father forbade any fuss; and obedience befits a wife.' / She spoke, and from the wicker basket the daughter revealed the cups / A bottle of cream and the tin jar full of sugar, / Placing them out in order on the grass ..." Johann Heinrich Voss, *Werke*, ed. Hedwig Voegt (Berlin: Aufbau, 1976), 102-3 (=1795 ed. of *Luise*).

is a masterpiece of parody. The literary unity is preserved by the use of local detail, and the associations of foreign trade, colonialism and the outside world are avoided. "Rheinwein" and "Römer" reinstate *German* identity-markers in the idyll — with the extra ironic twist, perhaps, that the distinctive wine-glasses of the Rhineland are named after the arch-enemy of the Teutonic tribes, the Romans.

The motif of the coffee in *Luise* however serves an additional function. The "wise old housewife" angers her family by excusing their humble fare as "kein gräflicher Schmaus" ("no noble feast") and then suggesting that they drink their coffee straight away:

'Trinken wir jetzt noch
Kaffee hier? Vornehme genießen ihn gleich nach der Mahlzeit.'[39]

Walter points out that common sense should prevail over Frenchified refinement, and that such food as they have enjoyed needs no apology:

'Herzlich danken wir, liebe Mama, für die schöne Bewirtung.
Machen Sie Karl nicht rot. Gut sein ist besser denn vornehm.
Säße bei solchem Mahle der Ländlichkeit selbst auch der Kaiser,
Unter dem Schatten der Bäum, in so traulicher lieber Gesellschaft,
Und er sehnte sich ekel zur Kost der französischen Köche
Und zum Gezier der Höflinge heim, so verdient' er zu hungern!
Wenn Mama es erlaubt, so gehen wir gleich nach dem Walde;
Und wenn der Kahn anlandet, dann kochen wir alle geschäftig
Unter dem hängenden Grün weißstämmiger Birken den Kaffee.'[40]

And the father takes the opportunity to make an angry protest at the false values of the courts:

Aber es schalt der Vater und rief die eifernden Worte:
'Ei mit der ungereimten Entschuldigung! ...
Es ist schändlich

---

[39] "'Shall we drink our coffee here, now? Fine people enjoy it straight after their meal.'" Voss, *Werke*, 92.

[40] "'Heartily we thank you, dear mama, for this fine food and drink. / But don't make Karl see red. It's better to be good than 'fine.' / If the Kaiser himself were to sit here in the countryside at such a meal, / Under the shade of the trees and in such close, dear company, / And still were to want that French fare / And the affected manners of his courtiers, then he would deserve to go hungry! / If mama is agreeable, we shall now go into the wood / And when the boat has been moored, then all together / We shall prepare the coffee / Under the hanging foliage of white-boughed birches.'" Voss, *Werke*, 92-93.

Wenn man Gottes Gaben aus Höflichkeit also verachtet!'[41]

The coffee-motive introduces a polemic against courtly society into the idyll. The apparently naive idealization of provincial middle-class values in the idyllic milieu is in fact politically tendentious. The parodic genius of Goethe's "Rheinwein" and "Römer," correcting Voss's model, lies in the unmasking of ideological and political aspects of the *bürgerliche Idylle*.

In her study of the idyll, Renate Böschenstein describes the difficulties Voss had in trying to create a vernacular literary language. His problem lay in bringing together dialect, the language of the people, and *Schriftdeutsch*, the written language, in such a way as to make his works accessible to a wide readership.[42] This problem is indicative of the tension in Voss's works between local and "national" self-definition. Dialect words or syntax are inserted to give the poetic text authenticity (in, for example, "gut sein ist besser denn vornehm"). Yet had Voss written in dialect, it would have been incomprehensible to large numbers of readers, and thus would have alienated the people whom he was trying to appeal to as (middle-class) "Germans."

Unlike Voss, Goethe does not misrepresent the political and social status of the German middle classes by glorifying political fragmentation as class identity, or by creating a false unity of provincial dialect and national culture. The home town can retain its idyllic quality only by remaining a provincial backwater in a pre-national setting. However in 1796, the town in *Hermann und Dorothea* is situated on the fault-line of post-revolutionary national development. In this new situation, the simple Vossian idyll could no longer function as the appropriate form of German middle-class literature.

---

[41] "But the father scolded and railed: 'Be done with your clumsy apologies! It is a disgrace to despise God's gifts for the sake of courteousness.'" Voss, *Werke*, 93. The German word "Höflichkeit" here is ambiguous, meaning "courtesy" and implying aristocratic or "courtly" manners.

[42] Voss added a glossary to the 1802 edition of his poems, cf. Renate Böschenstein, *Idylle* (Stuttgart: Metzler, 1967), 73.

# 3: The Revival of Traditional Values

### Disruption and Provocation

IF CANTOS ONE TO three represent the home town in its civic aspect, canto four, entitled "Euterpe" (the Muse of Flute-playing) reveals its roots in the village community or *Gemeinschaft*. Where the father's milieu is the town, the council and the public institutions, Hermann identifies with the estate, the cultivated land beyond the town wall, the idyllic garden and the spring. This canto is subtitled "Mutter und Sohn" ("Mother and Son"), and in it the interrelationships of parental and sexual love, pre- or pseudo-national feelings, individuation and socialization are represented.

In his long monologue in canto two, and in his dialogue with his mother in canto four, Hermann links for himself the formative events from his past with feelings of confusion and resentment in the present. He thereby articulates his memories of the town of his childhood with its traditional values (the town community as *Gemeinschaft*) against the modern home town and his father's ethos of progress.

As with the discussion of the innkeeper, problems arise with the use of terms such as "modernity," "tradition," and "progressiveness" in relation to Hermann. His change in attitudes is a change in orientation regarding received values. He takes up and radically reasserts those traditional values which his father is willing to sacrifice for the sake of progress. In the twenty years following the date of the action, the Germany with which the innkeeper identifies would be completely changed under the impact of Napoleon. The home town would exist within a vastly changed socio-political, and cultural environment, despite the innkeeper's attempts to retain its character as an ordered, forward-looking *Gemeinschaft*. For Hermann's generation the dialectic of development takes place within a wider context than the home town. Korff is mistaken in emphasizing the continuity of life-cycles from one generation to the next.[1] The crisis which Hermann experiences is one of European dimensions. It is no longer simply a question of the individual and the town community, as it had been for his parents after the fire. The frames of reference are wider, and, more importantly, have no precedent. The traditional values which Hermann revives and radicalizes at the end of the work are traditional in form only. In content, they presage the nationalism of the post-revolutionary era. This nationalism, with its roots in the early 1790s, emerged as a clearly definable social force in Germany only after Napoleon's defeat of Prussia

---

[1] Korff, 2:342.

in 1806.[2] Hermann's love of the idyllic past of his childhood is transformed from a nostalgic memory into a program for the future in the final canto:

'Denn es werden noch stets die entschlossenen Völker gepriesen,
Die für Gott und Gesetz, für Eltern, Weiber und Kinder
Stritten und gegen den Feind zusammenstehend erlagen.'

(IX, 308-10)[3]

On the subject of the re-emergence or radicalization of traditional values Barrington Moore writes:

> The assumption of inertia, that cultural and social continuity do not require explanation, obliterates the fact that both have to be recreated anew in each generation, often with great pain and suffering ... To speak of cultural inertia is to overlook the concrete interests and privileges that are served by indoctrination, education, and the entire complicated process of transmitting culture from one generation to the next.[4]

Interpreters have rarely asked how Hermann comes to emerge as the spokesman for the surcharged traditionalism, which contrasts so strongly with the attitudes of his father. Viktor Hehn and Wilhelm Scherer, in their nationalistic interpretations of *Hermann und Dorothea* in the nineteenth century, point out the tendentiousness of Hermann's statements in view of later developments of German nationalism.[5] Of course the strongly sympathetic response of these critics to Hermann's nationalism is no longer acceptable. However later interpreters from Korff to Borchmeyer and Lützeler, gloss over the hard lines of Hermann's final

---

[2] At the Peace of Basle (5 April 1795), Prussia surrendered its possessions on the left bank of the Rhine. A line of demarcation secured the neutrality of Northern Germany until 1806, cf. Sydney Seymour Biro, *The German Policy of Revolutionary France: A Study in French Diplomacy during the War of the First Coalition 1792-1797*, 2 vols. (Cambridge, Mass.: Harvard University Press, 1957), 1:312-64. Hans Mayer points out that this peace treaty was the first to be signed between the revolutionary government of France and a legitimate (i.e. *ancien régime*) European power, and that it introduced a period of uncertainty in Prussia and the surrounding states. Mayer, "Vergebliche Renaissance," 359. On the rise of national feelings in the Rhineland during the revolutionary period, see Blanning, *French Revolution*, 247-48.

[3] "'They are forever still praised, those peoples who with resolution / Fought for their God and their laws, for their parents, their wives and their children, / And at the hands of their enemies perished, still standing together.'"

[4] Barrington Moore, *Social Origins of Dictatorship and Democracy: Lord and Peasant in the Making of the Modern World* (Boston: Beacon, 1966), 486.

[5] Viktor Hehn, *Ueber Goethes Hermann und Dorothea* (1851), ed. Albert Leitzmann and Theodor Schiemann (Stuttgart: Cotta, 1893), 45-46; Wilhelm Scherer, *Geschichte der deutschen Literatur* (1883; Berlin: Weidmann, 1889), 572.

speech, which pre-empts the nationalist rhetoric of the period of the Wars of Liberation. Korff does not distinguish between the town ethos of the innkeeper and the new traditionalism of Hermann, and Borchmeyer, for example, citing canto nine, lines 313f., writes that Hermann represents "eine im privaten Kreis des Hauses und der Familie sich vollendende Bürgerlichkeit, die sich freilich bewußt in den Dienst des Gemeinwesens stellt."[6]

In the development of Hermann's character over the day of the action, the unresolved conflict between *Gemeinschaft* (the village origins of the home town) and *Gesellschaft* (the development within the town of more complex economic and social structures) becomes critical. When Hermann appears at the beginning of canto two, the reader has already received several reports about him, firstly from the father, and then just as he arrives, from the vicar. The father's remarks about his son prepare for a shy and withdrawn youth. However when he appears, the vicar recognizes a change in him:

Als nun der wohlgebildete Sohn ins Zimmer hereintrat,
Schaute der Prediger ihm mit scharfen Blicken entgegen
Und betrachtete seine Gestalt und sein ganzes Benehmen
Mit dem Auge des Forschers, der leicht die Mienen enträtselt;
Lächelte dann und sprach zu ihm mit traulichen Worten:
'Kommt Ihr doch als ein veränderter Mensch! Ich habe noch niemals
Euch so munter gesehn und Eure Blicke so lebhaft.'

(II, 1-7)[7]

He interprets this change in terms of his own enlightened Christianity. Hermann has experienced spiritual grace after the charitable act of distributing food and clothing to the suffering refugees:

'Fröhlich kommt Ihr und heiter; man sieht, Ihr habt die Gaben

---

[6] Korff, 350-51; "a middle-class identity which is developing to the fullest in the private sphere of the house and the family, but which at the same time consciously puts itself in the service of the community," Borchmeyer, "Weimar im Zeitalter der Französischen Revolution," 10; see also Paul Michael Lützeler, "Johann Wolfgang Goethe: *Hermann und Dorothea*," *Geschichte in der Literatur: Studien zu Werken von Lessing bis Hebbel* (Munich: Piper, 1987), 123-24.

[7] "Now when the landlord's well-favored son came into the parlour, / He was surveyed by the preacher with looks of intelligent interest / Which took in his appearance and his whole manner and bearing, / For men's looks were no riddle to this well-practised observer, / Who then smiled and with affable words accosted the young man: 'Why, what a change you have undergone, my young friend! I have never / Seen you in such good spirits before or looking so lively.'"

Unter die Armen verteilet und ihren Segen empfangen.'

(II, 8-9)[8]

However Hermann did not reach the refugees. He met only Dorothea and the woman in childbirth, due to his lateness in leaving and the number of townspeople returning home on the road (II, 13ff.), and his mood is far from cheerful or serene. The meeting with Dorothea and the confrontation with the outside world she represents has shocked and upset him.

This shock triggers a change of consciousness which prompts his spontaneous reading of his own "history" in canto two. This side of Hermann's character is new to his parents and friends. From the moment of entering the doorway of his parents' house, Hermann is the representative of a younger generation, whose experience of the new crisis (the approaching revolutionary armies) contrasts with his parents' memory of the old crisis (the fire). For Hermann the fire is a part of the home town history and a collective memory, which accompanied his childhood and adolescence. He points out to his parents that the fire, while destroying the town, also opened up a new life for them (V, 105-7). However the fire which had a liberating as well as a destructive moment for his parents, has determined his life up until the day of the action. The liberating aspect of the crisis for the parents was reduced to a didactic program for the son:

'Nicht einen jeden betrifft es,
Anzufangen von vorn sein ganzes Leben und Wesen;
Nicht soll jeder sich quälen, wie wir und andere taten,
O, wie glücklich ist der, dem Vater und Mutter das Haus schon
Wohlbestellt übergeben, und der mit Gedeihen es ausziert!'

(II, 161-65)[9]

Hermann's childhood and adolescence ran parallel to the rebuilding and improvement of the town under the leadership of his father as manager of public works (III, 33). However the patterns of individual development and civic rebuilding — the personal and the political — are not congruent. Hermann's early failure to show interest in his father's plans was interpreted as a sign of stupidity and obstinacy. This judgement, reinforced throughout the boy's life, has resulted in a resentment at the values of the new town (the *Gesellschaft*) which is only thinly veiled by the patina of idyll. The passive resistance with which Hermann protected himself throughout his childhood and adolescence is transformed on the day of the action into an adult consciousness.

---

[8] "'You seem happy and pleased with yourself, you have obviously been / Sharing out gifts among those poor folk and been given their blessing.'"

[9] "'To set up one's whole way of life like / That from the start, and begin with nothing, is not every man's lot. / Not every man must struggle as we did, and others have had to; / He is a fortunate fellow whose parents have handed him over / Their house all shipshape and ready, which he then improves as he prospers.'"

Hermann's father cannot understand why Hermann should want any closer contact with the refugees than that necessary to dispense alms. Hermann enters on his story conscious of this, and shifts the responsibility for meeting Dorothea by blaming his mother for taking so long to pack the food and old clothing:

'Mutter, Ihr kramtet so lange, die alten Stücke zu suchen
Und zu wählen; nur spät war erst das Bündel zusammen,'

(II, 13-14)[10]

He admits that he acted according to his heart's dictates in giving the food and clothing to Dorothea to distribute among the refugees. His narration of the events implies his strong emotional and sexual response to the refugee girl, a response which the mother and the vicar, but not the father, immediately perceive.

'Als ich nun meines Weges die neue Straße hinanfuhr,
Fiel mir ein Wagen ins Auge, von tüchtigen Bäumen gefüget,
Von zwei Ochsen gezogen, den größten und stärksten des Auslands,
Nebenher aber ging mit starken Schritten ein Mädchen,
Lenkte mit langem Stabe die beiden gewaltigen Tiere,
Trieb sie und hielt sie zurück, sie leitete klüglich.'

(II, 21-26)[11]

Dorothea's powerful presence stands in stark contrast to her sex for the inexperienced young man. She is associated with the power and strength of the animals, and he remembers her calmness in controlling them. Her independence and strength of character are striking in contrast to Hermann, who has little experience of the world, and who is easily dominated by his father and manipulated by his mother. Unsure of himself in this new situation, and with only his heart ("Herz") to guide him, Hermann stands in confusion before Dorothea. She is self-composed, but under no illusions about her status as a refugee in a foreign land. She refers to him as a foreigner ("ein Fremder") and makes it clear that she is a refugee driven by fate to ask for help in looking after the woman in childbirth, but loath to do so in the knowledge that she, as a refugee, may be given charity out of convenience or contempt rather than kindness:

'Noch nicht bin ich gewohnt, vom Fremden die Gabe zu heischen,
Die er oft ungern gibt, um loszuwerden den Armen;

---

[10] "'Mother, you rummaged around so long to find and sort out all / Those old things, it was late before the bundle was ready,'"

[11] "'Presently, as I was driving along the new highway, it happened / That I noticed a cart: it was made of good solid timber, / Drawn by a yoke of oxen, two big strong beasts from the Rhineland, / And beside it walked a young woman, stepping out briskly / And controlling the two huge beasts as she went, with a long stick, / Driving them on and holding them back with the skill of an expert.'"

Aber mich dränget die Not zu reden.'

(II, 30-32)[12]

Hermann recognizes in Dorothea and the refugees as a group, the members of a spiritual community, and extends to them trust and fellowship. His language with its pietistic coloring contrasts strongly with his father's and the apothecary's materialism, and with Dorothea's self-possessed pragmatism. The sexual moment of the meeting and his sympathy for the refugees elicit feelings which he expresses in terms of group identity, family, or a spiritual *Gemeinschaft*:

'Guten Menschen, fürwahr, spricht oft ein himmlischer Geist zu,
Daß sie fühlen die Not, die dem armen Bruder bevorsteht;'

(II, 44-45)[13]

This meeting brings together the three crises or turning-points of Hermann's life so far: the coming to sexual and emotional maturity, the psychological development into an adult responsible for his own actions, and the confrontation with the socio-political crisis of the Revolution. The personal history of this critical juncture in Hermann's life is provided in the early expository cantos, with the question of social and cultural identity coming to dominate the final canto and the complexion of the work as a whole.

### Alienation in the Home Town

The apothecary's pusillanimous reactions to the new crisis (II, 83-96) provoke an unusual response from Hermann. To the surprise of father and mother, he now speaks out:

'Lieber möcht' ich als je mich heute zur Heirat entschließen;
Denn manch gutes Mädchen bedarf des schützenden Mannes
Und der Mann des erheiternden Weibs, wenn ihm Unglück bevorsteht.'

(II, 102-4)[14]

The innkeeper interprets this to mean that Hermann has finally changed his attitude of passive resistance, and that he will marry and become a respectable *Bürger*. However he is mistaken. Sensing a conflict between father and son, the

---

[12] "'And I am still unaccustomed to begging from strangers, for I know / They often give with reluctance and just to get rid of the beggar. / But dire need compels me to speak.'"

[13] "'Now it is clear some angelic voice often speaks to good people / Making them feel in advance the plight of their poor human brethren;'"

[14] "'I am more ready than ever to take a wife in these dark days: / Many a good woman now is in need of a husband's protection, / And a man needs a woman to cheer him when evil times threaten.'"

mother points out that good things often come of bad. Just as the fire had brought them together twenty years earlier, so the crisis of the Coalition Wars and the knowledge that fellow Germans have been forced into exile, may bring happiness to Hermann:

'Sohn, fürwahr! du hast recht; wir Eltern gaben das Beispiel.
Denn wir haben uns nicht an fröhlichen Tagen erwählet,
Und uns knüpfte vielmehr die traurigste Stunde zusammen.
...
Darum lob' ich dich, Hermann, daß du mit reinem Vertrauen
Auch ein Mädchen dir denkst in diesen traurigen Zeiten
Und es wagtest, zu frein im Krieg und über den Trümmern.'
(II, 108-10; 155-57)[15]

But the father is not convinced:

'Die Gesinnung ist löblich, und wahr ist auch die Geschichte,
Mütterchen, die du erzählst; denn so ist alles begegnet.
Aber besser ist besser. Nicht einen jeden betrifft es,
Anzufangen von vorn sein ganzes Leben und Wesen;
Nicht soll jeder sich quälen, wie wir und andere taten,
...
Ja, mein Hermann, du würdest mein Alter höchlich erfreuen,
Wenn du mir bald ins Haus ein Schwiegertöchterchen brächtest
Aus der Nachbarschaft her, aus jenem Hause, dem grünen.
...
Nur drei Töchter sind da; sie teilen allein das Vermögen.'
(II, 159-63; 187-89, 192)[16]

Hermann rejects his father's materialism by leaving the room. His response to the suggestion that he take one of the rich neighbor's daughters for his wife, reflects

---

[15] '"Yes, my son, you are right, and your parents have set an example. / For it was not during happy days that we chose one another; / Rather, the bond between us was formed at a very sad moment. / ... / So I commend you, my Hermann, for your pure trust in the future / Which you show by that fact that you look for a bride in these sad times, / And would dare to get married despite the war and the ruins.'"

[16] '"It is a worthy intention, and that is indeed a true story, / My dear wife, that you've told us; for that is just how it all happened / But what is better is better. To set up one's whole way of life like / That from the start, and begin with nothing, is not every man's lot. / Not every man must struggle as we did, and others have had to; / ... / Yes, my dear Hermann, in my old age you would give me great pleasure / By bringing home to me soon a young daughter-in-law, one of those girls / From over there, the green house at the other side of the market. / ... / He's only got three daughters, they'll share his whole fortune between them.'"

a history of disillusionment with his father's philistine values. Certainly the innkeeper has a cynical view of human nature:

'Denn die Arme wird doch nur zuletzt vom Manne verachtet,
Und er hält sie als Magd, die als Magd mit dem Bündel hereinkam.
Ungerecht bleiben die Männer, und die Zeiten der Liebe vergehen.'

(II, 184-86)[17]

This last line is the famed "seven-footed monster" which the poet and translator Johann Heinrich Voss and his son identified with glee as proof of Goethe's inadequacy as a poet in classical meters. They did not see in it the ironic relationship of form and content, an expression of the disharmony of classical form and modern life.[18]

Hermann is influenced by the community-oriented pietism of his mother and the enlightened Christian optimism of the vicar. He is naturally disposed to trust rather than cynicism in his relations with others (although this trust has been repeatedly betrayed). The failure of his father to trust him has led to disappointment, internalization and deflection of emotional energies. His retreat to the farm, the stables and the company of farm-hands was his response to the authoritarian and insensitive personality of his father. In the down-to-earth environment of the farm he found a sense of community which he did not find in his class- or peer-group in the new town. The horses, which he bought as foals and trained with care are mentioned repeatedly.[19] However at the time of the action this adolescent private sphere of trust and animal warmth is no longer enough for him.

That the meeting with Dorothea and the refugees manifests more to Hermann than mere sexual awakening is clear from the way in which he speaks of it in his long monologues in canto two, and in the episodes from his childhood, which he recalls in canto four. Hermann's memories of childhood and adolescence reflect the conflict between the pietist-sentimental values inherited from his mother and the increasing sense of alienation from the town society, which he remembers as a close-knit community, and the loss of which he implicitly blames on his father. In the past he had been close to the children of the rich neighbor, just as he had to the other children, regardless of social status:

'Wir sind zusammen erzogen,
Spielten neben dem Brunnen am Markt in früheren Zeiten,

---

[17] "'For if she's poor, she'll end up as a woman despised by her husband / And treated just like a maid, who arrived like a maid with her bundle. / Men never treat women fairly, the season of love doesn't last long.'"

[18] For Cotta's planned complete edition (1808) Goethe requested Johann Heinrich Voss (son of the poet) to help him revise the hexameters of *Hermann und Dorothea*. See Gräf, 1/1:172-77; Ryder and Bennett, 440; and Schmidt, 86-87.

[19] I, 16; II, 62; IV, 5; V, 132-41, 150; VI, 296, 313.

Und ich habe sie oft vor der Knaben Wildheit beschützet.
Doch das ist lange schon her;'

(II, 199-202)[20]

The image of the fountain is central to his idyllic memory of the home town community. It is the focal point of his childhood memories in canto two and the place to which he returns to find Dorothea in the most lyrical and intimate section of the work in canto seven. Situated at the center of the town, it is a remnant of the home town as *Gemeinschaft*. It was the axis from which town community life radiated, and it contrasts with the modernized infrastructure of the new town with its '"wasserreichen, verdeckten, / Wohlverteilten Kanäle, die Nutzen und Sicherheit bringen'" (III, 29-30).[21] Hermann's father was largely responsible for the conception and rebuilding of the town. The fountain as symbol of the community is replaced by the pipes and canals of the sanitized and increasingly complex society. Hermann's memories of the town here, and his feelings for the countryside in canto four, express his desire for the restitution of the "pre-modern" environment. The fire destroyed everything but the core of the old town, the fountain and market. Those episodes which remain in Hermann's memory — the undifferentiated community of his childhood and the idyllic innocence of the fountain untouched by fire or change — are welded together into a repository of positive values, an internalized place of retreat from the values imposed by his father.

Hermann's clothing in canto two, like his father's dressing-gown in canto one, is used to symbolize changes in personal and social values. However where the father can pass from the less formal to the more formal with nothing more than a sense of nostalgia, Hermann cannot. The new clothes he wears in order to present himself at the rich neighbor's house, become a symbol of compromise, shame and loss of community values:

'Ich ging auch zuzeiten
Noch aus alter Bekanntschaft, so wie Ihr es wünschtet, hinüber;
Aber ich konnte mich nie in ihrem Umgang erfreuen.
Denn sie tadelten stets an mir, das mußt' ich ertragen:
Gar zu lang war mein Rock, zu grob das Tuch und die Farbe
Gar zu gemein und die Haare nicht recht gestutzt und gekräuselt.
Endlich hatt' ich im Sinne, mich auch zu putzen wie jene
Handelsbübchen, die stets am Sonntag drüben sich zeigen
Und um die halbseiden im Sommer das Läppchen herumhängt.
Aber noch früh genug merkt' ich, sie hatten mich immer zum besten;

---

[20] '"It's true we were brought up together, / Played together in days gone by, by the well in the square here, / And I would often defend them against my wilder companions. / But that's all long ago now;'"

[21] '"paved-over conduits, / Well laid out for safety and use and full of good water'"

Und das war mir empfindlich, mein Stolz war beleidigt; doch mehr noch
Kränkte mich's tief, daß so sie den guten Willen verkannten,
Den ich gegen sie hegte, besonders Minchen, die Jüngste.
Denn so war ich zuletzt an Ostern hinübergegangen,
Hatte den neuen Rock, der jetzt nur oben im Schrank hängt,
Angezogen und war frisiert wie die übrigen Bursche.
Als ich eintrat, kicherten sie; doch zog ich's auf mich nicht.'

(II, 204-20)[22]

It is the false values which upset Hermann in this episode, not the blow to his pride. Here (II, 215) as well as later (IV, 162-63) he refers to loss or the failure to recognize good will in the town. His expectation that the values of old acquaintance would be maintained and reciprocated is disappointed. In describing the visit he implicitly reproaches his father for his complicity in the destruction of traditional community values. The pejorative word "Handelsbübchen" ("silly young clerks") shows his resentment at the new social and class formations. His rejection of the new town and his identification with the unchanged farm life of the old community is a form of self-protection against the insistence that he become a good *Bürger* like his father. His use of the word expresses contempt and marks his first active rejection of paternal authority, after the passive resistance which characterized his earlier behavior — his refusal to excel at school or in business, and his interest in the farm rather than the town.

Hermann's attack is countered by his father's equally insulting use of the word, "Knecht" ("farm-hand," II, 248). The appearance of complacency and comfort which the father is at pains to cultivate in canto one, masking his unease at the presence of the refugees outside the town, breaks down completely in relation to his son. In this case the root of the problem is embarrassment at Hermann's failure to meet his expectations of public behavior as a successful *Bürger*. He does not have a son to parade before the other townspeople, as a representative of the new wealthy elite with the appropriate clothing and manners, who will marry upwards in social terms, and continue the family name. On the

---

[22] "'I've called on them sometimes, / As you wished me to do, just for old times' sake; but I must say / I never got any pleasure from talking to them, for I always / Had to put up with their finding fault for some reason or other. / Either my coat was too long or the cloth was too coarse and the color / Not at all chic, and my hair not properly trimmed and not curled right. / In the end I decided that I would make myself smart too, / Like those silly young clerks who are there on a Sunday / With their semi-silk coats flapping flimsily round them in summer. / But it was clear soon enough that the girls were still teasing me; that did / Hurt my feelings, it wounded my pride, and what made it more hurtful / Was their failure to understand my well-meaning gesture / And my good will towards them, especially Mina, the youngest. / Lately, for instance, at Easter, I paid them a call and was wearing / My new coat, which since then I've just left upstairs in a cupboard, / And with my hair done up, to look like the other young fellows. / When I came in, they giggled — but as I first thought, not about me.'"

contrary, his son's interests lie with the farm and his horses, he mixes with servants, he is not "modern," and he behaves like a peasant rather than a *Bürger*.

Hermann expresses his resentment through the rejection of the neighbor's daughters as potential marriage partners. The neighbor personifies the breakdown of home town (*Gemeinschaft*) values, and the penetration of modern, public attitudes into the family itself. For Hermann, this milieu has cut its roots in local culture and has lost touch with the values of the old community. The memory of the visit to the rich neighbor is loaded with the resentment at the modernization of town life, and with displaced aggression at his father for betraying these values:

'Minchen saß am Klavier; es war der Vater zugegen,
Hörte die Töchterchen singen und war entzückt und in Laune.
Manches verstand ich nicht, was in den Liedern gesagt war,
Aber ich hörte viel von Pamina, viel von Tamino,
Und ich wollte doch auch nicht stumm sein! Sobald sie geendet,
Fragt' ich dem Texte nach und nach den beiden Personen.
Alle schwiegen darauf und lächelten; aber der Vater
Sagte: 'Nicht wahr, mein Freund, Er kennt nur Adam und Eva?'
Niemand hielt sich alsdann, und laut auf lachten die Mädchen,
Laut auf lachten die Knaben, es hielt den Bauch sich der Alte.
Fallen ließ ich den Hut vor Verlegenheit, und das Gekicher
Dauerte fort und fort, so viel sie auch sangen und spielten.
Und ich eilte beschämt und verdrießlich wieder nach Hause,
Hängte den Rock in den Schrank und zog die Haare herunter
Mit den Fingern und schwur, nicht mehr zu betreten die Schwelle.
Und ich hatte wohl recht; denn eitel sind sie und lieblos,
Und ich höre, noch heiß' ich bei ihnen immer Tamino!'

(II, 221-37)[23]

The piano and music are status symbols, along with the ostentatious house, the Landau carriage (I, 56) and the thriving workshops, which make the neighbor the

---

[23] "'Mina was at the piano, her father was there, he was listening / To his dear daughters singing, and seemed in a very good temper. / I couldn't make out much of the songs they performed, but I kept on / Hearing them mention 'Pamina', and somebody else called 'Tamino'; / And I felt I must say something too, so when they had finished / I at once asked what the text had been, and about the two characters. / They were all silent at that, and smiled; but their father's reply was: / 'Why, young fellow, are Adam and Eve the last couple you've heard of?' / And at that they all burst out laughing, the girls and the boys all / Laughing their heads off together, the old man clutching his belly, / I was embarrassed so much that I dropped my hat, and the giggling / Never stopped, they went on and on giggling and singing and playing; / And I hurried back home in vexation and humiliation, / Hung up that coat in the cupboard and rumpled my hair with my fingers, / And took a vow that I'd never again set foot in that household. / And I think I was right! They're vain and heartless young women, / And I've been told that among them I still am nicknamed Tamino.'"

leading businessman in the region (I, 55), extending his trade links to the commercial centers of Strasbourg, Vienna, Frankfurt and Mannheim. The music, Mozart's *Magic Flute* in the form of the piano reduction, the clothing, even the carriage, carry associations with foreign or city cultures, which contrast with the home town. The description of the family entertainment shows the connections between the growth of the town and the appropriation of culture as a status symbol. The image of a daughter-in-law who can play the piano and conduct social occasions has impressed Hermann's father:

'Aber denke nur nicht, du wollest ein bäurisches Mädchen
Je mir bringen ins Haus, als Schwiegertochter, die Trulle!
...
Spielen soll sie mir auch das Klavier; es sollen die schönsten,
Besten Leute der Stadt sich mit Vergnügen versammeln,
Wie es Sonntags geschieht im Hause des Nachbars!'

(II, 263-64, 270-72)[24]

The father's plans for the marriage of his son to the rich neighbor's daughter (like the changing standards of dress in the town) can be seen in terms of Weber's *Vergesellschaftung*, the transition from simple communal, to more complex social patterns and expectations of behavior.[25] Personal emotions become interwoven with practical economic concerns and social aspirations, as the father puts pressure on his son to marry into a wealthy family. The name-calling which sticks so deeply in Hermann's memory epitomizes the *Vergesellschaftung* of the home town. This episode is especially injurious to Hermann's self-confidence, because his attempt to adopt the new fashions and social behavior — his compromise with change for the sake of his father — is ridiculed.

The snobbery of the neighbors is not merely an isolated incident. It is indicative of the changes in home town values:

Da versetzte die Mutter: 'Du solltest, Hermann, so lange
Mit den Kindern nicht zürnen; denn Kinder sind sie ja sämtlich.
Minchen fürwahr ist gut und war dir immer gewogen;
Neulich fragte sie noch nach dir. Die solltest du wählen!'
Da versetzte bedenklich der Sohn: 'Ich weiß nicht, es prägte
Jener Verdruß sich so tief bei mir ein, ich möchte fürwahr nicht

---

[24] "'But if you're thinking of bringing some peasant girl into my house / As my daughter-in-law, think again! I'll not have her, the baggage!/ ... / I'll expect her to play me the piano, the best and the finest / People in town shall come to my house and have a good time here, / Just as they have at our neighbor's house on a Sunday.'"

[25] Max Weber, *Wirtschaft und Gesellschaft: Grundriß der verstehenden Soziologie*, ed. Johannes Winckelmann, 5th rev. ed. (Tübingen: Mohr, 1980), 312-22; R. Bendix, *Nation-Building and Citizenship* (Garden City: Anchor Doubleday, 1969), 19f. and *Max Weber: An Intellectual Portrait* (Berkeley: University of California Press, 1977), 473-78.

Sie am Klaviere mehr sehn und ihre Liedchen vernehmen.'

(II, 238-44)[26]

Hermann's attitude towards his family home has become ambivalent. The old and new, *Gemeinschaft* and *Gesellschaft*, the private and the public are embodied in the figure of the father. In his public role Hermann's father is the progressive town councillor. As a private figure in the intimate sphere of home and family, however, he is the sentimental upholder of traditional community culture, symbolized in "Pantoffel und Mütze," "Römer" and "Rheinwein." Hermann inherits the crisis of his father's dual role. He finds himself torn between respect and love for the idyllic patriarch and contempt for the materialistic, upwardly mobile *Bürger*. On the one hand there is the father of his childhood memories, the paterfamilias and community leader, whom he defended against the sarcasm of his playmates:

'Vieles hab' ich fürwahr von meinen Gespielen geduldet,
Wenn sie mit Tücke mir oft den guten Willen vergalten;
Oftmals hab' ich an ihnen nicht Wurf noch Streiche gerochen:
Aber spotteten sie mir den Vater aus, wenn er Sonntags
Aus der Kirche kam mit würdig bedächtigem Schritte;
Lachten sie über das Band der Mütze, die Blumen des Schlafrocks,
Den er so stattlich trug und der erst heute verschenkt ward:
Fürchterlich ballte sich gleich die Faust mir; mit grimmigem Wüten
Fiel ich sie an und schlug und traf mit blindem Beginnen,
Ohne zu sehen wohin.'

(IV, 162-71)[27]

And on the other hand there is the father who humiliates him in front of friends and neighbors, and tries to force him to follow in his own footsteps in local politics:

Doch der Vater fuhr auf und sprach die zornigen Worte:

---

[26] "Then his mother said: 'Hermann, you should not go on being angry / With those children, for that after all is what they all are still. / Mina's a good girl really, I know that she always has liked you, / Lately she even was asking after you. She'd be a good choice!' / And her son still demurred: 'I don't know,' he said, 'that occasion / Made such a deep impression on me that I really would rather / Never again hear her singing her songs or playing the piano.'"

[27] "'I may say, from my playmates I had a great deal to put up with, / When they so often repaid me with spite for the good will I showed them. / Often I took no revenge for their tricks and their throwing things at me: / But if they ever made fun of my father, when on a Sunday / He would set forth from church at his dignified pace — if they then dared / Laugh at his cap and its ribbon, the pattern of flowers on that stately / Dressing-gown he used to wear, which we gave away only this morning — / Then my fist would be clenched in a fearsome rage, I went berserk / And would attack them and strike out at random, in a blind fury, / Not seeing who I was hitting.'"

'Wenig Freud' erleb' ich an dir! Ich sagt' es doch immer,
Als du zu Pferden nur und Lust nur bezeigtest zum Acker:
Was ein Knecht schon verrichtet des wohlbegüterten Mannes,
Tust du; indessen muß der Vater des Sohnes entbehren,
Der ihm zur Ehre doch auch vor andern Bürgern sich zeigte.'

(II, 245-50)[28]

The rich neighbor's house unambiguously represents all the negative aspects of the new, of wealth, progress, alienation of old values and stratification of the community. Hermann's hurt and resentment is preserved in the image of the complacent neighbor, Minchen at the piano and the "Handelsbübchen" all in one. It vents itself in an aversion to the episode as a whole — the people, the surroundings, and even the music — not merely to the individuals. It is in reaction to the memory of this episode and the father's outburst of fury, that Hermann seeks out his retreat under the pear tree, and begins to sort out his response to the critical happenings of the day.

The rich neighbor is a sarcastic snob, but what he says of Hermann is true. Hermann is naive. He belongs to the village community (with its simple, biblical stereotype) rather than to civic society (where "Tamino" from *The Magic Flute* represents the cultural sophistication of Vienna). The fountain is an image of patriarchal community life bound by unchanging moral and social laws. The childhood community around the fountain is timeless, unindividuated and untroubled by crisis or change. Repeatedly during the work, Hermann is drawn to the image of a patriarchal, ordered and uncritical community, the memory of which he cherishes from childhood, and which he will ultimately try to reinstate in response to his fear of change. In canto nine, this memory will be transformed into a vision of an armed, defensive, "idyllic" Germany — a Germany, the idyll of which consists in the maintenance of a series of inherited identity markers of *Deutschtum*, against political change and foreign influence. Hermann's idyll passed with childhood, and his story of the broken friendship with the children of the rich neighbor is an oblique critique of the type of society which has developed — and for which his father is blamed.

The mixture of retarding and progressive motives which Korff analyzes as liberal and moderately progressive in fact reveals conflicting and divergent tendencies. For Hermann the conflict polarizes into a negative image of the alienated town and a positive image of the idyllic traditional community. In canto two the motifs of Hermann's sexual and psychological development are linked with the socio-economic and cultural environment of the home town. Through the meeting with Dorothea and indirectly through the retold story of her first fiancé,

---

[28] "But his father lost patience and made this irascible answer: / 'Much joy I have of you, I must say! It's just as I always / Said when I saw you'd no liking except for the fields and the horses: / Even a farm-hand hired by a man like me of some substance, / Does what you do! But I am a father and I want a son here, / One who would make a good showing before other townsfolk, and do me / Credit!'"

this moment of convergence of individual and social identity within the home town will be linked with the socio-political developments of modern Europe. Hermann's father finds a compromise solution to the demands of the *Gesellschaft* by differentiating public and private spheres. Within the familial sphere, the old community values can at least appear to be maintained.

The plot of *Hermann und Dorothea* revolves around the Oedipal conflict between father and son, bordering on domestic crisis, but resolved finally through the agency of the mother into the happy end of the betrothal. The father-son conflict is an archetypal situation, linking the perennial themes of human nature to the contemporary history of the revolutionary period. The everyday nature of the "retarding" factor in *Hermann und Dorothea* (the father's objection to Dorothea) is important not as a glorification of the mundane, the non-political and the traditional, but as the linking matrix between the microcosm of personal identity and the macrocosm of European political development. History enters the art-work through the details of everyday life.

### Hermann's Transfigured Fatherland

Leaving the men discussing the prospects of the town, at the beginning of canto four, Hermann's mother goes out to look for her son. He is sulking by himself on the hill overlooking the property. Here, and in canto five he reveals how his sense of betrayal of community values within the town is deepened by the knowledge of revolutionary upheaval outside the town:

'Nein, das wilde Geschick des allverderblichen Krieges,
Das die Welt zerstört und manches feste Gebäude
Schon aus dem Grunde gehoben, hat auch die Arme vertrieben.
Streifen nicht herrliche Männer von hoher Geburt nun im Elend?
Fürsten fliehen vermummt, und Könige leben verbannet.'

(V, 96-100)[29]

The sexual and emotional attraction to Dorothea is the motive force behind this recognition. She comes from outside the town but is nevertheless German, and is in need of the love and protection which he can offer — a new experience for him. Most importantly, in view of his emotional ambivalence toward the town as both his home and the place of alienation and rejection, she is persecuted by forces which are *unambiguously* foreign. Hermann's first words to his mother express the seriousness of this apparently trivial crisis:

---

[29] "'No! This ruinous war with its wild reversals of fortune, / Which is destroying the world, which has shaken so many strong buildings / From their foundations already, has driven her too from her homeland. / Are there not men of high birth who have now become destitute wanderers? / Princes are fleeing disguised, and kings live banished in exile.'"

'Wahrlich, dem ist kein Herz im ehernen Busen, der jetzo
Nicht die Not der Menschen, der umgetriebnen, empfindet;
Dem ist kein Sinn in dem Haupte, der nicht um sein eigenes Wohl sich
Und um des Vaterlands Wohl in diesen Tagen bekümmert.
Was ich heute gesehn und gehört, das rührte das Herz mir;'

(IV, 72-76)[30]

Hermann emotionally links the fate of the individual to the common good of the fatherland. He imagines the fatherland as an idyllic, even paradisal garden, a transfigured image of his father's property:

'Und nun ging ich heraus und sah die herrliche, weite
Landschaft, die sich vor uns in fruchtbaren Hügeln umherschlingt;
Sah die goldene Frucht den Garben entgegen sich neigen
Und ein reichliches Obst uns volle Kammern versprechen.'

(IV, 77-80)[31]

In this image of the fatherland the language of pietism and *Empfindsamkeit* (sensibility) is merged with the peasant's attachment to the land. The imagery is charged with sexual energy in expressions such as "fruchtbaren Hügeln," "die goldene Frucht den Garben entgegen sich neigen," "volle Kammern," which reflect his emotional state. While the idealization of his environment is in no way objectionable or chauvinistic, it is followed by an outburst against the enemy, which is remarkable for its emotional and aggressive imagery. Idyllic images of the local environment, Oedipal and patriarchal structures, personal conflicts and projected fears are transfigured into a religiously charged sense of identity with the fatherland against a foreign enemy. The enemy which threatens the *Wunschbild* of his fatherland is exaggerated into a *Schreckbild* of superhuman proportions:

'Aber, ach! wie nah ist der Feind! Die Fluten des Rheines
Schützen uns zwar; doch ach! was sind nun Fluten und Berge
Jenem schrecklichen Volke, das wie ein Gewitter daherzieht!
Denn sie rufen zusammen aus allen Enden die Jugend
Wie das Alter und dringen gewaltig vor, und die Menge
Scheut den Tod nicht; es dringt gleich nach der Menge die Menge.
Ach! und ein Deutscher wagt in seinem Hause zu bleiben?

---

[30] "'Truly, that man must be stony-hearted indeed who in these days / Feels no distress at the pitiful plight of those fugitive people; / He must have no understanding or sense if he never has feared for / His own welfare in these sad times and for that of his country. / I was upset today by the things I have heard of and witnessed.'"

[31] "'So I went out and I saw the magnificent countryside round us: / Wide and fruitful it lies, with its hills and meandering valleys. / I saw our fields full of golden corn all ready for reaping, / And the abundant fruit that soon will be filling our store-rooms.'"

Hofft vielleicht zu entgehen dem alles bedrohenden Unfall?'

(IV, 81-88)[32]

Hermann's fantasy here, like the apothecary's image of the refugees in canto one, juxtaposes *Schreckbild* with *Wunschbild*, the apocalyptic hordes of the French with the paradisal fatherland. These juxtapositions disrupt continuity, bringing attention to the artificiality of the genre, and suggesting that the idyllic images *within* the work must not be confused with reality.

For Hermann the meeting with Dorothea and the realization of what is happening to the refugees creates a channel for long repressed aggression and resentment. His reaction to the imagined French armies in 1796 is nationalistic in a way that the Swiss Ulrich Bräker's reaction during the Seven Years' War, or the Prussian Tellheim's in Lessing's *Minna von Barnhelm*, for example, are not. Bräker and his fellow soldiers manifest the solidarity of a brutalized peasantry forced to fight for rulers who commanded no nationalistic or patriotic allegiance.[33] The dynastic wars of the eighteenth century did not cultivate the type of emotional response that Hermann expresses.

Hermann's patriotism in this canto is no longer the simple peasant's love of his land. Nor is it yet the nationalism which would develop in the next twenty years. It has elements of all of these. Werther's problems, as Georg Lukács points out, were rooted in the "fatal middle-class relations" under petty absolutism.[34] In the early 1770s there was no external enemy onto whom Werther could project the crisis of self and environment. In 1796, by contrast, the Revolution and the French aggression along the Rhine borders changed political and social relationships and provided an enemy onto whom internal and external tensions could be projected.

The difference in attitudes is indicative of changes in self-identity and national identity in the quarter century between the Seven Years' War and the revolutionary wars. The father, as representative of the older generation, feels no patriotic identification with the forces of the Coalition. However Hermann sees the war as a national phenomenon, where by "national" is meant a sense of the unity of ethnicity (i.e. Herder's concept of *Volk*), language (and *Sprachraum*) and cultural traditions and values, but not of socio-economic or political factors. In the absence of a political (i.e. state) identity, these feelings are expressed against the foreign enemy (the French) in primitive terms of inside-outside, *deutsch-fremd*.

---

[32] "'But alas! we are close to the enemy. We are protected / Still by the Rhine; but rivers and mountains, how long can they hold that / Terrible people at bay, whose armies advance like a storm-cloud? / For they are calling up men from all over the country, both young and / Old, they are pressing boldly and mightily forward, they all are / Heedless of death, each wave of their troops follows close on another. / How then dare any German remain at home and be idle? / How can he hope to escape from the general disaster that threatens?'"

[33] Ulrich Bräker, *Lebensgeschichte und Natürliche Ebentheuer des armen Mannes im Tockenburg*, ed. S. Voellmy (Basel: Diogenes, 1978), 188-91.

[34] H.A. 6:63; Lukács, *Goethe*, 45-46.

Studies of the origins of German nationalism focus on the debate on enlightenment, patriotism and *Deutschheit* among the intellectuals from the midcentury until Fichte's *Reden an die deutsche Nation* (*Speeches to the German Nation*), which is seen as the starting point of a qualitatively new form of German nationalism.[35] These studies pay relatively little attention to the generation of national feelings among the populace at a non-reflexive level.[36] The "national" feelings expressed by Hermann are closer to Herder's concepts of a cultural unity based on language-community than to earlier feudal-absolutist or dynastic concepts of the German nation. Hermann manifests such a "national" feeling for the first time in modern German literature on an emotional, rather than an intellectual, critical or self-reflexive level. The son of a wealthy *Bürger*, he identifies himself downward in terms of social class, as the spokesman for a sense of closeness to the land, which has its origins in a peasant consciousness, and which is used as the expression of "German" against "French" identity. Hermann's image of Germany and his loathing of the enemy echo the anti-French propaganda that was distributed among peasants and townspeople from 1792. This propaganda was designed to counter the promises of revolutionary liberation, and represent the French advances as military occupation.[37] The images with which Hermann shores up his feelings of outraged patriotism draw together various motifs. The defense of the fatherland is represented as an apocalyptic battle of good against evil, in terms of the most primitive values of the *Gemeinschaft*, the tribe protecting itself against rape and pillage:

'im innersten Busen
Regt sich Mut und Begier, dem Vaterlande zu leben
Und zu sterben und andern ein würdiges Beispiel zu geben.
Wahrlich, wäre die Kraft der deutschen Jugend beisammen,
An der Grenze, verbündet, nicht nachzugeben den Fremden,
O, sie sollten uns nicht den herrlichen Boden betreten
Und vor unseren Augen die Früchte des Landes verzehren,

---

[35] Epstein, 29-237 and passim; John Gagliardo, *Reich and Nation: The Holy Roman Empire as Idea and Reality, 1763-1806* (Bloomington: Indiana University Press, 1980), passim; Friedrich Meinecke, *Weltbürgertum und Nationalstaat*, ed. Hans Herzfeld, vol. 5 of *Werke* (Munich: Richard Oldenbourg, 1962), 9-57; Reinhold Aris, *History of Political Thought in Germany from 1789 to 1815* (London: Allen & Unwin, 1936), 21-166.

[36] Cf. Valjavec, *Die Entstehung der politischen Strömungen*, 328-42, and Theo Stammen and Friedrich Eberle, eds., *Deutschland und die Französische Revolution 1789-1806* (Darmstadt: Wissenschaftliche Buchgesellschaft, 1988), 5-7, 15-25; and Groote, passim.

[37] See Grab, *Eroberung*, 16-50, 58-85; Blanning, *Mainz*, 210-334; Blanning, *French Revolution*, 90-92, 207-54, 317-36; Epstein, 494-96; A. Sorel, *Europe and the French Revolution: The Political Traditions of the Old Regime*, ed. and trans. Alfred Cobban and J.W. Hunt (London: Collins, 1969), 433-70.

Nicht den Männern gebieten und rauben Weiber und Mädchen!'

(IV, 95-102)[38]

Hermann's wish to serve the fatherland betrays his desire for an alternative not merely to the imagined misery and subservience to French domination (IV, 94), but also to his present sense of the loss of traditional community values in the home town. His desire for martyrdom is both a self-justification and a reproach to his father. To join the ranks of soldiers defending the fatherland would be to rebel against his father, who had forbidden him to go, and whose property he must remain at home to manage. Yet at the same time the defense of the fatherland would express his attachment to a broad patriarchal world-view which, on a personal level in the relationship with his father, is problematic.

When questioned by his mother, he admits that his long-standing resentment of his father had come to a head with the demand that he marry one of the rich neighbor's daughters:

'Alles, fühl' ich, ist wahr; ich darf es kühnlich behaupten.
Und doch tadelt Ihr mich mit Recht, o Mutter, und habt mich
Auf halbwahren Worten ertappt und halber Verstellung.'

(IV, 134-36)[39]

He seeks a restoration of the old patriarchal values of the town community in the defense of the other father, the "fatherland," as both a reproach and a pledge to the father who has denied him any sense of self-esteem, both within the town (by dominating his future) and beyond it (by forbidding him to fight). His resentment of his father and the values he has come to stand for, finds potential redemption in the defense of the fatherland, perceived as the repository of the values of family and community which have been eroded in the home town:

'Sehet, Mutter, mir ist im tiefsten Herzen beschlossen,
Bald zu tun und gleich, was recht mir deucht und verständig;
Denn wer lange bedenkt, der wählt nicht immer das Beste.
Sehet, ich werde nicht wieder nach Hause kehren! Von hier aus
Geh' ich gerad' in die Stadt und übergebe den Kriegern

---

[38] "'This I feel in my innermost soul, and my spirit has moved me / To this undaunted desire: to live for my fatherland and to / Die for it, and to give others a worthy and noble example. / Truly I say, if the strength of our German youth were assembled / On our frontier, resolved to yield no ground to the stranger, / Why, no enemy then would set foot on our glorious country; / We should not see them devouring the fruits of our soil and our labor / They should not rule our men or make off with our women and daughters!'"

[39] "'All this I feel to be true, so I know I may boldly assert it! / Nevertheless you are right to reproach me, mother, for I have / Not told the whole truth, the half was pretence, and it did not deceive you.'"

Diesen Arm und dies Herz, dem Vaterlande zu dienen.
Sage der Vater alsdann, ob nicht der Ehre Gefühl mir
Auch den Busen belebt und ob ich nicht höher hinauf will!'

(IV, 103-10)⁴⁰

Blind action is justified as the response to the conflict between personal and social values (IV, 105). The war will be the cause for an imagined new community of German youth reasserting the values of the old idyllic Germany.

The Revolution was the turning point at which French Enlightenment became explicitly national. After 1792 the behavior of the revolutionary armies provoked hostile responses in the German territories, especially in the upper Rhineland.⁴¹ In *Hermann und Dorothea* the interrelationships of enlightened progress, revolutionary liberation and national self-determination are revealed in the confrontation of German idyll and French Revolution. For Hermann this conflict takes the form of the "non-political" idyllic German *Gemeinschaft* defending itself against revolutionary French *Gesellschaft*.

The German "national" response was in fact a series of regional responses which occurred during the period of the Coalition and Napoleonic Wars and which were consolidated into a sense of identity in terms of language, culture and ethnicity (i.e. as a "Volk"). This "national" response began in the Rhineland, as the first point of entry of the French armies into Germany, and was shared by other territories when and insofar as they were affected or threatened. Intellectuals of the later national movement looked back on these responses as the beginnings of a German answer to French revolutionary nationalism, and Fichte in particular framed his analysis of the effects of the Revolution in terms of a "national" Germany in the *Reden an die deutsche Nation* in 1806. In the later 1790s the rhetoric of modern nationalism had begun to develop. This expressed a mixture of regional, religious and cultural responses to the threat from outside in the terminology of Germany as a "nation." But in the absence of a nation-state structure these responses remained "pre-national." Only after the Napoleonic reforms had created the larger political units for a national Germany from the multiplicity of states and cities of the Holy Roman Empire did these "pre-national" responses consolidate into a broader phenomenon.⁴²

---

⁴⁰ "'See, in the depths of my heart, dear mother, I now am determined / Soon and at once to do what good sense and good conscience command me; / For when one ponders too long one does not always choose the right action. / So you see, I shall not return home! I shall go from this place straight / Into the town, and there I shall offer myself to the army / In our fatherland's cause, and with hand and heart I will serve it. / Then let us see if my father will say that I too have some wish to / Better my station in life, that I too have some feeling of honor!'"

⁴¹ Sorel, 464.

⁴² See Blanning, *French Revolution*, 247-54, and A.J.P. Taylor, *The Course of German History: A Survey of the Development of German History since 1815* (1945; London: Methuen, 1982), 30f.

## The Inadequacy of *Gemeinschaft*: The Mother

The characterization of the mother as "die gute, verständige Hausfrau" ("the wise, good mother") and exaggeration of her housewifely virtues, as she walks through the vegetable garden, parody the mother in Voss's *Luise*:

> [sie] freute sich jegliches Wachstums,
> Stellte die Stützen zurecht, auf denen beladen die Äste
> Ruhten des Apfelbaums wie des Birnbaums lastende Zweige,
> Nahm gleich einige Raupen vom kräftig strotzenden Kohl weg:
> Denn ein geschäftiges Weib tut keine Schritte vergebens.
> (IV, 11-15)[43]

She makes light work of the snakes in this Garden of Eden, but cannot find Hermann, who has secluded himself beneath the pear-tree on the hill above the property. Her search for him from the yards to the town wall, the vineyards and the fields, becomes a symbolic survey of the family's holdings and influence in the community:

> Also war sie ans Ende des langen Gartens gekommen,
> ...
> Aber nur angelehnt war das Pförtchen, das aus der Laube,
> Aus besonderer Gunst, durch die Mauer des Städtchens gebrochen
> Hatte der Ahnherr einst, der würdige Burgemeister.
> (IV, 16, 19-21)[44]

She discovers Hermann in an image of idyllic and rustic harmony:

> Zwischen den Äckern schritt sie hindurch auf dem Raine den Fußpfad,
> Hatte den Birnbaum im Auge, den großen, der auf dem Hügel
> Stand, die Grenze der Felder, die ihrem Hause gehörten.
> Wer ihn gepflanzt, man konnt' es nicht wissen. Er war in der Gegend
> Weit und breit gesehn, und berühmt die Früchte des Baumes.
> Unter ihm pflegten die Schnitter des Mahls sich zu freuen am Mittag
> Und die Hirten des Viehs in seinem Schatten zu warten;

---

[43] "[She] was glad as she saw all the things that were growing; / Straightened as she went by the props that supported the burdened / Apple-tree's branches, and the well-laden boughs of the pear-tree; / Picked as she passed some grubs from the sprouting leaves of the cabbage; / For a well-occupied wife never takes a step to no purpose." Cf. *Luise*: "dem Weibe geziemt der Gehorsam" ("obedience befits a wife").

[44] "Thus she walked through the whole of the garden and came to its far end, / ... But from the arbor a little gate led, which her family's worthy / Forebear, the burgomaster, had made by favor and privilege / Here in the little town's wall; and it now stood ajar."

Bänke fanden sie da von rohen Steinen und Rasen.

(IV, 52-59)⁴⁵

With her sensitivity and common sense, she unravels the tangle of misunderstanding to resolve the conflict. She sees through Hermann's fantasies of self-sacrifice for his fatherland, just as in canto nine she, and not the vicar, stops Dorothea from leaving the house. She realizes that Hermann has fallen love with the unknown refugee girl, and that his father's cynicism has upset him. Characterized as a maternal figure, as wife and mother, she is free of masculine experiential and behavioral responses:

'Denn die Männer sind heftig und denken nur immer das Letzte,
Und die Hindernis treibt die Heftigen leicht von dem Wege;
Aber ein Weib ist geschickt, auf Mittel zu denken, und wandelt
Auch den Umweg, geschickt zu ihrem Zweck zu gelangen.'
...
'Stehen wie Felsen doch zwei Männer gegeneinander!
Unbewegt und stolz will keiner dem andern sich nähern,
Keiner zum guten Worte, dem ersten, die Zunge bewegen.'

(IV, 148-51; 229-31)⁴⁶

She is ironically distanced here, as earlier on her walk through the idyllic garden, by the triteness with which her words are reported. She too belongs to the older generation, for whom individual identity and social roles are not problematic. She cannot fully comprehend the expansion of Hermann's personal feelings of hurt into general feelings of patriotism.⁴⁷ At this point she prevents Hermann from joining the militia — a rash step which they both know he would soon regret. At

---

⁴⁵ "On she walked through the separate fields, by the path on the unploughed / Border, making her way to the great pear-tree on the hill-top; / It was the boundary-mark of the land that belonged to her husband. / Nobody knew who had planted it there; one could see it from far and / Wide, and the fruit of this tree was famous all over the district. / Under its shade the reapers would sit enjoying their dinner, / And the herdsman would sit there too looking after the cattle, / For there was soft grass there, and rough stone benches to rest on."

⁴⁶ "'Men always think in extremes, for they are so headstrong by nature / And so easily rush off their course when they meet with a hindrance. / But a woman is skilful, she thinks of ways, she will even / Take a roundabout way in the skilful pursuit of her purpose. / ... / Here's how it is, when two men like rocks confront one another! / Both unyielding and proud, neither willing to make a concession, / Each refusing to open his lips and speak the first kind word.'"

⁴⁷ On the psychological roots of pietism see Gerhard Kaiser, *Pietismus und Patriotismus: Ein Beitrag zum Problem der Säkularisation*, 2nd rev. ed. (Frankfurt am Main: Athenäum, 1973), passim, and Robert Minder, *Glaube, Skepsis und Rationalismus: Dargestellt auf Grund der autobiographischen Schriften von Karl Philipp Moritz* (Frankfurt am Main: Suhrkamp, 1974), 40-49.

the same time however the interchange reveals a weakness of character in Hermann, in view of which his final speech in canto nine becomes questionable. His inability to rebel against or even challenge his father face to face is revealed:

'Darum lasset mich gehn, wohin die Verzweiflung mich antreibt!
Denn mein Vater, er hat die entscheidenden Worte gesprochen,
Und sein Haus ist nicht mehr das meine, wenn er das Mädchen
Ausschließt, das ich allein nach Haus zu führen begehre.'

(IV, 224-27)[48]

Hermann's patriotic fantasies are a vicarious rebellion against the father he dares not question in reality. The fabrication of an adolescent dream of national brotherhood projects exaggerated sexual and Oedipal conflicts onto the foreign enemy. As the basis for his statement of a national program in the final lines of the work, it is unconvincing. His mother sees only part of the change in him. She does not see the extent to which his fantasies of self-sacrifice and national solidarity fulfil a group need, which marriage alone will not resolve. Although confused and contradictory here, Hermann's thoughts are tendentious. By the end of the work his patriotism will have consolidated alongside his love for Dorothea. His final speech is more strong-willed and self-composed than his words in canto four. Uncontained by any narrative commentary at the end of the work it breaks out of the ironic-parodic form, pointing forward to the nationalism of the post 1806 period.

Excursus: Language and the Nation in Eighteenth-Century Germany

The term, *Vaterland* as used generally in the later eighteenth century did not yet signify a broad political or national identity. The Grimm Brothers cite the use of the word as "the land possessed by the father" from early times, and locate the wider use of the word from Luther's time onwards as: "the land in which my father lived, and to which I consider myself to belong; often — although not necessarily — meaning the same as 'land of birth,'" The use of the word to signify "not only the home of a single individual, but also of a people, or ethnic region" is traced back only as far as Heinrich Heine.[49] In the 1790s this word still denoted the region where one was born or lived, expressing through the emotive value of the word "father" the sense of attachment to the land, which only gradually would be extended to the nation as a whole.

---

[48] "'So let me go my way now, where despair is driving my footsteps! / For my father today spoke words that can not be unspoken, / And his house can no longer be mine, if he says he will close its / Doors to the only girl I desire to bring home here and marry.'"

[49] Jacob and Wilhelm Grimm, *Deutsches Wörterbuch*, 33 vols. (Leipzig, 1854; repr. Munich: DTV, 1984), 25:27.

Before the Revolution there had been little consensus as to what a German identity might be.[50] As Goethe pointed out in "Literarischer Sanskulottismus," Germany was a conglomeration of petty absolutist territories with various overlapping religious, linguistic and cultural identities. In the second half of the century especially there had been considerable discussion among the intelligentsia of the possibility, the nature and the value of a German "nation."[51] Political commentators such as Schubart, Schlözer, and Möser, used concepts of a German nation to criticize the dependence of petty absolutism on French cultural models. Among certain sections of the intelligentsia of the mid eighteenth century, a form of Roman "patriotism" was propagated in the absence of a German national identity. Goethe objected to this "Römerpatriotismus" in his early review of Sonnenfels's *Ueber die Liebe des Vaterlandes*. Sonnenfels had tried to enlist the ancient Roman concept of patriotism in the cause of the Habsburg dynasty.[52] This concept was also used by writers such as Joh. Wilh. Gleim and Ewald von Kleist in the cause of Prussia during the Seven Years' War, in order to glorify Friedrich II.[53] For some middle-class writers, the story of the Roman patriot, Cincinnatus, was used to link concepts of *Bürgertugend* to patriotism and service to one's country.[54] This story could be used by those writers who felt a sense of patriotism (perhaps hearkening back to the Holy Roman Empire of the German Nation) in spite of their moral and political objections to petty absolutism.[55] Gerhard Schulz writes that modern concepts and definitions of the Holy Roman Empire of the German Nation, Germany, "Germanness," and national culture do not reflect the reality of the situation in the late eighteenth century. The political unity of the German nation had no place in the national memory, since it had last existed in people's minds as a political reality in the late middle ages. And neither were the far-reaching political changes imaginable, which would allow Germany to become a cohesive nation-state in the eighteenth century.[56] Gerhard Kaiser points out that

---

[50] Schulz, 21ff.

[51] Krauss, *Perspektiven und Probleme*, 149-211.

[52] See ch. 1, fn. 12.

[53] Johann Wilhelm Ludwig Gleim, "Siegeslied nach der Schlacht bei Lowositz, den 1. Oktober 1756," *Preußische Kriegslieder in den Feldzügen 1756 und 1757 von einem Grenadier, Anakreontiker und preußisch-patriotischen Lyriker*, ed. Franz Muncker, *Deutsche National-Litteratur* vol. 45, ed. Joseph Kürschner (Stuttgart, n.d.; repr. Tokyo: Sansyusya, 1974), 244-48.

[54] Cincinnatus had withdrawn from a political system of which he disapproved, but was willing to help his country in its hour of need.

[55] Joh. Heinr. Merck's Oheim in the *Geschichte des Herrn Oheims*, vol. 1 of *Werke*, ed. A. Henkel (Frankfurt am Main: Insel, 1968), and Lessing's Odoardo Galotti, the "rauher Degen" who has withdrawn to his estate in Sabionetta, would also come into this category.

[56] Schulz, 22-23.

the growth of nation-states which characterized western European development since the Renaissance did not occur in Germany. Two types of patriotism developed as a result of the socio-political structure of German petty absolutism and the intensification of political thinking in the later eighteenth century: the renewal of particularist patriotism and a strengthening of the sense of cultural nationhood.[57]

In the early seventeenth century Martin Opitz had attempted to cultivate a German literary language and culture by showing, for example, the differences between German and classical prosody. These foundations of a German national literature were built upon during the eighteenth century by Gottsched and others in societies such as the *Deutsche Gesellschaft*.[58] The idea of a German national literature continues through Klopstock and Voss in the later eighteenth century.[59] The ambivalence of Goethe and Schiller to the concept of a German national literature and culture without a German nation is expressed in the distichs:

Das Deutsche Reich:
Deutschland? Aber wo liegt es? Ich weiß das Land nicht zu finden;
   Wo das gelehrte beginnt, hört das politische auf.

and

Deutscher Nationalcharakter:
Zur Nation euch zu bilden, ihr hoffet es, Deutsche, vergebens;
   Bildet, ihr könnt es, dafür freier zu Menschen euch aus![60]

In the second half of the eighteenth century especially, the concept of Germany as a *Kulturnation* had gained currency among intellectuals. Weimar classicism, with its roots in the thinking of Winckelmann and Wieland came to occupy the central position in this concept. German intellectuals knew of the national movements in North America and elsewhere from the mid 1770s onward, and sympathized with enlightened concepts of the republic and free state since Rousseau.[61] These influences were felt most strongly in Herder's ideas of language and culture as the

---

[57] Kaiser, *Pietismus und Patriotismus*, 33.

[58] Kohn, *Idea of Nationalism*, 346.

[59] Voss's attempts to weld classical prosody to German verse stands in direct lineage to Opitz's creation of a literary language, and is parodied by Goethe in the disjunction between hexameter and spoken stress-units in *Hermann und Dorothea*.

[60] "The German Empire: Germany? Where is it? I don't know where to find this country. The 'intellectual' Germany begins where the 'political' Germany ends." And "German National Character: You Germans, you hope in vain to become a nation. Why don't you become individuals instead — you can do that and be freer as well." W.A. I, 5, 218.

[61] Schulz, 30.

criteria of national identity, which paved the way for the whole of the linguistic community, and not merely a section (whether the nobility, middle classes, intellectuals, or peasants), to comprise the "nation." Groote writes:

> It was not by any means the cultivated language of the highly educated, but rather the originality and truth of the common language, to which people felt attached. ... Praiseworthy characteristics were soon discovered ... among the people ("Volk") itself which spoke the language. Whether in criticism or praise, one began to identify oneself with the people.[62]

Herder distrusted the concept of the state (i.e. as the absolutist state or the nation-state), but formulated a broad concept of the nation as a unity in terms of its language, ethnicity ("Volk"), cultural traditions, territory, and independence or freedom from oppression.[63] However the unity of "nation" and "state" which the French Revolution introduced to Europe, and which became paradigmatic during the nineteenth century, aroused Herder's contempt.[64] Hans Kohn writes:

> In the Western World, in England and in France, in the Netherlands and Switzerland, in the United States and in the British dominions, the rise of nationalism was a predominantly political occurrence; it was preceded by the formation of the future national state, or, as in the case of the United States, coincided with it.[65]

In the German states, this welding together of the political state with the emotional, cultural and linguistic complex of the "fatherland" did not occur during the eighteenth century. Rather than the socio-political concept of nationalism, German nationalism substituted "the infinitely vaguer concept of the 'Volk'" as described by Herder.[66]

---

[62] Groote, 12; see also John Gagliardo, *From Pariah to Patriot: The Changing Image of the German Peasant, 1770-1840* (Lexington: University Press of Kentucky, 1969), 144-45.

[63] Johann Gottfried Herder, "Haben wir noch jetzt das Publikum und Vaterland der Alten?" *Sämtliche Werke*, ed. Bernhard Suphan, 33 vols., (Berlin, 1877-1913; repr. Hildesheim: Olms, 1967-1968), 1:13-28; *Briefe zur Beförderung der Humanität*, 5te. Sammlung (1794), *Sämtl. Werke*, 17:211. Cf. also Kohn, 429; Fishman, *Language and Nationalism*, 3-29; Isaiah Berlin, *Vico and Herder: Two Studies in the History of Ideas* (London: Hogarth, 1976), 149ff.; M. Barnard, ed. and trans., *J.G. Herder on Social and Political Culture* (Cambridge: Cambridge University Press, 1969), 17-32; M. Barnard, *Herder's Social and Political Thought: From Enlightenment to Nationalism* (Oxford: Clarendon Press, 1965), 54-87; Robert Ergang, *Herder and the Foundations of German Nationalism* (New York: Columbia University Press, 1931; repr. New York: Octagon Books, 1966).

[64] Kohn, *Idea of Nationalism*, 429.

[65] Kohn, *Idea of Nationalism*, 329.

[66] Kohn, *Idea of Nationalism*, 331.

Language is the means by which patriotism, and emotional and psychological conflicts are interlinked. Hermann's language is quite different from that of the other characters. When recounting the meeting with Dorothea (I, 11-81), he uses the word "Herz" ("heart") or its cognate "herzlich" five times, and makes many references to Providence and the power of good deeds. August Langen in *Der Wortschatz des deutschen Pietismus* identifies "Herz" and its cognates as key expressions of German pietism.[67] Pietism had been the most important resource for the development of a broad and flexible vocabulary to express emotional and psychological states of mind from the early eighteenth century onward.[68] Langen and Eric A. Blackall in particular have shown how pietism encouraged the development of German as a medium for the expression of emotions, states of mind, feelings and perceptions in literature from the early decades of the century.[69] With its vagueness, its surcharges of emotion and its development of a vocabulary for psychological and emotional states and feelings, the language of pietism influenced literary language in Germany from the early years of the eighteenth century, and had affected everyday language by the last quarter of the century. Pietistic self-expression flowed over from the religious contexts of the conventicle, the letter and the diary into the wider usage of everyday life. By the 1790s the language-consciousness of Werther was no longer unique to a generation of young middle-class intellectuals. It had become the language of a new generation, twenty years younger than Werther, and belonging to a quite different stratum of the middle classes.

Werther's discovery of "Wahlheim" is a result of his need for escape from an outside world which presents irresolvable conflicts for him. At the beginning of the book he finds himself in a provincial town, which he finds unpleasant, although the surrounding countryside is beautiful: "Die Stadt selbst ist unangenehm, dagegen rings umher eine unaussprechliche Schönheit der Natur."[70] Likewise Hermann rejects the modernized town out of a sense of betrayal of community values, and opts for the idyllic garden and the spring outside the town. Idyllic nature serves as a place of refuge for both characters. Rousseauian ideas of rejection of corrupted civilization influence both Werther and Hermann, although the former is able to articulate his feelings within a cultural and intellectual context.

---

[67] August Langen, *Der Wortschatz des deutschen Pietismus*, 2nd enl. ed. (Tübingen: Niemeyer, 1968), 372-73, 452.

[68] Hans Eggers, *Deutsche Sprachgeschichte*, 2 vols. (Reinbek bei Hamburg: Rowohlt, 1986), 2:302-8.

[69] See Eric Blackall, *The Emergence of German as a Literary Language 1700-1775* (Cambridge: Cambridge University Press, 1959), 343ff.; Hans Sperber, "Der Einfluß des Pietismus auf die deutsche Sprache," *DVjs* 8 (1930): 497-515, and "Beiträge zur Geschichte der deutschen Sprache im 18. Jahrhundert," *Zeitschrift für deutsche Philologie* 52 (1927): 331-45.

[70] "The town itself is unpleasant, although the natural surroundings are indescribably beautiful." H.A. 6:8.

The rediscovery of idyll by the young generation in 1796 however is very different to that of 1774. Werther's flight to idyll comes as a result of the lack of options available for a creative, educated, young middle-class professional in a petty absolutist German state. His suicide is an indication of the wretchedness of society as well as of radical utopianism.[71] Where Werther's crisis ends in suicide, Hermann's results in a socio-political program. The former's response to the internal developments in the home town and the external upheavals of the Revolution amount to a rejection of large-scale politics and modernity. The home town in its progressive aspect (i.e. as *Gesellschaft*) is rejected in favor of an idyll (*Gemeinschaft*) which has become surcharged with fear of the French. Hermann's "language of the heart" will not simply die away as Werther's letters do, without resonance, in increasingly alienated monologues. On the contrary, it will find resonance in Germany over the following decades as an idyll charged with religious energies and collective historical memories. Werther's inwardly turned aggression is turned outward in *Hermann und Dorothea*, in an image of Germany, which pre-empts the nationalism of Hermann's contemporaries after 1806.

---

[71] See Goethe's comments on Werther's suicide, H.A. 9:583.

# 4: The Crisis of Enlightenment

SO FAR THE REFUGEES have functioned as a counter-image to the home town in the story. For the innkeeper and the apothecary their misery and disorder bring to mind fears and insecurities dating back to the time of the fire. For Hermann they incite fears of an invading enemy and dreams of a new future in which he, with the resurgent youth of Germany (IV, 98), would play a heroic role. The classical idyll since Vergil had made use of the motif of the "wider world," the sphere of politics, war, and social change, in contrast to which idyllic life is provincial, uneventful and happy. In counterpoint to the father, mother, and son in the home town are the less easily categorized figures of the judge, Dorothea and her first fiancé, all of whom experience personal crisis and social change on the broader plane of European politics. The motif of the "wider world" and the contrast with the idyllic haven is expanded in *Hermann und Dorothea*, to express the relationships between individual perception, social identity and socio-political change.

## The Failure of Freedom: The Judge

The judge appears only at the end of canto five and the beginning of canto six, reporting on the Revolution in France, and linking the history of the refugees to the Revolution and the Coalition Wars, as well as supplying information about Dorothea and her first fiancé to the vicar and apothecary. He first appears as patriarch and arbiter, sorting out squabbles and conflicts among the refugees:

Stärker fanden sie bald das Gedränge. Da war um die Wagen
Streit der drohenden Männer, worein sich mischten die Weiber,
Schreiend. Da nahte sich schnell mit würdigen Schritten ein Alter,
Trat zu den Scheltenden hin; und sogleich verklang das Getöse,
Als er Ruhe gebot und väterlich ernst sie bedrohte.

(V, 193-97)[1]

The threatening men and screaming women represent a community on the verge of breakdown, where individual is pitted against individual for survival. The

---

[1] "Soon the crowd became thicker, for round the wagons a quarrel / Had broken out: the men were uttering threats, and the screaming / Women joined in. But now an old man of dignified bearing / Strode up at once to the quarrelsome group, and as he rebuked them, / Calling for silence with fatherly sternness, the hubbub abated."

enjambment of the participial adjective "Schreiend" at the beginning of line 195 disrupts the rhythm, which is then restored in lines 196 to 197, as the judge restores order. The judge is identified by the vicar as an Old Testament prophet:

'Ja, Ihr erscheint mir heut als einer der ältesten Führer,
Die durch Wüsten und Irren vertriebene Völker geleitet.
Denk' ich doch eben, ich rede mit Josua oder mit Moses.'

(V, 225-27)[2]

Like the innkeeper at the time of the fire, he is a leader and pillar of support for an otherwise fragmented community. Here however the similarity with Hermann's father ends. For where Hermann's father as leader could rebuild within the old forms, the judge cannot. The fire was an internal disaster, bounded by the walls of the town. It symbolizes the destruction of the old forms within a confined area. The town has been rebuilt, reformed and modernized. Against this, the Revolution and the Coalition Wars symbolize a more profound upheaval, where the old foundations have been entirely destroyed, and cannot be rebuilt. The judge has only the archetypal refugee identity of the Old Testament Jews to draw upon. He is a charismatic patriarch in a situation where all paradigms of self-identity other than the Old Testament have been destroyed. He characterizes his people and their experiences in terms of Old Testament models. Their sufferings have been sent down upon them in order that they learn forbearance and cooperation:

'Hat uns,' rief er, 'noch nicht das Unglück also gebändigt,
Daß wir endlich verstehn, uns untereinander zu dulden
Und zu vertragen, wenn auch nicht jeder die Handlungen abmißt?
Unverträglich fürwahr ist der Glückliche! Werden die Leiden
Endlich euch lehren, nicht mehr wie sonst mit dem Bruder zu hadern?
Gönnet einander den Platz auf fremdem Boden und teilet,
Was ihr habet, zusammen, damit ihr Barmherzigkeit findet!'

(V, 198-204)[3]

They must learn from their past, and experience is subsumed into the form of the parable, expressed in Lutheran language. The imagery of the refugee community

---

[2] "'Yes; when I see you today I take you for one of those ancient / Leaders of exiled peoples through wildernesses and wandering: / For I feel I am speaking to Joshua now or to Moses.'"

[3] "'Have our misfortunes still,' he exclaimed, 'not taught us their lesson? / Have you not yet at long last learnt to bear with each other, to make peace / Even when one of you thoughtlessly does his neighbor a mischief? / Fortunate men, to be sure, are not reconciled soon; but will you not / Learn from your long-shared troubles to give up dissension and wrangling? / You are on foreign ground now, you must live and let live, you must share out / What you have with your brothers: the merciful shall obtain mercy.'"

as brothers on foreign ground echoes Dorothea's earlier self-identification in meeting Hermann (II, 30ff.), and contrasts with Hermann's acceptance of the refugees as "brothers" (II, 45).

The interchange between the vicar and the judge in cantos five and six reflects the meeting of two world-views, which are separated not by the Revolution of 1789, but by the experiences of 1792. The vicar is the mouthpiece for the naive, superficial and dogmatic enlightenment, popularized by the philosopher, Christian Wolff and satirized by Voltaire in the figure of Pangloss in *Candide*, who sees a divine plan or manifestation of theodicy in even the worst events. He addresses the judge with a parable of the loss of innocence, which uses an image of agrarian idyll, drawing on the theme of the expulsion from Eden:

'Vater, fürwahr! wenn das Volk in glücklichen Tagen dahinlebt,
Von der Erde sich nährend, die weit und breit sich auftut
Und die erwünschten Gaben in Jahren und Monden erneuert,
Da geht alles von selbst, und jeder ist sich der Klügste
Wie der Beste; und so bestehen sie nebeneinander,
Und der vernünftigste Mann ist wie ein andrer gehalten:
Denn was alles geschieht, geht still, wie von selber, den Gang fort.'

(V, 210-16)[4]

When the harmony between individual and nature is disrupted, man's need for divine guidance shows itself. The vicar posits an enlightened God, who speaks through reason to reveal the hidden divine logic:

'Aber zerrüttet die Not die gewöhnlichen Wege des Lebens,
...
Ach! da sieht man sich um, wer wohl der verständigste Mann sei,
Und er redet nicht mehr die herrlichen Worte vergebens.'

(V, 217, 221-22)[5]

In response to the vicar's presumptions about the refugee experience, the judge posits a dour Old Testament religiosity. However he is not simply a fundamentalist as the "enlightened" vicar presumes during the conversation. On the contrary, his attitudes are the result of disillusionment. His experiences can be seen in terms

---

[4] "'Truly, good father, when times of ease are enjoyed by the people, / When they are fed by the plentiful earth which opens its treasures / Far and wide, and renews its gifts as the years and the months pass: / Then we need have no cares, for each man makes his own judgements / Wisely and well, and thus they can live at peace with each other, / And the good sense of rational men is taken for granted / As the natural course of events moves quietly onwards.'"

[5] "'But when disaster disturbs the accustomed ways of our life,/ ... / Why it is then that we take a look round us in search of a wise man, / And when he speaks, his excellent words are no longer wasted.'"

of the "crisis of enlightenment" described in the introduction: disappointment at the failure of the Revolution to bring about a political utopia, and recognition that the revolutionary enthusiasm of the French could turn into nationalist fervor and ruthless exploitation (i.e. "occupation" rather than "liberation"). In order to comprehend this experience, he has taken recourse to non-political, apocalyptic and fundamentalist religious categories.

The vicar's well-meaning but limited and unimaginative "enlightenment" is incapable of comprehending these experiences. His words prompt the judge to remember the parable of the Jews in the desert:

Und es versetzte darauf mit ernstem Blicke der Richter:
'Wahrlich, unsere Zeit vergleicht sich den seltensten Zeiten,
Die die Geschichte bemerkt, die heilige wie die gemeine.
Denn wer gestern und heut in diesen Tagen gelebt hat,
Hat schon Jahre gelebt: so drängen sich alle Geschichten.
...
O, wir anderen dürfen uns wohl mit jenen vergleichen,
Denen in ernster Stund' erschien im feurigen Busche
Gott der Herr; auch uns erschien er in Wolken und Feuer.'

(V, 228-32, 235-37)[6]

The judge does not merely liken the refugee experience to the Exodus; it is a new Exodus, where the appearance of God to the believers in the desert indicates a religious and national-cultural mission. Fundamentalist categories of thought have here been revised in response to experiences which the judge cannot comprehend in any other way. The strangeness of the times, the "unerhörte Begebenheiten" ("unprecedented events") of the revolutionary experience, and the "new epoch of world history" can only be understood by comparing it to the unique moments of biblical history.[7] In comparison with the present, all other stories of mankind become one and the same ("so drängen sich alle Geschichten"). Hence he retells his experiences using religious rather than political imagery. The chiliastic expectations of the Revolution led to disillusionment and rejection when it was realized that the ideal, enlightened constitutional monarchy or republic would not be realized. The beginnings of the Revolution are seen as the dawning of a new age of democracy and liberation from absolutist tyranny, which would disperse the old order of absolutist despotism:

---

[6] "And the judge with a serious air made the following answer: / 'Truly our times may well be compared with the rarest of epochs / That human history, sacred or worldly, has ever recorded. / For any man who has lived through these last few days has already / Lived for many a year; so thick and fast have events come. / ... / Oh, indeed, we may well compare ourselves to those others / Who in a grave hour saw the Lord God in a fiery bush: for / He has appeared before us in clouds and pillars of fire too.'"

[7] See ch. 2, fn. 31.

'Denn wer leugnet es wohl, daß hoch sich das Herz ihm erhoben,
Ihm die freiere Brust mit reineren Pulsen geschlagen,
Als sich der erste Glanz der neuen Sonne heranhob,
Als man hörte vom Rechte der Menschen, das allen gemein sei,
Von der begeisternden Freiheit und von der löblichen Gleichheit!
Damals hoffte jeder sich selbst zu leben; es schien sich
Aufzulösen das Band, das viele Länder umstrickte,
Das der Müßiggang und der Eigennütz in der Hand hielt.'

(VI, 6-13)[8]

Likewise his respect for the early leaders of the Revolution, men like Lafayette and Mirabeau, who acted against their class interests in the name of liberty, reveals a naive view of the motivations and the issues at stake in the early days of the Revolution:[9]

'Schauten nicht alle Völker in jenen drängenden Tagen
Nach der Hauptstadt der Welt, die es schon so lange gewesen
Und jetzt mehr als je den herrlichen Namen verdiente?
Waren nicht jener Männer, der ersten Verkünder der Botschaft,
Namen den höchsten gleich, die unter die Sterne gesetzt sind?
Wuchs nicht jeglichem Menschen der Mut und der Geist und die Sprache?'

(VI, 14-19)[10]

As the French troops approached with the propaganda of liberation, their German neighbors in the left-bank territories were at first enthusiastic and receptive. The excitement and hope of the early revolutionary period are portrayed in an image of the community as idyllic, free and responsible for its own government:

'Und wir waren zuerst als Nachbarn lebhaft entzündet.
Drauf begann der Krieg, und die Züge bewaffneter Franken
Rückten naher;

---

[8] "'For what man can deny that his soul was moved and uplifted / And that his heart was beginning to beat more freely and purely / Then, as the first light broke in that dawn, the new light of that sunrise, / When we first heard of the Rights of Man that were common to all men, / When we first sang Equality's praises, and Freedom inspired us! / Every man hoped then for freedom to live his own life, and the bondage / Which enslaved so many a people, which idle self-interest / Had imposed and maintained, now seemed at last to be easing.'"

[9] Cf. Goethe, *Campagne in Frankreich*, H.A. 10:317.

[10] "'For in those days of urgent demand for change, did the nations / Not all look to the world's chief city, which so long had been so, / And now merited more than ever that name of distinction? / Were not the names of those men who had first proclaimed the new message / Highly exalted and praised to the stars as the equals of any? / And did not all men acquire a new courage and eloquent spirit?'"

...
Jedem das Seine versprechend und jedem die eigne Regierung.
Hoch erfreute sich da die Jugend, sich freute das Alter,
Und der muntere Tanz begann um die neue Standarte.
So gewannen sie bald, die überwiegenden Franken,
Erst der Männer Geist mit feurigem, munterm Beginnen,
Dann die Herzen der Weiber mit unwiderstehlicher Anmut.'

(VI, 20-22, 25-30)[11]

However this idyll was shattered by the realization that the political movement had a momentum of its own, against which the village community is powerless. Revolutionary expectation and disappointment are imagined in sexual and utopian imagery which implies the elation, but also the brevity of the revolutionary enthusiasm:

'O, wie froh ist die Zeit, wenn mit der Braut sich der Bräut'gam
Schwinget im Tanze, den Tag der gewünschten Verbindung erwartend!
Aber herrlicher war die Zeit, in der uns das Höchste,
Was der Mensch sich denkt, als nah und erreichbar sich zeigte.
Da war jedem die Zunge gelöst; es sprachen die Greise,
Männer und Jünglinge laut voll hohen Sinns und Gefühles.'

(VI, 34-39)[12]

The judge's disillusionment with the Revolution mirrors that of many of the German intellectuals who rejected their earlier revolutionary sympathies in the early to mid 1790s. One after another they either denied or realigned their views of the Revolution, withdrew to non-political spheres of literature and philosophy, turned their backs on literature altogether, or recanted in favor of the old order.

The poets Klopstock and Voss were among the most notable of these writers. In the years from 1789 to 1796 their attitudes changed from euphoric celebration to apocalyptic disappointment. In "Die Etats Généraux," ("The Estates General," 1788) and "Kennet Euch Selbst" ("Know Thyselves," 1789) Klopstock used the image of the Revolution as the dawning of a new age: "Der kühne Reichstag

---

[11] "'And among us, as a neighboring people, the flame was soon kindled. / Then the war broke out, and the marching armies of Frenchmen / Were drawing nearer, ... / Promising each man his due and a government of his own choosing. / There was rejoicing then by the young folk and by the old folk; / Gleeful dancing began all around the new tricolour standard. / Thus before long the victorious French were accepted among us: / First they won over the minds of our men with their fire and their boldness, / Then, with their charm which none could resist, the hearts of our women.'"

[12] "'Ah, how glad is the time of betrothal, the bride and her bridegroom / Dancing together, awaiting the day of the union they long for! / But more splendid than this was that time when the noblest of projects / Man can conceive seemed to be within reach and near to fulfillment. / We were all orators then: there were speeches by old men, speeches / By mature men and speeches by boys, full of wisdom and passion.'"

Galliens dämmert schon."[13] Like the judge, he sees this image as unique in world history: "so durchwandre die Weltannalen, und finde / Etwas darin, das ihr ferne nur gleicht."[14] Most important in "Kennet Euch Selbst" is the utopian image of the post-revolutionary situation, after the political storm has passed:

Ach ich frag' umsonst; ihr verstummet, Deutsche! Was zeiget
Euer Schweigen? bejahrter Geduld
Müden Kummer? Oder verkündet es nahe Verwandlung?
Wie die schwüle Stille den Sturm,
Der vor sich her sie wirbelt, die Donnerwolken, bis Glut sie
Werden, und werden zerschmetterndes Eis!
Nach dem Wetter, atmen sie kaum die Lüfte, die Bäche
Rieseln ...
Alles ist reg', und ist Leben, und freut sich! die Nachtigall flötet
Hochzeit! liebender singet die Braut!
Knaben umtanzen den Mann, den kein Despot mehr verachtet!
Mädchen das ruhige, säugende Weib.[15]

The imagery of idyll and dance is closely comparable to that used by Goethe's judge. Like the judge, Klopstock questions and ultimately turns against his earlier pro-revolutionary stance after 1792 in "Die Jakobiner" ("The Jacobins," 1792) and "Der Erobrungskrieg" ("The War of Conquest," 1793):

Jetzo lag an der Kette das Ungeheuer, der Greuel
Greuel! itzt war der Mensch über sich selber erhöht!
Aber, weh uns! sie selbst, die das Untier zähmten, vernichten
Ihr hochheilig Gesetz, schlagen Erobererschlacht. [16]

---

[13] "Dawn is already breaking over Gaul's bold parliament." Friedrich Gottlieb Klopstock, *Ausgewählte Werke*, ed. Karl August Schleiden (Munich: Hanser, 1962), 140.

[14] "Seek through the annals of the world and find therein anything even faintly comparable." Klopstock, 140.

[15] "I ask in vain. Germans, you are silent? What does / This silence signify? timeworn patience, or / Weary grief? Or does it presage timely change? / Like the humid lull before the storm, / Which drives the molten thunder clouds on until they hail down in shattering ice! After the storm, the air is free to breathe, the streams trickle ... / Everything stirs and is lively and joyous! The nightingale trills / accompaniment to the wedding! / The bride sings more lovingly! / Boys dance around the man, whom no tyrant holds longer in contempt! / Girls dance around the quiet, suckling wife." Klopstock, 141.

[16] "Now the monster lay in chains. Abomination! / Horror! And the human being was raised above himself! / But woe to us! they themselves, who tamed the monster, now are destroying their own holy laws and waging wars of conquest," Klopstock, 150. Also "An la Rochefoucaulds Schatten": "in der Dämmerung dort seh ich ein blutig Gewand." ("In the dusk there I see a bloodied robe") Klopstock, 147.

The images of storm, twilight, and the monstrous or bestial and the tone of abhorrence and outrage is echoed in the judge's words:

'Aber der Himmel trübte sich bald. Um den Vorteil der Herrschaft
Stritt ein verderbtes Geschlecht, unwürdig, das Gute zu schaffen.
Sie ermordeten sich und unterdrückten die neuen
Nachbarn und Brüder und sandten die eigennützige Menge.
Und es praßten bei uns die Obern und raubten im großen,
Und es raubten und praßten bis zu dem Kleinsten die Kleinen;'

(VI, 40-45)[17]

The experiment in enlightenment has failed: man is no better than a marauding animal, and civil unrest, brutality and selfishness are the order of the day. Seeing his hopes for enlightened progress dashed, the judge reverts to a harsh, fundamentalist world view:

'Nichts ist heilig ihm mehr; er raubt es. Die wilde Begierde
Dringt mit Gewalt auf das Weib und macht die Lust zum Entsetzen.
Überall sieht er den Tod und genießt die letzten Minuten
Grausam, freut sich des Bluts und freut sich des heulenden Jammers.
...
Möcht' ich den Menschen doch nie in dieser schnöden Verirrung
Wiedersehn! Das wütende Tier ist ein besserer Anblick.
Sprech' er doch nie von Freiheit, als könn' er sich selber regieren!
Losgebunden erscheint, sobald die Schranken hinweg sind,
Alles Böse, das tief das Gesetz in die Winkel zurücktrieb.'

(VI, 62-65, 76-80)[18]

After the sexual imagery of revolutionary hope and euphoria, the judge expresses his disillusionment in images of natural cataclysm and destruction. The lateral imagery of equality and harmony in the dance is replaced by the vertical imagery of the storm in the heavens and the fight for power and superiority. The image of

---

[17] '"But this unclouded weather soon changed. A depraved generation, / Men unworthy to do great things, were struggling for power now. / They began murdering each other, and we, their new brothers and neighbors, / Fell under tyrannous rule. A self-seeking rabble was sent here: / We had their overlords squandering and pillaging here on a large scale, / While on the pettiest scale their underlings pillaged and squandered."'

[18] '"Nothing is sacred to them, they will simply seize it; in wild lust / They must take women by force, they must make a horror of pleasure; / Everywhere they see death, and gloat cruelly over the dying's / Final moments, delighting in blood and in screams of affliction."'

the idyllic community around the freedom tree gives way to that of the natural world of storms and animal instincts.[19]

### The Critique of Dogmatic Enlightenment: The Vicar

The vicar meanwhile has found more arguments against the judge's pessimism:

'Wolltet Ihr aber zurück die traurigen Tage durchschauen,
Würdet Ihr selber gestehen, wie oft Ihr auch Gutes erblicktet,
Manches Treffliche, das verborgen bleibt in dem Herzen,
Regt die Gefahr es nicht auf, und drängt die Not nicht den Menschen,
Daß er als Engel sich zeig', erscheine den andern ein Schutzgott.'
(VI, 84-88)[20]

In the calamities that have befallen the refugees the vicar seeks proof of human goodness, not of the corruption of human nature. However the judge's metaphor of the melted gold and silver found after a fire highlights the difference between his understanding of human nature and the vicar's:

Lächelnd versetzte darauf der alte, würdige Richter:
'Ihr erinnert mich klug, wie oft nach dem Brande des Hauses
Man den betrübten Besitzer an Gold und Silber erinnert,
Das geschmolzen im Schutt nun überblieben zerstreut liegt.
Wenig ist es fürwahr, doch auch das wenige köstlich;
Und der Verarmte gräbet ihm nach und freut sich des Fundes.'
(VI, 89-94)[21]

---

[19] The image of revolutionary liberation as the setting free of a wild animal, or "Untier" is used in many anti-revolutionary writings of the period, and is established in the classical German literary tradition in Schiller's "Das Lied von der Glocke" (1800, beg. 1791): "Freiheit und Gleichheit! hört man schallen, / Der ruh'ge Bürger greift zur Wehr, / ... / Da werden Weiber zu Hyänen / Und treiben mit Entsetzen Scherz, / Noch zuckend, mit des Panthers Zähnen / Zerreißen sie des Feindes Herz." ("Freedom and equality! ring out / And the peaceful citizen reaches for his arms / ... / Then women turn into hyenas / and amuse themselves with atrocities / While it is still beating, with their panther teeth / they tear apart the enemy's heart." Friedrich Schiller, *Sämtliche Werke*, ed. Fritz and Walter Strich, 13 vols. (Berlin: Tempel, n.d.), 1:225.

[20] "'But if you were to look back on these sad days, and to survey them, / You would admit it yourself: there was often some good to be found there, / Many a virtue that also lives in man's heart, but lies hidden/ If no peril has roused it, no urgent need has compelled him / Into some act that makes other men think him a god or an angel.'"

[21] "Then the old Judge of dignified bearing smiled and made answer: / 'Often indeed, as you wisely remark, when a house has been burnt down, / One may remind its sorrowing owner of pieces of molten / Gold and silver that still lie scattered under its ruins. / Not much will have survived, it is true, but that little is precious, / And the poor man now searches and digs and is glad when he finds it.'"

Where the vicar sees human nature in enlightened terms as "open" and dynamic, the judge sees it as unchanging and determined. Where the vicar focuses — albeit superficially — on the process of development of human nature and history, the judge can see only the basic substance, which can be modelled but not changed. His analogy also links the sufferings of the refugees with the inhabitants of the town after the fire. His cynical analogy of the survivors overjoyed at finding remnants of melted gold and silver, contrasts strongly with the father, who was spurred on by the fire to rebuild and to plan for the future.

Nevertheless, the patriarch good-humoredly takes the vicar's point. He is reminded of the surprising achievements of people in extraordinary situations, and in this context cites Dorothea's heroic act in protecting herself and the girls from the raiding soldiers:

'Ja, ich will es nicht leugnen, ich sah sich Feinde versöhnen,
Um die Stadt vom Übel zu retten; ich sah auch der Freunde,
Sah der Eltern Lieb' und der Kinder Unmögliches wagen;
Sah, wie der Jüngling auf einmal zum Mann ward, sah, wie der Greis sich
Wieder verjüngte, das Kind sich selbst als Jüngling enthüllte.
Ja, und das schwache Geschlecht, so wie es gewöhnlich genannt wird,
Zeigte sich tapfer und mächtig und gegenwärtigen Geistes.'

(VI, 97-103)[22]

The vicar, like Hermann, is an untried and inexperienced character, "ein Jüngling, näher dem Manne" ("A young man still, but maturing," I, 79). While his influence is ultimately for the good, his tendency to substitute moral platitudes or enlightenment dogma for experience suggests a belief in progress which is unshaken only because untested. He is always ready to proffer advice that all is for the best. His view of human nature compares favorably with the cynicism of the judge, but, as he lacks experience, his judgements lack conviction. In the passage above, for example, the judge suggests circumstances which could be seen to justify the vicar's views about progress in human affairs. The irony of this interchange is that the judge's recognition carries the weight of experience, where the vicar's dogma does not.

Against Dorothea's first fiancé, who, as the judge tells us (VI, 187-89), attempted to translate revolutionary ideals into praxis, the vicar has repudiated any form of action, because of his intellectual insecurity in distinguishing chance from the will of God (the problematic question of Enlightenment theodicy). His enlightenment, in contrast to that of the fiancé, is superficial. In apologizing for the

---

[22] "'Yes, I will not deny I have seen sworn enemies make their / Quarrels up when their town was endangered; I have seen love for / Friends or children or parents do feats of impossible daring, / Seen boys grow in a moment to manhood, or old men regain their / Youth, or young children reveal themselves as boyish and manly. / Even the weaker sex, as it is our custom to call it, / Has given proof of strength and of presence of mind and of valor.'"

status quo, it becomes itself a form of "idyll," of intellectual inactivity, where ultimately no moral choices are necessary, as "all is for the best." The vicar represents the type of enlightened character that Goethe satirized in, for example, "Mittler" in Die Wahlverwandtschaften (Elective Affinities). His tendency to play the moderator in any situation, to avoid conflict by always opting for the golden mean, and to place endless faith in a naively optimistic reading of human nature, render him slightly comical as a character without personality, a colorless mediator. His attitudes reflect the popularized enlightenment of Christian Wolff, and indeed he is the only figure from the home town who belongs to the Protestant middle-class intelligentsia. At the end of the canto he takes the reins of the carriage, to the consternation of the apothecary. He reassures his passenger by telling him that he used to drive his protégé, the baron, in a carriage through the busy streets of Strasbourg when he was a tutor at court:

'Denn geschickt ist die Hand schon lange, den Zügel zu führen,
Und das Auge geübt, die künstlichste Wendung zu treffen.
Denn wir waren in Straßburg gewohnt, den Wagen zu lenken,
Als ich den jungen Baron dahin begleitete;'

(VI, 304-7)[23]

This is a nostalgic and idealized image of enlightened absolutism, the alliance of the intelligentsia and the ruling classes, which for Goethe had begun to fade by the mid 1780s.[24] For Goethe in 1796 the attitudes of the vicar are obsolete. Moreover his complacency and his snobbery (in making a menial task appear elevated to the apothecary) round off the portrait of his "enlightenment" as superficial, dogmatic, and unconvincing.

In a time of crisis and upheaval the judge has reverted to an ideology of the past in an attempt to cope with the new experiences of the present. With historical change has occurred a *Tendenzwende* or change in consciousness. The Old Testament morality, which had been criticized as belonging to a past stage of human development by Enlightenment thinkers, such as Lessing in *Die Erziehung des Menschengeschlechts* (*The Education of Mankind*, 1780), has become newly relevant in the judge's response to the problems created by the Revolution.

The biblical stories provided the shared general mythology for German popular culture during this period. The story of the national mission, the flight of the Jews from Egypt in search of the promised land, and the creation of a nation from the religious community, brings together themes of ethnicity, religion and national identity. The characterization of the judge as an Old Testament prophet

---

[23] "'my hands are long skilled and my eyes are long practised / Managing horses; there's no fancy turn that I can't negotiate. / When I went with the young baron to Strassburg, we were well used to / Driving carriages, I was driving one day after day there;'"

[24] The "necklace affair" of 1785 symbolized to Goethe the failure of enlightened absolutism in France, and his departure for Italy a year later was a result of frustration at the failure of enlightened reforms in Weimar. See Mayer, *Goethe*, 16-24.

brings these themes into the story of *Hermann und Dorothea*. The need for spiritual authority and the urge toward a collective identity finds an outlet in the imagery of the Old Testament patriarch and the Exodus of the Jews. In canto nine the surcharged traditional values of family, God and Germany have a comparable function for Hermann. Like the judge, he will respond to revolution and social disruption with the call for moral and national leadership along traditional lines. The idea of the nation will have become a form of theodicy. In the light of this change in attitudes, it is the vicar's dogmatic enlightenment, his *Vernunftreligion* and superficial rationalism, not the patriarchal moralism of the judge or the traditionalism of Hermann, which is a spent force in Germany after 1792.[25]

The judge, like Hermann, is shown to be responding to forces over which he has no control. He represents an important aspect of patriarchal German culture, but is shown through parody, to be a powerful but disillusioned and potentially dangerous leader. (Parody, as defined in the introduction, indicates an attitude of authorial ambivalence through the quotation of pre-existent material — in this case the language of Klopstock, in a new context.) Goethe was writing in 1796, not in 1806, when the demagogic aspect of this type of charismatic personality was becoming more evident in the aftermath of Napoleon and the later Coalition Wars. The ironic ambivalence in the characterization of the judge highlights the contradiction between the innocence of individual character and the complexity of history.

---

[25] Kant reformulated the concept of enlightenment for the post-revolutionary period as a critical category in the *Kritik der reinen Vernunft* (1781/87).

# 5: The Critical Idyll

## Perception and Reality in the Idyll

IN HIS DISCUSSION OF the generic aspects of the idyll, Frank Rainer Max rejects the concept of an idyllic paradigm, and identifies instead the structural and thematic elements which constitute the genre.[1] Max characterizes the traditional idyll as idealized, artificial and selective, quoting Goethe's own description of the genre in "Wilhelm Tischbeins Idyllen," as presenting "natural human life-situations, unspoilt by anything disagreeable, impure, or repugnant." This does not however limit the modernization of idyllic conventions, for example in Voss's "Der siebzigste Geburtstag," where "the traditional *locus amoenus* is transformed into a cosy living-room" and coffee and tobacco constitute the simple joys of everyday life.[2]

In reference to Goethe's early works Max mentions the inclusion of outside perspectives on the idyll (in "Der Wanderer," *Werther* and *Hermann und Dorothea*) but does not consider this to alter the idyllic core of the latter work in particular. Goethe places the idyll in the context of European history, where it is conscious of and resigned to its existence as an anachronism.[3] Renate Böschenstein points out the function of "non-idyllic" historical themes in the genre since Vergil as a foil to the clarity and harmony of the idyllic world.[4] Vergil, for example, represented the idyllic world as a place where human life could continue undisturbed by the upheavals of contemporary politics.[5]

Far from maintaining the *bürgerlich* milieu as the untroubled inner space of the idyll, however, Goethe as we have seen, draws attention to conflicts and inner anxieties in both Hermann and his father, which affect their relationships with each other and which are reflected onto their "idyllic" environments. Moreover the

---

[1] Frank Rainer Max, "Die Idylle," *Formen der Literatur in Einzeldarstellungen*, ed. Otto Knörrich (Stuttgart: Kröner, 1981), 193.

[2] Max, 197-98.

[3] Max, 198.

[4] Renate Böschenstein, "Idylle," *Fischer Lexikon: Literatur II*, 2 vols., ed. Wolf-Hartmut Friedrich and Walther Killy (Frankfurt am Main: Fischer, 1965), 1:294.

[5] Böschenstein, "Idylle," 1:295.

refugees bring the results of the Revolution to the attention of the inhabitants of the town. And Dorothea's story of her first fiancé, the German Jacobin who died in Paris, brings the consciousness of the Revolution into the middle-class family enclave. In this work the concept of the idyll itself has become problematic.

The second meeting of Hermann and Dorothea takes place at the spring outside the village where the refugees have settled down for the night:

Von dem würdigen Dunkel erhabener Linden umschattet,
Die Jahrhunderte schon an dieser Stelle gewurzelt,
War mit Rasen bedeckt ein weiter grünender Anger
Vor dem Dorfe, den Bauern und nahen Städtern ein Lustort.
Flachgegraben befand sich unter den Bäumen ein Brunnen.
Stieg man die Stufen hinab, so zeigten sich steinerne Bänke,
Rings um die Quelle gesetzt, die immer lebendig hervorquoll,
Reinlich, mit niedriger Mauer gefaßt, zu schöpfen bequemlich.

(V, 151-58)[6]

The scene is presented as a *locus amoenus* complete with ancient linden trees, lawn and stone-stepped spring, which is associated with life and good health (VII, 20, 144). Ernst Robert Curtius writes of the *locus amoenus*:

The *locus amoenus* (pleasance) ... from the Empire to the sixteenth century ... forms the principal motif of all nature description. It is ... a beautiful shaded natural site. Its minimum ingredients comprise a tree (or several trees), a meadow, and a spring or brook.[7]

The motifs of the lovers' meeting by the spring, of the reflection of their images in the water, and of gossiping in the coolness of the shade by the spring belong to both the Classical and the Biblical traditions, from which writers such as Geßner drew their inspiration. Like the idyllic images in canto four of the reapers (IV, 56-57) and the shepherds (IV, 58-59), this idyllic set piece is stylized to the point of artificiality. The spring is an alternative to the town fountain with which Hermann's memories of the community of his childhood are associated, and which has been discredited by its associations with the new town and his father's

---

[6] "There was a meadow not far from the village, a shadowy greensward, / Wide and verdant, encircled by linden-trees, tall and majestic, / Which for centuries now had grown at this place: and the village / People and folk from the nearby town all loved to resort there. / Under the trees was a well, in a shallow hollowed-out basin, / And at the foot of the steps, where the spring-water gushed never-ceasing, / Benches of stone stood round it, a low wall neatly enclosed it; / Here it was pleasant to sit, and the clear water easy to draw from."

[7] Ernst Robert Curtius, *European Literature and the Latin Middle Ages*, trans. Willard Trask (New York: Harper, 1963), 195.

materialism. The *locus amoenus* has been displaced from the home town into the countryside which Hermann had idealized in canto four.

The description of the spring occurs in canto five, after Hermann has driven the vicar and the apothecary to the outskirts of the refugee camp, so that they can inquire about the girl with whom he has fallen in love. The narrative at the end of canto five and in canto six follows the events in the refugee camp, with the vicar, the judge and the apothecary. At the beginning of canto seven the narrative reverts to Hermann who has returned to his horses by the spring. The canto begins with an extended Homeric simile:

Wie der wandernde Mann, der vor dem Sinken der Sonne
Sie noch einmal ins Auge, die schnellverschwindende, faßte,
Dann im dunkeln Gebüsch und an der Seite des Felsens
Schweben siehet ihr Bild; wohin er die Blicke nur wendet,
Eilet es vor und glänzt und schwankt in herrlichen Farben:
So bewegte vor Hermann die liebliche Bildung des Mädchens
Sanft sich vorbei und schien dem Pfad ins Getreide zu folgen.
Aber er fuhr aus dem staunenden Traum auf, wendete langsam
Nach dem Dorfe sich zu und staunte wieder; denn wieder
Kam ihm die hohe Gestalt des herrlichen Mädchens entgegen.
Fest betrachtet' er sie; es war kein Scheinbild, sie war es
Selber.

(VII, 1-12)[8]

Hermann's preoccupation with Dorothea has "dazzled" him so that wherever he looks the shining image blots out everything. However his *mental* image of Dorothea is confused by the *real* image, as Dorothea herself appears on the road, heading for the spring to fetch water. The simile introduces the theme of the subjective nature of perception, at a point in the work where perceptions of the Revolution and the home town have become diverse and contradictory.

Lines one to seven, describing the way in which the images of Dorothea conflict in Hermann's perception, are written in regular hexameters. However as Hermann adjusts his perception, realizing that Dorothea is in fact approaching, the lines become irregular. The hexameters are broken by caesurae and enjambment until in line 12 the grammatical sense closes at the beginning of the metrical unit: "... sie war es / Selber. ..." Dorothea's appearance is ambiguous. On the one hand

---

[8] "As when a wayfaring man who has fixed his gaze on the sinking / Sun once more as it vanishes fast beneath the horizon, / Sees then on the cliff-face, on the shadowy wood, its reflected / Image still floating before him, and no matter which way he looks, it / Speeds on ahead of him, gleaming and shimmering in radiant colors: / So before Hermann's eyes the charming shape of the girl moved / Gently past him, and seemed to be taking the path through the cornfields. / But from his wondering dream he suddenly started, and turning / Round to look back at the village, he wondered again, for again that / Noble and splendid maidenly figure was walking towards him. / Gazing intently, he saw that it was no trick of his eyesight: / It was the girl herself."

it is she, but on the other hand she appears in an idyllic setting like Rebecca with water-jugs to fetch water from the spring. The disjunction between Hermann's mental image, her actual appearance, and the *mise en scène* as fetcher of water from the spring, finds expression in the conflict of grammatical sense and metrical form.

In contrast to Hermann's hesitant and stuttering speech, Dorothea's lines are characterized by the harmony of meaning, grammatical structure and metrical rhythm. Hermann's confusion is a result of the conflict of expectations arising from his memory of Dorothea, his recognition of her when she unexpectedly appears, and the role in which she appears. His rather poetic expectation that she has come to fetch water from this spring because of its medicinal value is undercut by her down-to-earth, practical reason — that the refugees have muddied the fountains and troughs in the village (VII, 30-34). Here, as throughout the work, the regularity of Dorothea's hexameters expresses her calmness, level-headedness and purposefulness in responding to new situations.

The suggestion of biblical idyll in Dorothea's appearance with the water-jugs is developed in the meeting with Hermann by the spring:

Also sprach sie und war die breiten Stufen hinunter
Mit dem Begleiter gelangt; und auf das Mäuerchen setzten
Beide sich nieder des Quells. Sie beugte sich über, zu schöpfen;
Und er faßte den anderen Krug und beugte sich über.
Und sie sahen gespiegelt ihr Bild in der Bläue des Himmels
Schwanken und nickten sich zu und grüßten sich freundlich im Spiegel.
'Laß mich trinken,' sagte darauf der heitere Jüngling;
Und sie reicht' ihm den Krug. Dann ruhten sie beide, vertraulich
Auf die Gefäße gelehnt;

(VII, 37-45)[9]

The naive idyll of the courting of Rebecca in the Book of Genesis is echoed in this section of *Hermann und Dorothea*.[10] However in the modern idyll tensions manifest themselves which are not present in the biblical model: through the mirroring of the naive model the modern idyll is rendered *sentimentalisch*. Dorothea asks Hermann why he has come to the spring, and he replies that he has come to offer

---

[9] "Thus she spoke, and so she came down to the foot of the wide steps / With her companion, and there on the little wall round the well-spring / They both sat; then she stooped down over the water to draw some, / And he, taking up one of her jugs, did the same, leaning over. / There in the blue of the sky they saw their images mirrored / And in the tremulous surface they nodded and smiled at each other. / Then the boy, with his spirits rising, said: 'Give me a drink!' She / Held out her jug to his lips. So they rested, leaning against their / Pitchers, friendly and close;"

[10] Mose 1, 24, 15-17 (Genesis, 24, 15-17). Goethe wrote the essay, "Israel in der Wüste," in mid April, 1797 — i.e. before finishing *Hermann und Dorothea*. In this essay he referred to the "pure patriarchal being" of the books of Moses (H.A. 2:223), to "the triumph of faith" of the first book and the "lack of faith" of books two to five (H.A. 2:208).

her employment in his father's house. His speech flows smoothly as he describes the life at home:

'Denn ich lebe beglückt mit beiden liebenden Eltern,
Denen ich treulich das Haus und die Güter helfe verwalten
Als der einzige Sohn, und unsre Geschäfte sind vielfach.
Alle Felder besorg' ich: der Vater waltet im Hause
Fleißig; die tätige Mutter belebt im ganzen die Wirtschaft.'

(VII, 56-60)[11]

He naturally makes no reference to his father's domineering attitudes or his frustration at the materialism and snobbishness of town life. However the regularity of the lines is disturbed as Hermann mentions his father, with the caesura in the middle of line 59 (a metrical indication of the displacement of emotions) and the enjambment of the end of the clause, "der Vater waltet im Hause / Fleißig" running on to the beginning of line 60.[12] Mention of his busy mother restores the regularity of meter. Hermann's description of the patriarchal family is idealized. It is yet another version of idyll in the work, but it is undercut by the broken rhythm of the meter. Hermann's stylization of his home life in this section marks an important stage in his progression from the transfigured image of the fatherland in canto four to the defensive "idyll" of his speech at the end of canto nine.

## History and Literary Form: The Function of the "Idyllic" in *Hermann und Dorothea*

The Homeric simile of the dazzling image of the sunset is unique in the work. It draws attention to the theme of disjunction between individual perception and historical reality, examples of which have been identified throughout this analysis. Moreover it gives a clue to the function of the "idyllic" — i.e. of idyllic elements as well as of the idyll as a generic model — for the work as a whole.

We have seen in cantos one and two how the father rebuilt his home town after the crisis of the fire twenty years earlier, and how the same crisis led to the apothecary's debilitating fear that work and good deeds can only end in death. In canto four the father's property is an idyllic garden of Eden from which Hermann in his frustration desires expulsion, and the Rhineland countryside becomes an expanded and transfigured image of the fatherland for the boy, who can no longer identify with the town of his father. For the vicar the world is a Wolffian theodicy,

---

[11] "'I have the great good fortune to live with my two loving parents; / I am their eldest son, so I do my duty and help them / Run their house and their land and the whole extent of our business. / I look after the fields, and my father's in charge of the house; both / He and my mother work hard, she's the life and soul of the whole place.'"

[12] On the psychological and linguistic effects of rhythmic and metrical variations in verse, cf. Ivan Fonàgy, "Communication in Poetry," *Word* 17 (1961): 194-218.

where everything that happens, no matter how bad, can somehow be justified as part of God's plan. The judge shrewdly recognizes the fallacy in the vicar's thinking, but he too sees the world in terms of a paradigm. In his newly acquired role of Old Testament prophet, he sees man as inherently wicked and in need of moral guidance. Likewise for the Germans living in the left bank provinces, the first years of the Revolution brought the promise of an idyllic utopia (VI, 34ff.), and the fiancé of Dorothea, believing that the political ideal had been realized in Paris, went there only to become a victim of the Terror.

Individual characters' perceptions, expectations and views are undercut by juxtaposition of contrasting attitudes, by the use of irony and parody as "modes of ambivalence," and by irregularities, caesurae, enjambment, tension and breaks in meter: the juxtaposition of the father and the apothecary, the vicar and the judge and, in canto nine, Hermann and the first fiancé; the ubiquitous parody of Voss's style and language, especially in the wine-drinking scene (canto one) and the mother's search for Hermann in the idyllic garden (canto four); the ironic breaking of the meter when idyllic consciousness and reality come into conflict, for example when Hermann idealizes the patriarchal family-relationships at home, analyzed above, or when the content of the lines is incompatible with the expected (traditional) content of the idyllic hexameter, for example in the famed "seven-footed monster."[13] In this last example, as in many others both in the authorial narrative and the direct speech of the characters, the hexameters begin to break down altogether, so that the effect is of prose in verse lines rather than verse hexameters. Idyllic motifs and episodes in this work are fragmented, disjunctive and open-ended, where traditionally the idyll is unified, harmonious, and confined to the small world.

The diversity and fragmentation of the idyllic motifs gives them a contrastive function, which can be described in terms of "norm" and "norm-break," or of the traditional, continuous and expected versus the new, disjunctive and unexpected. The norm of the idyllic clichés is broken by irony, juxtaposition, and metrical irregularity. The contrastive and comparative function of these literary-idyllic motifs can be analyzed in terms of the literary *topic*. Ernst Robert Curtius reintroduced the concept of *topoi* from the classical rhetorical tradition into modern literary studies as the "stockroom" of ancient rhetoric, in which "ideas of the most general sort ... could be employed in every kind oratory and writing.[14] Curtius adds that "to poetic *topoi* belongs the beauty of nature in the widest sense — hence the ideal landscape with its typical equipment. So too dreamlands and dream ages."[15] While *topoi* are timeless in that they concern "basic relations of existence,"

---

[13] Cf. ch. 3, fn. 18.

[14] Curtius, 79.

[15] Curtius, 82.

the style of expression of the *topoi* is historically determined.[16] The appearance and historical context of certain *topoi* then becomes important:

> Now there are also *topoi* which are wanting throughout Antiquity down to the Augustan Age. They appear at the beginning of late Antiquity and then are suddenly everywhere. ... They have a twofold interest. First ... we can observe in them the *genesis of new topoi*. Thus our knowledge of the genetics of the formal elements of literature is widened. Secondly, these *topoi* are indications of a changed psychological state. ... Thus our understanding of the psychological history of the West is deepened, and we approach spheres that the psychology of C.G. Jung has explored.[17]

Walter Veit adds to the definitions of Curtius the view of the *topic* as literary argument, a cliché, which by reformulating an older idea, implicitly alters its meaning in the new context, but also retains its formulaic character in the horizon of meaning.[18] The literary *topic*, then, potentially brings a historical level to the relationship of the poetic image to reality.[19] In his excursus, "Jest and Earnest in Medieval Literature," Curtius sketches the use of *topoi* for comic effect to debunk serious or revered subjects, namely rulers, saints and serious literary forms.[20] In this latter sub-section in particular, Curtius comes closest to suggesting the potential use of *topoi* in literature as parody of traditional, sacred or revered subjects. While he does not use the term, parody, it is clear that the debunking humor of the medieval mock-epics and saints' lives arises from their comic "quotation" in normally serious contexts — an example of the historicity of the *topic*, emphasised by Veit. Eighteenth-century mock-epics such as Thümmel's *Wilhelmine* and Wieland's *Oberon* make use of the parodic quotation of *topoi*, clichés and set pieces for their comic effect.

In *Hermann und Dorothea* the *topic* of the idyllic environment, the *locus amoenus*, appears throughout the work in different forms. Even the genre of the work (with its self-conscious stylization) as an idyll is a literary *locus amoenus*, a refuge from the *misère* of literary relationships in Germany in the mid 1790s. (This was Goethe's implied criticism of Voss.) This idyllic element or *topic* thereby becomes self-reflexive, critical and contrastive. As in the innkeeper's and the apothecary's perceptions of the home town, the idyll is shown to be subjective and selective, a state of mind. The father wants to know nothing of the refugees who are passing by, since they are symptomatic of forces which could damage the home town more

---

[16] Curtius, 82.

[17] Curtius, 82.

[18] Walter Veit, "Topos," *Fischer Lexikon: Literatur II*, 2 vols., ed. Wolf-Hartmut Friedrich and Walther Killy (Frankfurt am Main: Fischer, 1965), 2:569.

[19] Veit, 569-70.

[20] Curtius, 417-35.

radically than the fire. The Vossian overtones in the characterization of the mother and the exaggeration of the images of natural abundance in the garden in canto four, culminating in the kitschy platitude, "Denn ein geschäftiges Weib tut keine Schritte vergebens" ("For a well-occupied wife never takes a step to no purpose," IV, 15), make it difficult to read this section "straight." Hermann's patriotic love of his fatherland is so heavily laden with symbolism revealing a state of adolescent sexual frustration that it too must be explicated in terms of the character and preoccupations of the perceiver. Linked by association with his heroic decision to fight for the fatherland in canto four moreover, this idyllic image of the fatherland becomes slightly ludicrous, as Hermann has already shown himself incapable of making a decision — let alone of carrying it out. Readers and critics of the work have tended to identify Hermann's views with Goethe's. However the discrepancies between character, sentiment and form here, as elsewhere, show such an identification to be untenable. The judge's memories of the early stages of the Revolution are expressed in terms of the village idyll, of the dance around the "freedom tree" and the expectation of the golden age.[21] However this idyll was soon shattered, as the judge ruefully remembers, and the euphoria of the occupied Rhineland population turned into cynicism and despair (VI, 40ff.).

Goethe's and Schiller's discussions of form are relevant to the quotation of idyllic images, motifs and moods in the work. They used terms such as "bürgerliche Idylle," "Idylle," "idyllisches Epos," and "das epische Gedicht," and in the elegy, "Hermann und Dorothea," Goethe refers to his intention "Homeride zu sein, auch nur als letzter."[22] The formal ambiguity of the work — as idyll, epic, mock-epic, idyllic epic, parody (i.e. *parothia*, the epigonal hexameters of the post-Homeric poets) — reflects the problematic nature of the German idyll in the age of the French Revolution. "Idyll" has been expanded beyond the particular literary forms of the Bible, classical antiquity, Geßner and Voss, to include all forms of provincial, "small world" consciousness, over and against which revolutionary France represents an intrusive and destructive "greater world." In this context the middle-class idylls of Voss, Geßner, Maler Müller and others had lost the progressive impetus of the pre-revolutionary period. The fiction of German provincial autonomy, or of the cultural independence of the German middle classes, which was an integral part of the genre as reformulated by Voss, could not be maintained after 1792.

The Revolution introduced new categories of political experience and rendered existing ones obsolete or questionable. In "Das Märchen" Goethe had intimated the impossibility of perpetuating the literary forms of the pre-revolutionary period in

---

[21] VI, 24-27, 34-37. Cf. Curtius, 90; and Walter Veit, "Toposforschung: Ein Forschungsbericht," in *Toposforschung*, ed. Max L. Baeumer (Darmstadt: Wissenschaftliche Buchgesellschaft, 1973), 192-95.

[22] Goethe to Schiller, beginning of July 1796, W.A. IV, 11, 324; Goethe to Christiane, 9 September 1796, W.A. IV, 11, 189; Goethe to Heinrich Meyer, 18 March 1797, W.A. IV, 12, 72; "to be a Homeric epigone, even if I'm the last," J.W. Goethe, "Hermann und Dorothea," H.A. 1:198, l. 30.

the post-revolutionary situation. The hope expressed in the late works of Voss and Klopstock, and reflected in the attitudes of the judge in *Hermann und Dorothea*, that German socio-political relationships would return to a transfigured pre-revolutionary state, were an escape into idyllic false consciousness. The utopian civic image which ends "Das Märchen" had not been created in reality. Goethe's solution was to produce a work which both drew attention to the relationships of false consciousness in characters such as Hermann, his father and the vicar, and refused to create an alternative where there was — as yet — none. In *Hermann und Dorothea* the "fragments" of earlier idyllic discourses are pieced together and juxtaposed into a text which is epic/idyllic, absolutist/middle-class, classical/modern, closed/open, and parodic/ironic.

# 6: The Paradigm of Individual Identity

## Dorothea and Ruth

THE CHARACTERIZATION OF DOROTHEA, like that of the judge, has strong Old Testament associations. Where the Books of Moses, Joshua and the Judges tell the stories of the nation (*Volk*) and its leaders, the Book of Ruth tells the personal and individual fate of the refugee. Ruth's answer to Naomi is paradigmatic of the emigré's acceptance of the new homeland and new relationships: "Wo du hin gehst, da will ich auch hin gehen; wo du bleibst, da bleibe ich auch. Dein Volk ist mein Volk, und dein Gott ist mein Gott."[1] The Book of Ruth presents an alternative paradigm to the national mission of the Tribes of Israel in the previous books of the Old Testament.[2]

Far from romanticizing or idealizing her future, Dorothea pragmatically evaluates her situation:

'Euer Antrag war kurz; so soll die Antwort auch kurz sein.
Ja, ich gehe mit Euch und folge dem Rufe des Schicksals.
Meine Pflicht ist erfüllt, ich habe die Wöchnerin wieder
Zu den Ihren gebracht, sie freuen sich alle der Rettung;
Schon sind die meisten beisammen, die übrigen werden sich finden.
Alle denken gewiß, in kurzen Tagen zur Heimat
Wiederzukehren; so pflegt sich stets der Vertriebne zu schmeicheln.'

(VII, 80-86)[3]

---

[1] "... whither thou goest, I will go; and where thou lodgest, I will lodge: they people shall be my people, and thy God my God ..." Ruth, I, 16.

[2] In the "Noten und Abhandlungen zu besserem Verständnis des west-östlichen Divans" Goethe writes, "gedenken wir des Buches Ruth, welches ... als das lieblichste kleine Ganze betrachtet werden kann, das uns episch und idyllisch überliefert worden ist," H.A. 2:128.

[3] "'Your proposition was brief, and so you shall have a brief answer. / Yes I will go with you, sir, and since fate seems to send me this summons / I will obey it. My duty is done here; the woman in childbed / Has rejoined her own people, they all rejoice in her rescue. / Most of them now are together again, the rest will be found soon. / All of them think, I am sure, that before long they will be back home, / For that is always the flattering belief of the wandering exile.'"

The parallel with Ruth is all the stronger in that Dorothea, as we discover later, is attracted to Hermann (IX, 149-59) — she does not see in him merely stability and employment in a time of crisis. Her directness in confronting her situation, and making a decision and acting on it, contrasts with Hermann. He talks of actively facing up to his fate:

'Selber geh' ich und will mein Schicksal selber erfahren
Aus dem Munde des Mädchens, ...'

(VI, 277-78)[4]

However he does not confront Dorothea honestly, but prevaricates until others act for him in canto nine.

The judge in his role as Old Testament patriarch leads the refugees and maintains the belief that they will eventually return to their homeland. Dorothea, like Ruth, accepts the unlikelihood of return, and the necessity of adjusting to a new home. She has come to value personal and family ties above those of community and ethnicity. As in the Book of Ruth, this is a "female" paradigm — and it proves stronger than the "male" paradigms represented by Hermann's father, the vicar, the judge, Hermann — or the first fiancé. Just as it was the mother who did not lose heart after the calamity of the fire (II, 127-28), so it is Dorothea here who shows greater ability than the men in coming to terms with crisis and upheaval.

Against the Panglossian optimism of the vicar and the bitterness and disillusionment of the judge, Dorothea represents an ethos of self-help and practicality in an otherwise hopeless situation:

'Aber ich täusche mich nicht mit leichter Hoffnung in diesen
Traurigen Tagen, die uns noch traurige Tage versprechen:
Denn gelöst sind die Bande der Welt; wer knüpfet sie wieder
Als allein nur die Not, die höchste, die uns bevorsteht?'

(VII, 87-90)[5]

She faces realities squarely where the male characters base their perceptions and decisions on idyllic, idealized or utopian hopes for the future. The father's home town, Hermann's fatherland, the vicar's theodicy, the judge's fundamentalism, and the political idealism of Dorothea's first fiancé fail to come to terms with reality. In attempting to control destiny, they create perspectives which in a period of upheaval are artificial and unrealistic. Dorothea is the only character who responds

---

[4] "'I will go to her myself, I myself will learn what my fate is / From her own lips;'"

[5] "'But I am not deceiving myself with any such easy / Hope in sad days like these, which presage even sadder to follow. / For the bonds of the world have been loosed, nothing now can reforge them, / Nothing except the supreme ordeal that still lies before us!'"

to the crisis of the Revolution by not pre-empting the future. Of all the characters, including the judge, she alone has been tested by the Revolution and has come to terms with the helplessness of the individual in the face of historical events. In this respect she is the opposite of the apothecary, who is paralyzed by fear of loss of his material possessions.

In canto seven Dorothea expresses her sense that the world order has been disrupted (VII, 89). Through a comparable motif of upheaval of the established order by the Revolution, the judge comes to speak of Dorothea's heroic act in protecting a group of girls from soldiers (VI, 104-18). For the judge this episode has become part of the *Heilsgeschichte* of the revolutionary period. He sees Dorothea as a latter-day Judith, as the virgin turned slayer and liberator.[6] The motifs of heroism, virginity, sex, castration and death in the Judith legend are echoed in the judge's retelling of Dorothea's heroic act. The details of the slain rapist bleeding at her feet come as a shock in the midst of the idyll:

'Und so laßt mich vor allen der schönen Tat noch erwähnen,
Die hochherzig ein Mädchen vollbrachte, die treffliche Jungfrau,
...
Da überfiel den Hof ein Trupp verlaufnen Gesindels
Plündernd und drängte sogleich sich in die Zimmer der Frauen.
Sie erblickten das Bild der schön erwachsenen Jungfrau
Und die lieblichen Mädchen, noch eher Kinder zu heißen.
Da ergriff sie wilde Begier; sie stürmten gefühllos
Auf die zitternde Schar und aufs hochherzige Mädchen.
Aber sie riß dem einen sogleich von der Seite den Säbel,
Hieb ihn nieder gewaltig; er stürzt' ihr blutend zu Füßen.
Dann mit männlichen Streichen befreite sie tapfer die Mädchen,
Traf noch viere der Räuber; doch die entflohen dem Tode.'
(VI, 104-5, 108-17)[7]

The father, the vicar and the judge have identifiable characteristics as representatives of their class, profession or experiences, and the ironic and parodic associations from contemporary life and literature render them recognizable as

---

[6] Cf. Klopstock's description of Charlotte Corday as "die erhabne / Männin," ("the lofty virago") in "Mein Irrtum" ("My Error") written after Corday's execution in July 1793.

[7] "'And above all there was one fine deed I would here like to mention, / Done by a bravehearted girl, a noble and excellent maiden, / ... / They were surprised at the farm by some soldiers, a runaway plundering / Rabble, who forced their way to the women's quarters at once, and / There set eyes on this maiden, a beautiful woman she'd grown to, / And on the charming young girls, little more than children they still were. / Then they were seized by passionate lust, they attacked in a brutal / Frenzy the girls who stood trembling with fear, and the bravehearted maiden. / But she immediately snatched the sword of one of them from its / Scabbard, and struck him dead at her feet, and as he lay bleeding / She dealt more mighty blows, most valiantly freeing the victims. / Four more of the marauders she wounded, who fled with their bare lives.'"

types. For Dorothea however there is no such "prototype." Nor is she made the object of irony or parody in the way the other characters are. Her language is her own. Hermann, the judge, the father, the vicar and the apothecary by contrast, try to subsume experience into world-views or ideologies. Hence the pervasive quality of parody — of "quotation" of literary styles such as those of Voss and Klopstock, or of cultural and intellectual movements, as in the figures of the vicar and the judge. Dorothea's experiences have forced her to abandon preconceived frameworks of identity for an ethos of practical day to day living which is neither cynical nor idealistic, but is simply self-help, a means of coming to terms with a world which no longer offers traditional frameworks. Where the judge for example remembers the political idealism of Dorothea's first fiancé, Dorothea remembers his recognition that the world is in a state of flux, and that neither goods nor preconceived ideas can protect the individual in a time of historical upheaval.

Dorothea has been forced to come to terms with the conflicting demands of the individual, the group, the community, and the *Volk* (i.e. the "nation" in Herder's sense). Her confidence and clear-sightedness stand out in contrast to Hermann's inexperience, the judge's hardened pessimism, the vicar's superficiality, the father's pettiness and even her dead lover's idealism. Her attitude to the other refugees is refreshingly honest. She does not idealize them (or herself) into a patiently suffering community of exiles. She is critical of their selfishness (VII, 30-36) and their short-sightedness (VII, 86-88). Her practical intelligence sees what is needed, but she is not willing to martyr or sacrifice herself unnecessarily. She has learnt the lesson which her dead fiancé forced upon her. Her decision is firm and pragmatic:

'Ungern lass' ich euch zwar; doch jeder ist diesmal dem andern
Mehr zur Last als zum Trost, und alle müssen wir endlich
Uns im fremden Lande zerstreun, wenn die Rückkehr versagt ist.'

(VII, 153-55)[8]

Dorothea is the only character who experiences all three spheres of the poem: the revolutionary upheavals at home, the wretchedness of the refugee situation, and, finally, the peace and material well-being of the home town. The irony of Dorothea's fate is that after being deserted by her lover in the euphoria of the first revolutionary period, fleeing the revolutionary annexation of her homeland, surviving the attack of the marauding soldiers and maintaining humanity and order among the refugees, she ends up in such a narrow environment and with a future husband, who, while good, honest, loving and trustworthy, is clearly no match for her in intelligence, personality or experience. This is perhaps the point of the mock-portentous symbolism of the storm and her turned ankle in canto eight. In the final canto this potential conflict is resolved at least in part through

---

[8] "'Though I am sorry to leave you, in such days we all bring each other / Burdens rather than comfort; and in the end, in these foreign / Lands we must all be scattered and part, if we cannot return home.'"

the motif of the two rings, and through Dorothea's remembrance of her dead lover.

Dorothea does not appear in the story until canto seven. Before that we hear of her from the others, firstly Hermann, and then the judge, the vicar and apothecary. She speaks relatively little in the work, and when she does, it is generally in relation to her immediate concerns with the refugees. At the end most of her speech is devoted to the memory of her dead fiancé. In terms of imagery she, like the innkeeper, is a bringer of water, but not in the sense of the new town with its drains and canals (III, 29-30). She is associated with the water from the spring outside the village:

Und sie reichte das Wasser herum. Da tranken die Kinder
Und die Wöchnerin trank mit den Töchtern, so trank auch der Richter.
Alle waren geletzt und lobten das herrliche Wasser;
Säuerlich war's und erquicklich, gesund zu trinken den Menschen.

(VII, 141-44)[9]

She asks the refugees to think of her in future days when quenching their thirst at pure springs:

'Freunde, dieses ist wohl das letzte Mal, daß ich den Krug euch
Führe zum Munde, daß ich die Lippen mit Wasser euch netze;
Aber wenn euch fortan am heißen Tage der Trunk labt,
Wenn ihr im Schatten der Ruh' und der reinen Quellen genießet,
Dann gedenket auch mein und meines freundlichen Dienstes,
Den ich aus Liebe mehr als aus Verwandtschaft geleistet.'

(VII, 146-51)[10]

This image of purity and freshness is central in Goethe's work, from the patriarchal springs of the Old Testament referred to the essay "Alttestamentliches," to the chemical analogy in *Die Wahlverwandtschaften*.[11]

---

[9] "So she distributed water: the children drank it, the mother / Of the new baby drank with her daughters, the magistrate drank too. / Everyone's thirst was quenched, and they praised the splendid clear water; / It had a mineral content that made it refreshing and wholesome."

[10] "'Friends, this may be the last time I shall hold a jug to your thirsty / Lips, the last time I shall come from the well for you, bringing you water. / But henceforth, in the heat of the day, when you take your refreshment, / Or when you rest in the shade and enjoy the clear bubbling springs there, / Then remember me too, and remember my well-wishing service, / Which I performed for you more out of love than because you are kinsfolk.'"

[11] The essay, "Alttestamentliches" was written in Spring 1797 and included in the "Noten und Abhandlungen zu besserem Verständnis des west-östlichen Divans"; on the image of spring-water in *Die Wahlverwandtschaften*, see John Milfull, "The Idea of Goethe's *Wahlverwandtschaften*," *Germanic Review* 47 (1972): 83-94.

## Dorothea and Iphigenie

"Hat denn zur unerhörten Tat der Mann / allein das Recht?"[12]

In canto five when they are trying to talk the father into accepting the refugee girl as his daughter-in-law, both the vicar and the mother unwittingly play on her name (which they do not yet know). "Dorothea" means literally "gift of the gods":

'Nun ist er kommen, der Tag; nun hat die Braut ihm der Himmel
Hergeführt und gezeigt;'
(The mother, V, 46-47)

'die Gaben
Kommen von oben herab in ihren eignen Gestalten.'
(The vicar, V, 69-70)[13]

Like Goethe's other "gift from the gods," Iphigenie, Dorothea has experienced extraordinary events. She has suffered the *Tantalidengeschichte* of the Revolution, and the attack by marauding soldiers, only to find herself transported to the idyllic provincial backwater of the home town far from the political upheavals of the *polis*. The classicism of *Iphigenie auf Tauris* does not belong in the modern story of Dorothea. The *deus ex machina* of the plot, the resolution of the real and the ideal, whereby a happy ending is created out of a potential tragedy, is undercut by irony in *Hermann und Dorothea*. *Iphigenie* was Goethe's last attempt to internalize enlightenment, to humanize the real world through literature. In *Hermann und Dorothea* the classical deities have been banned to the sphere of ornamentation and mock-classicism. Lending their names to the cantos, they have no inner relevance to the story. Their classical presence does little to resolve the contradictions and conflicts of the modern era.

Dorothea experiences the degeneration of social ties to the most primitive instincts of aggression and domination: war-time rape of women and children. This experience is comparable to that of human sacrifice in *Iphigenie*. However Dorothea reverses the roles, where Iphigenie transcended them. In the first instance Iphigenie is transferred to the shores of Tauris by Artemis to save her from sacrifice in Aulis. In Tauris she then brings about the cessation of human sacrifice and ultimately, through her strength of character, her civilization and her goodness, convinces Thoas, the king of the Taurians, to allow her, Orest and the other Greeks freedom to return home. She moves from center to periphery, and

---

[12] "Do men alone have the right to unprecedented deeds?" Goethe, *Iphigenie auf Tauris*, V, iii, 1893-94, H.A. 5:59.

[13] "'Well, that day has now come; now heaven has found him his sweetheart, / Brought her and showed her to him;'" "'good gifts / Come from above to us, wearing a shape that is not of our choosing.'"

back again, changing both worlds for the better. Dorothea does not and cannot act to embody enlightenment in this way. She has no choice but to reverse sacrifice into self-defense and kill her attacker. In doing so she is separated from the fragile ideality of Iphigenie and is placed in a modern world from which there is no return to the "home" of pre-revolutionary enlightenment. Moreover her experience contrasts with that of her first fiancé, whose life ended tragically in Paris, as he chose death rather than to sacrifice his ideals.

The critical reception of Dorothea is one of the most interesting aspects of the work's history. Wilhelm von Humboldt incurred Goethe's irritation and set the tone for succeeding generations of interpreters by criticizing the episode in which Dorothea kills one of her attackers. For Humboldt, the Prussian gentleman and propagator of the ideals of *Bildung* and *Ordnung*, this action overstepped the bounds of womanhood. Dorothea has fared little better ever since, despite the fact that even the judge regards her action as heroic and praiseworthy. Even modern critics have shown little interest in rescuing Dorothea in the name of feminism.

### Dorothea in the Home Town

The image of the sunset behind gathering clouds at the beginning of canto eight echoes the dazzling sunset of canto seven:

Also gingen die zwei entgegen der sinkenden Sonne,
Die in Wolken sich tief, gewitterdrohend, verhüllte,
Aus dem Schleier bald hier, bald dort mit glühenden Blicken
Strahlend über das Feld die ahnungsvolle Beleuchtung.
'Möge das drohende Wetter,' so sagte Hermann, 'nicht etwa
Schloßen uns bringen und heftigen Guß; denn schön ist die Ernte.'

(VIII, 1-6)[14]

The portentous sunset and gathering storm however are undercut by the mock-epic context. The texture of *Hermann und Dorothea* cannot support imagery of this symbolic weight. The parodic use of epic motifs and techniques here as elsewhere renders the text ambiguous.[15] This same imagery had been used by Klopstock in relation to the Revolution in "Kennet Euch Selbst," and in the context of the time it has strong symbolic overtones. Yet Hermann's practical response — that the storm threatens the harvest — almost comically deflates the symbolism. Is the

---

[14] "So together they walked towards the west and the sunset. / Deeply the sun was veiling its face in threatening storm-clouds, / Though it still gleamed here and there, its fiery eye was still flashing, / Glinting across the fields, as a luminous omen of thunder. / 'This is dangerous weather,' said Hermann, 'I hope we shall not have / Violent rain or hail, for the harvest should be a fine one.'"

[15] E.g. Hermann with the horses, I, 16-17; the poet's direct address to his characters, VI, 298; and the address to the Muses, IX, 1.

reader meant to take the symbolism of the gathering storm seriously or not?¹⁶ The question is impossible to answer — perhaps the point of the formulation is that the poet himself cannot answer it. Unlike the old man with the lamp in "Das Märchen," the poet does not necessarily know whether the moment for historical change has come, or whether the winds of change will "blow over" and be forgotten. Writing the *Campagne in Frankreich* from his notebook entries in the early 1820s, Goethe could look back over thirty years since the Cannonade of Valmy to make his famous statement on the importance of the period: "From this place and time a new epoch of world history is beginning."¹⁷ However in the last year of the First Coalition War, before either side had emerged as the stronger, and before Napoleon had appeared to give direction to post-revolutionary France, it was impossible to know whether new political relationships would take effect in Europe, or whether the old relationships would resume.

Hence ambiguity dominates this canto. After the sun has sunk behind the clouds and the moon come out, allowing Dorothea to see clearly the details of the town, the image of storm again threatens the idyllic summer night:

'Aber laß uns nunmehr hinab durch Weinberg und Garten
Steigen; denn sieh, es rückt das schwere Gewitter herüber,
Wetterleuchtend und bald verschlingend den lieblichen Vollmond.'
(VIII, 77-79)¹⁸

In the hurry to reach home before the storm breaks, Dorothea twists her ankle following Hermann down the steps through the vineyard:

Aber sie, unkundig des Steigs und der roheren Stufen,
Fehlte tretend, es knackte der Fuß, sie drohte zu fallen.
...
Doch sie verhehlte den Schmerz und sagte die scherzenden Worte:
'Das bedeutet Verdruß, so sagen bedenkliche Leute,
Wenn beim Eintritt ins Haus nicht fern von der Schwelle der Fuß knackt.
Hätt' ich mir doch fürwahr ein besseres Zeichen gewünschet!'
(VIII, 89-90, 99-102)¹⁹

---

¹⁶ Ryder and Bennett, 436-37.

¹⁷ See ch. 2, fn. 31.

¹⁸ "'But come along now, we must go down through the vineyard and garden. / Look, the storm's drawing nearer, I think it's going to be heavy; / Lightning's flashing, and soon the clouds will have covered the full moon.'"

¹⁹ "But there were some rough steps, and the pathway was unfamiliar, / And she stumbled, missing her foothold; / ... / But she made light of the pain, and smiled and jestingly spoke thus: / 'It's an unfortunate sign (or so wise people have told me) / Stumbling and twisting one's foot just before first crossing the threshold: / I must say, I could really have done with a luckier omen!'"

Dorothea's foot now is her weak point.[20] That she falls however also reflects on Hermann's ability as leader. The symbolism of leading ("lenken," "Lenker") and guiding occurs throughout the poem in, for example, Hermann's control over the horses and carriage in the narrow streets of the home town, the vicar's driving among the crowds of Strasbourg, Dorothea's driving of the oxen and, at a different level, of the father's leadership of the town and the judge's leadership of the refugees. This imagery ranges from the comic and the trivial ("Was der Junge doch fährt, und wie er bändigt die Hengste!" I, 16) to the elevated and biblical tone of the judge as leader of the refugees in the wilderness in canto six.[21] Dorothea's fall too is presented in mock-heroic dimensions:

Und so fühlt' er die herrliche Last, ...
Trug mit Mannesgefühl die Heldengröße des Weibes.

(VIII, 96, 98)[22]

This treatment of a motif which has been of importance throughout the work again leaves the reader perplexed. The potential seriousness of this moment of intimacy is broken by exaggerated grammatical fragmentation:

Und es hörte die Frage, die freundliche, gern in dem Schatten
Hermann des herrlichen Baums, am Orte, der ihm so lieb war,

(VIII, 57-58)[23]

The canto heading, "Melpomene," after the muse of tragedy, linked with the subtitle "Hermann und Dorothea," enforces the general ambiguity as to how seriously the reader is meant to take the signs of warning for the future. Moreover, if these are portents, what do they portend? The coming of the French Revolution to Germany? Or a symbolic "slip" on Dorothea's part in deciding to settle in the provincial home town after all she has experienced?

At this point in the story Dorothea stands midway between the revolutionary idealism of her first fiancé and the home town consciousness of Hermann. However she herself has known an alternative to both the *Gemeinschaft* of the town

---

[20] The apothecary's comments on Dorothea's foot earlier suggest a hint of voyeuristic eroticism (V, 175-76 and VI, 144-45). Goethe is perhaps parodying similarly suggestive or erotic motifs in *Luise*, e.g. "kühlender Seewind / Hauchte zurück das Gewand, das die trippelnden Füsse des Mägdleins / Rauschend umwallt'" (*Werke*, 100) or "... es erhob Luis den Saum des weißen Gewandes, / Zeigend den Unterrock und schimmernde Strümpf in der Dämmrung." (*Werke*, 117).

[21] "'Look at the boy, how he drives! He can handle the stallions, I must say!'"

[22] "Thus his splendid burden he felt, ... / And with masculine strength he bore her magnificent stature."

[23] "Hermann listened with joy as she made her kindly enquiry, / Here in the shade of that splendid tree, in this place that he loved,'"

and the *Gesellschaft* of the modern city. In a short episode which contrasts with Hermann's traumatic experience of snobbery and social ineptness at the house of the rich neighbor in canto two, Dorothea remembers the social environment of her childhood:

'Und der äußeren Zierde bin ich von Jugend nicht fremde.
Unsere Nachbarn, die Franken, in ihren früheren Zeiten
Hielten auf Höflichkeit viel; sie war dem Edlen und Bürger
Wie den Bauern gemein, und jeder empfahl sie den Seinen.
Und so brachten bei uns auf deutscher Seite gewöhnlich
Auch die Kinder des Morgens mit Händeküssen und Knichschen
Segenswünsche den Eltern und hielten sittlich den Tag aus.
Alles, was ich gelernt und was ich von jung auf gewohnt bin,
Was von Herzen mir geht — ich will es dem Alten erzeigen.'

(VIII, 41-49)[24]

The everyday politeness among all classes of society contrasts with the uneasy social relations of the home town, characterized by the boorishness of the father, the snobbery of the rich neighbor, the vicar's complacency, the apothecary's miserliness, Hermann's social ineptitude, and the insensitivity of the townspeople, who treat the refugees' misery in canto one as the excuse for a Sunday outing. Dorothea's memories contrast too with the behavior of the refugees themselves, preoccupied with their own survival. The image of the German children copying the behavior of the French introduces a theme of socio-cultural interchange between French and German, which is an alternative to the aping of French culture by the German nobility and aristocracy on the one hand, and the aggressive rejection by the *Bürger* on the other.

---

[24] "'And from my childhood I've been accustomed to airs and to graces, / For the French were our neighbors, and they in that earlier epoch / Set much store by politeness, and not the nobility only: / Townsfolk and peasants as well, and they made their families learn it. / So we Germans were used to it too, and the children each morning / Came to wish their parents good health, and made little curtsies, / Kissing their hands, and passed the whole day in seemly behavior. / All that I learnt as a child and have practiced ever since childhood / So that it comes from my heart — all this I'll show to your father.'"

# 7: The Story of the Salzburg Protestants

### Göcking's Source Story

GOETHE WROTE OF *HERMANN und Dorothea*: "Der Gegenstand selbst ist äußerst glücklich, ein Sujet, wie man es in seinem Leben vielleicht nicht zweimal findet."[1] Goethe's source was discovered in 1809 and later documented by E.F. Yxem: Gerhard Gottlieb Günther Göcking's *Vollkommene Emigrationsgeschichte von denen aus dem Erzbistum Salzburg vertriebenen ... Lutheranern*.[2]

Göcking's anecdote runs as follows. As the Protestant exiles from Salzburg pass by a provincial German town (Erfurt), a young woman meets a local youth. He falls in love with her and, when he meets her again shortly afterwards, offers her employment as a servant in his parents' household — this being a pretext for keeping her in the town. The young man's father has been pestering him for some time to find himself a wife. The boy has already told his father after first meeting the girl that he intends to bring her home as his bride and that if the father rejects her because she is a refugee, then he will never marry. When the girl arrives home with the boy, the father makes a remark about the marriage and upsets the girl, who does not know that the father is expecting to meet his future daughter-in-law, and not a servant, and who assumes that he is treating her with contempt. The misunderstanding is resolved and even the father is won over when the refugee girl brings out of her bosom a purse containing 200 ducats as her dowry.

Göcking's refugee girl has been persecuted by the Salzburg Catholics, but having been willing to sacrifice all, even her family ties, for her faith, and having suffered the hardships of migration, she finds happiness as the wife of an Erfurt *Bürgerssohn*. Göcking wrote his history as the Protestant response to the Catholic victimization of the Salzburg Protestants in 1731. Archbishop Firmian of Salzburg, in a position of relative political power at the time of the "Pragmatic Sanction" for the accession of Maria Theresia, chose to exercise his constitutional right as a prince of the Holy Roman Empire, to compel his subjects to either adopt Catholicism or leave Salzburg.

---

[1] "The subject-matter itself is a stroke of luck — a plot, the likes of which one would scarcely find twice in a lifetime." Goethe to Heinrich Meyer, 28 April 1797, Gräf, 1/1:122.

[2] Gerhard Gottlieb Günther Göcking, *Vollkommene Emigrationsgeschichte von denen aus dem Erzbistum Salzburg vertriebenen ... Lutheranern* (Frankfurt am Main and Leipzig, 1734). The relevant parts are pp. 404f. and 671f. Cf. E.F. Yxem, *Über Goethes Hermann und Dorothea* (Berlin, 1836), 41-50; Hehn, *Ueber Goethes "Hermann und Dorothea,"* 52, 158; Seidlin, 113-15.

This exercise of political and religious authority was a late manifestation of the terms with which peace was established after the Peasants' Wars (Peace of Augsburg, 1555), and which was re-affirmed at the end of the Thirty Years' War (Peace of Westfalia, 1648).[3] Archbishop Firmian's action exemplified the complex interrelationships of politics and religion in the Holy Roman Empire until the revolutionary period. The history of development of modern religious and political identities under German petty absolutism underpins Göcking's naively told story of refugee Protestants. In the tale of Providence Göcking consolidates the belief that God helps those who help themselves into a representative story of German Protestantism.

## The Transposition from 1731 to 1796

According to both Schiller and Böttiger, Goethe had been thinking out ideas for *Hermann und Dorothea* from as early as 1792.[4] Over the same time, as Privy Councillor to the Duke of Saxe-Weimar, he had a detailed knowledge of political developments affecting his own and the other northern German states. He accompanied Karl August on the French Campaign from August to October 1792, and after spending the winter of 1792/3 back in Weimar, he was present at the siege of Mainz during the summer of 1793. After his return, he was kept up to date on events closer to the Rhine by friends, acquaintances and family. His mother, for example, had remained in Frankfurt during the French occupation, and kept him informed of events there.

Goethe's comments on the relationship between the historical events and his personal and creative life from this time onward are of relevance to *Hermann und Dorothea*. In the "Jahresheft" for 1792 he notes the itinerary of the campaign in France, remarking on the altered relationships with his old friends in Mainz (including Georg Forster), Düsseldorf and Münster. In 1793 he notes how *Reineke Fuchs* became a sort of "unheilige Weltbibel," and how his scientific work afforded creative support over the previous two years:

> Und so hielt ich für meine Person wenigstens mich immer fest an diese Studien, wie an einem Balken im Schiffbruch; denn ich hatte nun zwei Jahre unmittelbar und persönlich das fürchterliche Zusammenbrechen aller Verhältnisse erlebt.[5]

The imagery of the survival of shipwreck, or of landing after a sea-voyage occurs at the end of both *Torquato Tasso* and *Hermann und Dorothea*. Just as Dorothea

---

[3] I.e. the ius reformandi, "cuius regio, eius religio."

[4] Gräf, 1/1:86f., 96.

[5] "unholy Bible of the world," W.A. I, 35, 22. "And so I, for myself, held on fast to these studies, as to a beam in a shipwreck; for I had now been experiencing for two years, directly and personally, the most terrible collapse of all relationships," W.A. I, 35, 23.

excuses her emotionally fragile state at the end of *Hermann und Dorothea* with the image of the "endlich gelandeten Schiffer" ("one who has long been at sea," IX, 295), so Goethe here uses the image of the floating remains of the shipwreck, to which he has clung for survival.[6] He mentions his own literary-patriotic reactions to the French expansion into Germany — and at this later stage offers a justification for having written the plays of the early 1790s, *Der Bürgergeneral* and *Die Aufgeregten*.[7] The next year, which he had hoped would lead to an improvement of the situation, turned out worse:

> Doch wie sollte man sich erholen, da uns die ungeheuern Bewegungen innerhalb Frankreichs jeden Tag beängstigten und bedrohten, ... da die äußern Kriegstaten der im Innersten aufgeregten Nation unaufhaltsam vorwärts drängten, rings umher die Welt erschütterten und alles Bestehende mit Umschwung, wo nicht mit Untergang bedrohten.[8]

While other German states were drawn in and out of war with France, Prussia was neutral after signing the Peace of Basle (5 April 1795).[9] Goethe describes life under these conditions as like living in "einer traumartigen, schüchternen Sicherheit im Norden" and in a state of "eingeschläferten Fürchtsamkeit."[10] He also draws attention to a publication of the time which stirred up anti-French feeling:

> Bei großen Begebenheiten, ja selbst in der äußersten Bedrängnis, kann der Mensch nicht unterlassen mit Waffen des Wortes und der Schrift zu kämpfen. So machte ein deutsches Heft großes Aufsehen: Aufruf an alle Völker Europens; es sprach den siedenden Haß gegen die Franzosen aus,

---

[6] The symbolism in this canto is undercut by realistic touches. Dorothea may also here be making an excuse for her limping.

[7] "Einem tätigen produktiven Geiste, einem wahrhaft vaterländisch gesinnten, und einheimische Literatur befördernden Manne wird man es zugute halten, wenn ihn der Umsturz alles Vorhandenen schreckt, ohne daß die mindeste Ahnung zu ihm spräche was denn Besseres, ja nur anderes daraus erfolgen solle. Man wird ihm beistimmen wenn es ihn verdrießt, daß dergleichen Influenzen sich nach Deutschland erstrecken, ... In diesem Sinne war *Der Bürgergeneral* geschrieben, ingleichen *Die Aufgeregten* entworfen, sodann *Die Unterhaltungen der Ausgewanderten*." W.A. I, 35, 24.

[8] "Yet how was one to have recovered, when every day the monstrous upheavals in France frightened and threatened us ... when the belligerent external acts of this internally agitated nation pushed relentlessly forward, shaking the very foundations of the world, and threatening the existing order with revolution, if not downfall." W.A. I, 35, 25-26.

[9] See ch. 3, fn. 2.

[10] "a dreamlike, timorous security in the north," W.A. I, 35, 26; "drowsy fearfulness." W.A. I, 35, 67.

in dem Augenblicke da sich die ungebändigten Feinde mächtig gegen unsere Grenzen näherten.[11]

At the same time however, the pro-French parties were active:

> Um aber den Wechselstreit der Meinungen aufs höchste zu treiben, schlichen französische revolutionäre Lieder im Stillen umher; sie gelangten auch zu mir, durch Personen denen man es nicht zugetraut hätte.[12]

These passages are indicative of the general sense of confusion of politics, ideologies and patriotism over the period in which Goethe was working on *Hermann und Dorothea*. In view of this, the relocation in time from 1731 to late August 1796 is significant.

The expulsion of the Salzburg Protestants was the result of the consequent, if belated, application of the central formative law of the Holy Roman Empire after the Peace of Augsburg. Goethe's story occurs at the end of August 1796, after three years of various allied and French victories and consequent crossings and recrossings of the Rhine, at the time when Baden, Bavaria and Württemberg had signed peace treaties with the French, and shortly before the decisive battles of Amberg, Würzburg and Altenkirchen (early September 1796), led by Archduke Karl, which drove the French troops under Jourdan back across the Rhine.[13] In October 1792 Goethe had expressed his fears that Germany was facing another Thirty Years' War, when he compared the political situation in that year to that of 1618. And later he regarded the Cannonade of Valmy (September 1792) as the turning-point of a new epoch in world history.[14]

Goethe's reworking of the simple tale of religious fortitude is set in a less clearly defined socio-political context than his source. The action of *Hermann und Dorothea* takes place at a time when the fate of the German Rhine territories was in the balance, and when Napoleon's campaign in Italy was at its height. Göcking's story is devotional literature (*Erbauungsliteratur*) told in the traditional form of the providential tale. In Goethe's story the banality of the plot contrasts with the complexity of the socio-historical context.

---

[11] "During the great events, yes, even in the most extreme distress, people cannot refrain from fighting with words and writing. At that time a German pamphlet caused a great sensation: Call to all peoples of Europe. It expressed seething hatred of the French at the very moment when the unbeaten enemies were approaching our borders with all their might." W.A. I, 35, 26.

[12] "French revolutionary songs crept around stealthily, driving the war of opinions to an extreme; they even reached me, through the agency of persons, of whom one would not have thought such things." W.A. I, 35, 26.

[13] On the political situation in late August 1796, see: Helmerking, 74-76; Biro, 2:602-700; Saine, *Black Bread — White Bread*, 385-86.

[14] See Introduction, fn. 5 and ch. 2, fn. 31.

The question underlying Goethe's recasting of the plot is: how will the providential tale of love turn out in the post-revolutionary context? Goethe transposed the story into 1796, in the form of a mock-epic with a happy ending, using parody to signal ambivalence regarding the future. He thereby implicitly questions whether the situation in 1796 is another episode of the history of discontinuities of the Holy Roman Empire (i.e. like that of his source), or the turning-point for new, far-reaching changes in German life. Would change be for better or for worse? Another Thirty Years' War, or a new (and better) epoch in world history? The literary ambiguity of *Hermann und Dorothea* reflects the historical ambiguity of 1796. The source material is reworked in such a way as to reflect the historical ambiguity of the situation in 1796 — as another episode in the history of religious and political conflict in the Holy Roman Empire, or as the turning-point for new developments, which would engender new literary forms. Goethe's solution to the literary problem of representing this period was to use established German narrative traditions in a form which was at once traditional (*Erbauungsliteratur, Idylle*) and new (ironic parody).

A related aspect of the transposition from 1731 to 1796 is the change in sociocultural identities. In Göcking's source story the protagonists are identified in terms of religion. In Goethe's version identities are problematic. The father's, Hermann's and the first fiancé's images of Germany and of themselves as Germans are very different, ranging from the local patriotism of the father, to Hermann's incipient nationalism, to the revolutionary cosmopolitanism of the first fiancé.

This aspect introduces the theme of the Revolution as both culmination of the Enlightenment and beginning of modern nationalism. The events in Mainz in 1792/3 (on which Dorothea's experiences are probably based) revealed the "other face" of revolutionary liberation as national aggression.[15] The Mainz revolutionaries, especially Georg Forster, found themselves in this dilemma, as they realized that their liberators were becoming oppressors, and when they were condemned by their countrymen as traitors after 1793. From 1792 onwards, it became increasingly clear that republican liberation could be much the same as national occupation, when carried out with force from outside. This recognition contributed to the growth of a sense of nationality which exceeded feudal-absolutist, dynastic boundaries.

Thinkers of the French Enlightenment, such as Rousseau, had given strong emphasis to the ideas of freedom and ethnic and national identity — if for the most part in idealized and abstract form — as well as to republicanism. However the events of the period of revolutionary expansion discredited these enlightenment ideals in Germany. The German territories were the first to experience the force of the Revolution as occupation as well as liberation. National oppression occurred simultaneously with liberation from absolutism, as liberation from outside, rather than as self-liberation from below.

---

[15] August Gassner, *Goethe und Mainz* (Bern: Peter Lang, 1988), 137.

In the 1780s Goethe had turned his attention to the cultural heritage of the south of Europe (i.e. in *Iphigenie, Torquato Tasso,* the works inspired by his experience of Italy). In the 1790s the political inheritance from the west predominated (*Unterhaltungen deutscher Ausgewanderten, Hermann und Dorothea, Wilhelm Meisters Lehrjahre*). The American Revolution was an important formative influence on *Wilhelm Meister,* and the economic and political developments in France are central to the former works. In the early to mid 1790s, in response to the sense of the breakdown of the feudal-absolutist order, Goethe was preoccupied in creative terms with the adaptation and reformulation of literary forms and genres. During the revolutionary period the socio-political situation was changing so quickly that mimetic reflection into the literary fiction was impossible. Parody, irony, symbolism, and "modes of ambivalence" predominate from this period onward, as the expression of Goethe's sense of the end of the old world and the need for change to come to grips with the new.

# 8: The Restitution of Idyll?

CANTO NINE BRINGS *HERMANN und Dorothea* to a close. Hermann and his new bride return home and after some misunderstandings are betrothed by the vicar. The canto consists of five episodes: the mock-epic invocation of the Muses and description of the parents and friends waiting for the arrival of the young couple (IX, 1-14); the apothecary's anecdote of how his father taught him patience (IX, 15-54); the entry of Hermann and Dorothea and the confusion about Dorothea's role in her new home (IX, 55-248); her remembrance of her first fiancé (IX, 249-96); and Hermann's final speech (IX, 297-318). Each of these episodes brings together earlier themes from the work, concerning the interrelationships between individual consciousness and social identity.

### Life and Death in the Idyll

The apothecary tells the anecdote about his grim, pious father while he, the vicar and the parents are impatiently awaiting the arrival of Hermann and Dorothea. The spring outside the town reminds the apothecary of an episode when, as a child, he was impatiently waiting for a carriage to take the family on a picnic there. His father admonishes him with a parable linking pleasure with death for the restless and sensitive child:

'Siehst du des Tischlers da drüben für heute geschlossene Werkstatt?
...
Aber bedenke dir dies: der Morgen wird künftig erscheinen,
Da der Meister sich regt mit allen seinen Gesellen,
Dir den Sarg zu bereiten und schnell und geschickt zu vollenden;
Und sie tragen das bretterne Haus geschäftig herüber,
Das den Geduld'gen zuletzt und den Ungeduldigen aufnimmt
Und gar bald ein drückendes Dach zu tragen bestimmt ist.'

(IX, 32, 35-40)[1]

---

[1] "'Look over there: though it's closed today, that's the carpenter's workshop, / ... / just remember this: there will come a day, sooner or later, / When they will all be at work, the master and every apprentice, / Skilfully making a coffin for you, which they'll punctually finish, / And there will be no delay when that small wooden house is delivered, / Everyone's house in the end; whether they've been impatient or patient, /

This early experience is engraved in the apothecary's memory. It manifests itself in a negative attitude to life, in which all urges toward procreation, self-fulfillment and creativity are negated by the consciousness that they mark off the stages toward death:

'Rennen andere nun in zweifelhafter Erwartung
Ungebärdig herum, da muß ich des Sarges gedenken.'

(IX, 44-45)[2]

With his faculties of fantasy and imagination paralyzed, he cannot, as Hermann realized earlier (II, 97ff.), comprehend such qualities as generosity of spirit — or for that matter of material generosity either (VI, 206ff.). This anecdote completes the characterization of the apothecary in the work. His emotional paralysis stems from the same type of religious background as the father's obsession with rebuilding the town as a model environment, without thought for the inner lives of its inhabitants. The apothecary is the product of a fatalistic Calvinism, which, unlike the innkeeper's "Protestant ethic," finds no release in work or good deeds. The apothecary's symbolic, formative experience of death in terms of a paralyzing and claustrophobic fear, narrated at the beginning of this final canto reintroduces themes of activity and inactivity, progress and stagnation in the home town.

His anecdote draws a predictable response from the vicar, who feels that this display of pessimism cannot be let by unchecked. However his platitude does not come to grips with the apothecary's problematic consciousness of happiness, personal fulfillment and death:

'Zeige man doch dem Jüngling des edel reifenden Alters
Wert und dem Alter die Jugend, daß beide des ewigen Kreises
Sich erfreuen und so sich Leben im Leben vollende!'

(IX, 52-54)[3]

Here, as throughout the work, the vicar displays a superficiality and lack of conviction which reflects the degeneration of enlightenment from a critical and imaginative way of thinking into empty dogma. His words reflect the institutionalized enlightenment of Christian Wolff as taught in the Protestant theological schools of the northern German universities. He cannot come to terms with the complex issues of everyday life, let alone the political, ethical and social questions thrown up by the approach of the revolutionary armies into German territory.

---

It will receive them, and heavy's the roof it must very soon carry.'"

[2] "'Now, when I see other folk waiting anxiously, running around and / Fussing and fretting, I think of those words, and remember my coffin.'"

[3] "'let a young man / Rather be taught the value of late years nobly maturing, / And let the elderly look at the young, that both may take pleasure / In the eternal cycle, and life be fulfilled in its living!'"

### The Final Retarding Moment

The vicar's homily is interrupted by the arrival of Hermann and Dorothea. Hermann, having invited Dorothea to return with him as hired domestic help rather than as his bride, is in a quandary. He whispers to the vicar to save him from the mess he has got himself into, but by then his father has already offended Dorothea:

> 'Mit Freuden erfahr' ich, der Sohn hat
> Auch wie der Vater Geschmack, der seinerzeit es gewiesen,
> Immer die Schönste zum Tanze geführt und endlich die Schönste
> In sein Haus als Frau sich geholt'
>
> (IX, 78-81)[4]

Under the impression that Dorothea has come as his future daughter-in-law, he openly appraises her, and suggests that she is an opportunist:

> 'Aber Ihr brauchtet wohl auch nur wenig Zeit zur Entschließung?
> Denn mich dünket fürwahr, ihm ist so schwer nicht zu folgen.'
>
> (IX, 84-85)[5]

She, insulted and confused, defends herself without any help yet from Hermann or the vicar. Only now does Hermann signal to the vicar to intervene:

> Eilig trat der Kluge heran und schaute des Mädchens
> Stillen Verdruß und gehaltenen Schmerz und Tränen im Auge.
> Da befahl ihm sein Geist, nicht gleich die Verwirrung zu lösen,
> Sondern vielmehr das bewegte Gemüt zu prüfen des Mädchens.
>
> (IX, 108-11)[6]

Line 109, with its three spaced emphases focuses on Dorothea's humiliation. The vicar, who alone knows the full story and is in a position to clear things up, deliberately allows the misunderstanding to reach an extreme, with no positive result other than that Dorothea breaks down:

---

[4] "'Well, my child, I'm delighted — delighted to learn that my son has / Taste as good as his father's, who used to show his in the old days; / I always danced with the best-looking girls, and ended by fetching / Home as my wife the best-looking of all,'"

[5] "'But I dare say you didn't need long to make your decision, / For I'll wager my son has a way with him as a wooer!'"

[6] "And that wise man moved close to the girl and observed her protesting / Silence, her barely restrained distress, and the tears she was shedding. / Yet some instinct advised him not yet to resolve the confusion, / But instead to try out the girl's troubled heart and to test her."

'Und nun soll im Hause mich länger
Hier nichts halten, wo ich beschämt und ängstlich nur stehe,
Frei die Neigung bekennend und jene törichte Hoffnung.
Nicht die Nacht, die breit sich bedeckt mit sinkenden Wolken,
Nicht der rollende Donner (ich hör' ihn) soll mich verhindern,
Nicht des Regens Guß, der draußen gewaltsam herabschlägt,
Noch der sausende Sturm. Das hab' ich alles ertragen
Auf der traurigen Flucht und nah am verfolgenden Feinde.
Und ich gehe nun wieder hinaus, wie ich lange gewohnt bin,
Von dem Strudel der Zeit ergriffen, von allem zu scheiden.
Lebet wohl! ich bleibe nicht länger; es ist nun geschehen.'
(IX, 171-81)[7]

She retains her integrity (IX, 179ff.), and is about to leave. The vicar, having brought about this situation, is now powerless to rectify it. Not he but the mother steps in to clear up the misunderstanding:

Aber die Mutter ergriff mit beiden Armen das Mädchen,
Um den Leib sie fassend, und rief verwundert und staunend:
'Sag', was bedeutet mir dies? und diese vergeblichen Tränen?
Nein, ich lasse dich nicht; du bist mir des Sohnes Verlobte.'
(IX, 184-87)[8]

Even now, when misunderstanding threatens everything, Hermann does not act to clarify the situation. He lets Dorothea fend for herself in the new environment, against the insensitivity of his father and the spitefulness of the vicar in letting the confrontation here, and the later misunderstanding about the two engagement rings, take its full course.[9] Hermann still has not learnt his lesson. Instead of asking Dorothea whether she is already engaged, he even at this late stage stays silent, although he has been painfully aware of the ring since the meeting at the

---

[7] "'And this house shall no longer detain me / Now, where I merely am standing with shame and misgiving before you, / Frankly confessing my love and that foolish hope I have cherished. / Neither the night which lowering clouds are covering over, / Nor (for I hear it) the roll of the echoing thunder shall stop me, / Nor the torrents of rain that will fall out there like a deluge, / Nor the howl of the storm; for already I know and have borne all / This, on my sorrowful flight with the enemy closely pursuing. / Now I go out again into it all, what I long have been used to, / Seized by the whirl of the times, to be parted from everything. Farewell, / All of you! I cannot stay; the whole thing is over and done with.'"

[8] "But Hermann's mother stood in her way and embraced her with both arms / Holding her fast, and exclaimed to the girl in bewildered amazement: / 'Tell me, what does all this mean? and why are you shedding these vain tears? / No, I shall not let you go! for you are betrothed to my dear son.'"

[9] Cf. Ryder and Bennett, 435.

spring (VII, 101; IX, 252). Hermann's story is one of "retardation" in the extreme. His passivity repeatedly creates situations in which others act for him: Dorothea, not he, took the food and clothing and distributed them to the refugees; his mother went in search of him and helped him work out a strategy to overcome his father's prejudices against the refugee girl; he talked of joining the soldiers at the front against the French, but did not enlist in the army; the vicar and apothecary located the girl and found out about her; he did not propose to Dorothea, but merely offered her the position of housemaid, leaving to her the decision whether to settle in the town or follow the refugees into an uncertain future.

Irritated at the crying women, the father threatens to go to bed, whereupon Hermann finally demands some respect, and chides the vicar for his provocative behavior:

'Vater, eilet nur nicht und zürnt nicht über das Mädchen!
Ich nur habe die Schuld von aller Verwirrung zu tragen,
Die unerwartet der Freund noch durch Verstellung vermehrt hat.
Redet, würdiger Herr! denn Euch vertraut' ich die Sache.
Häufet nicht Angst und Verdruß; vollendet lieber das Ganze!
Denn ich möchte so hoch Euch nicht in Zukunft verehren,
Wenn Ihr Schadenfreude nur übt statt herrlicher Weisheit.'

(IX, 200-6)[10]

Embarrassed at Hermann's unexpected forthrightness, the vicar excuses himself on the basis that the truth would not have come out had he not provoked the situation. He urges Hermann to speak up for himself: "'Rede darum nur selbst! was bedarf es fremder Erklärung?'" ("'So why don't you speak for yourself? You don't need someone else to explain it!'" IX, 211). He and the apothecary alone had heard the story of Dorothea's first fiancé from the judge (VI, 186-90), and he is still the only one who knows both about the ring and Hermann's pretext for bringing Dorothea home. Instead of helping Dorothea to explain the story of her first lover, he waits until the betrothal, and only at the point of putting the second ring on her finger, asks for an explanation.

Before the actual betrothal takes place however, Dorothea approaches the father and apologizes for her behavior. In doing so she exemplifies the everyday "politeness" which she had described in canto eight as typical of the French (VIII, 40-49). After removing the rings from the father's and mother's hands, the vicar says with unconscious irony:

---

[10] "'Father, wait just a little! it's not her fault, don't be angry; / It's entirely my doing that there is this misunderstanding, / And now our friend's unexpected dissembling has only increased it. / Reverend sir, now speak! It's to you I entrusted this matter; / Now make an end of it. Why do you stir up dismay and annoyance? / It will be harder for me to respect you so much in the future / If you prefer making mischief to showing the wisdom you're famed for.'"

'Noch einmal sei der goldenen Reifen Bestimmung,
Fest ein Band zu knüpfen, das völlig gleiche dem alten.'

(IX, 243-44)[11]

He is of course referring to the marriage of Hermann's parents. However the ring on Dorothea's finger is still a disturbing mystery to Hermann. The question of Dorothea's first engagement is left until the very last moment, so that Dorothea's remembrance of her first fiancé occurs during the actual betrothal, with Hermann's final speech following directly after, although the beliefs of the first fiancé and of Hermann, both coming within the last sixty lines of the work, are opposed in terms of ideals and ideologies.

## The Tragedy of Revolutionary Enlightenment

The story of the first fiancé has already been told by the judge in canto six as a tragic episode in Dorothea's life (VI, 186-90). Now she requests leave to devote a moment to his memory herself:

Aber sie sagte darauf: 'O, laßt mich dieser Erinnrung
Einen Augenblick weihen! Denn wohl verdient sie der Gute,
Der mir ihn scheidend gab und nicht zur Heimat zurückkam.
Alles sah er voraus, als rasch die Liebe der Freiheit
Als ihn die Lust, im neuen, veränderten Wesen zu wirken,
Trieb, nach Paris zu gehn, dahin, wo er Kerker und Tod fand.'

(IX, 256-61)[12]

Dorothea focuses her attention on her lover's political idealism rather than on the Revolution as a political event. Her use of the word "rasch" suggests a judgement of over-hastiness in devoting himself to a political movement which was still an unknown quantity to him.[13] She does not dwell on his experiences and sufferings in Paris, but rather on the heightened state of euphoria in which he deserted his

---

[11] "'Let these gold rings once more be put to their purpose, / Forming a bond of wedlock as firm as that of these parents.'"

[12] "But she replied: 'Oh, now for a moment let me remember / That dear friend who gave me this ring, for he truly deserves it. / It was his parting gift, and he never returned to his homeland. / He foresaw what would happen: his passion for freedom was driving / Him, his desire to serve in a new and changed situation, / All too rashly to Paris, to suffer prison and death there.'"

[13] The accusation of over-hastiness was levelled at Georg Forster by Goethe and Schiller in the distich, "Unglückliche Eilfertigkeit: Ach, wie sie 'Freiheit' schrien und 'Gleichheit,' geschwind wollt ich folgen, / Und weil die Trepp mir zu lang deuchte, so sprang ich vom Dach." ("Unfortunate Haste: Oh, how they cried out: 'Freedom' and 'Equality!' I wanted to follow as fast as I could, / And since the stairs seemed too far, I jumped from the roof.") W.A. I, 5, 254. See Rödel, 110-12.

old life, on his deeply felt ideals, and on his recognition that the Revolution had disrupted for good the traditional patterns of life. Dorothea quotes his final words to her in a long passage (IX, 262-89), which brings him and his ideals into the home town:

'Lebe glücklich,' sagt' er. 'Ich gehe; denn alles bewegt sich
Jetzt auf Erden einmal, es scheint sich alles zu trennen.
Grundgesetze lösen sich auf der festesten Staaten,
Und es löst der Besitz sich los vom alten Besitzer,
Freund sich los von Freund: so löst sich Liebe von Liebe.
Ich verlasse dich hier, und wo ich jemals dich wieder
Finde — wer weiß es? Vielleicht sind diese Gespräche die letzten.'

(IX, 262-68)[14]

The Revolution is experienced by him as hope and euphoria on a level superseding even love. It transforms the engagement ring which he gives to Dorothea into a parting gift, signalling the greater attraction of the love of freedom.

While the revolutionaries in Paris styled themselves as Roman republicans, they remained aware of socio-economic and political realities, despite their costumery. There were millennial currents among sections of the French revolutionary intelligentsia, but they remained marginal to the central sociopolitical issues of control of resources and political power. Most of the politically inexperienced intellectuals in the German territories, however, had no conception of the everyday reality of the Revolution. Their Revolution was an enlightened *deus ex machina*, a utopian hope springing from an intolerable but omnipotent political system. This is reflected in the words of the fiancé. The Revolution as millennial happening overrides all the earthly concerns: of history ("alles bewegt sich / Jetzt auf Erden einmal"), politics ("Grundgesetze lösen sich auf der festesten Staaten"), social relations ("es scheint sich alles zu trennen"), material relations ("es löst der Besitz sich los vom alten Besitzer"), personal relations ("Freund sich los von Freund"), and sexual-emotional relations ("so löst sich Liebe von Liebe"). The religious element of his hopes and the alienation in terms of social and national identity are revealed in his belief that man is at best "a foreigner" on earth, especially at this point in history:

'Nur ein Fremdling, sagt man mit Recht, ist der Mensch hier auf Erden;
Mehr ein Fremdling als jemals ist nun ein jeder geworden.
Uns gehört der Boden nicht mehr; es wandern die Schätze;

---

[14] "'Farewell, may you be happy,' he said, 'I am leaving; for all things / Now are in sudden upheaval, a time of partings has come now. / Constitutions dissolve, even those most firmly established; Old possessions are falling away from their former possessors, / Bonds are loosed between friends, and so lover from lover is parted. / Here I leave you, and who can tell when I ever again shall / Find you? For now we are talking together perhaps for the last time.'"

Gold und Silber schmilzt aus den alten heiligen Formen;
Alles regt sich, als wollte die Welt, die gestaltete, rückwärts
Lösen in Chaos und Nacht sich auf und neu sich gestalten.
Du bewahrst mir dein Herz; und finden dereinst wir uns wieder
Über den Trümmern der Welt, so sind wir erneute Geschöpfe,
Umgebildet und frei und unabhängig vom Schicksal.'

(IX, 269-77)[15]

The religiously charged image of the "Fremdling" is linked to the disintegration of the old feudal-patriarchal forms of the Holy Roman Empire and the *ancien régime* in France.[16] In the imagery of the melting gold and silver he supplies a counter-image to the facile dialectic of the vicar and the cynicism of the judge in canto six (VI, 81ff.). The individual and the Revolution are subsumed into an apocalyptic vision where all is to be lost or won. In the figure of the first fiancé, the spiritually lonely pietist-Protestant individual and the enlightenment cosmopolitan (*Weltbürger*) are transfigured into the revolutionary.[17]

The altruism of the first fiancé is important because of its cultural, religious and psychological roots, rather than its utopianism. His political judgement is naive, the product of inexperience, and his euphoria a result of enlightened idealism and despair at once. He imagines the reunited couple rising up from the rubble and ashes of the old world, as the free, re-formed beings of a new, enlightened world order, released from the internal compulsion of false *Bildung* ("education," or "formation") and the external compulsion of fate. This image combines the Christian myth of paradise regained with the enlightened myth of the supersession of negative psychological, social and historical determinants. After the millennial euphoria has given way to sobriety in revolutionary Paris, however, he is left stranded and despairing. The prophetic fatalism of the fiancé's words expresses desperation and frustration beneath the revolutionary euphoria:

'Denn was fesselte den, der solche Tage durchlebt hat!
Aber soll es nicht sein, daß je wir, aus diesen Gefahren
Glücklich entronnen, uns einst mit Freuden wieder umfangen,
O, so erhalte mein schwebendes Bild vor deinen Gedanken,
Daß du mit gleichem Mute zu Glück und Unglück bereit seist!

---

[15] "'Man is only a stranger on earth, it has rightly been said so, / And as never before we are strangers now in these last days. / For the ground no longer is ours, wealth wanders in exile, / Gold and silver are melted down from their ancient and sacred / Forms, it seems the whole world is in flux, that its shape is dissolving / Back into chaos and night, and perhaps it will take on a new shape. / May your heart remain mine, and if we should meet again one day / Somewhere among the world's ruins, we shall undergo a renewal / Into some other life, and be free, so that fate cannot touch us.'"

[16] Schmidt notes the echo of Psalm 119, l. 19 in the fiancé's expression, "Nur ein Fremdling ...," Schmidt, 38.

[17] Cf. Erich Fromm, *The Fear of Freedom* (London: Routledge & Kegan Paul, 1966), 63.

Locket neue Wohnung dich an und neue Verbindung,
So genieße mit Dank, was dann dir das Schicksal bereitet.
Liebe die Liebenden rein und halte dem Guten dich dankbar.
Aber dann auch setze nur leicht den beweglichen Fuß auf;
Denn es lauert der doppelte Schmerz des neuen Verlustes.
Heilig sei dir der Tag; doch schätze das Leben nicht höher
Als ein anderes Gut, und alle Güter sind trüglich.'

(IX, 278-89)[18]

Dorothea refers to her first fiancé as "der Gute" ("the good one," IX, 257) and "der Edle" ("the noble one," IX, 290) and his words evoke a powerful impression of idealism and nobility of character. Hermann, for all his honesty, inarticulate sensitivity and goodness, does not share these characteristics. The words of the first fiancé occupy a special place in the text. The quality of the verse lifts it from its ironic-parodic context.[19] The models of the Bible, the Homeric epics, classical idyll, Voss and Klopstock are superseded by lines of originality and beauty. There are no parodic signals here, simply the echoes of a tragic history of German idealism and revolutionary politics.

The first fiancé is represented less as a revolutionary than as a character for whom the relationship between the ideal and the praxis of revolutionary enlightenment in the ethical, moral and political spheres is problematic and contradictory. The reason for this lies not in intellectual hypocrisy, as with so many other German intellectuals of the revolutionary period, but rather in the disparity between the moral and idealist orientation of the German Enlightenment and the political and practical nature of French revolutionary enlightenment.

The first fiancé tries to resolve his frustration at the political stagnation of Germany through a morally and intellectually inspired belief in revolution as practical enlightenment. However the revolutionary dialectic had advanced beyond this position, as the fiancé discovered in Paris. The culmination of

---

[18] "'For what force could bind any who live through such days as the present? / But if it is not to be, if we do not escape from these perils / By some good chance, and with joy return to each other's embraces: / Then let my image still hover before you, oh think of me often / And with equal resolve be prepared for good and ill fortune. / If one day you are drawn to a new home and a new marriage / Then accept what fate has in store for you, gladly enjoy it, / Love those sincerely who love you, and gratefully cherish your husband; / But even then, as you travel this earth, still tread on it lightly, / For a redoubling of grief lies in wait for you, threatening new loss. / May you give thanks for that day, but do not be deluded, or value / Life more than other possessions, for every possession is transient.'"

[19] Ryder and Bennett, 441.

enlightenment in revolution led not to the idealization of politics, but rather to the "politicization" of enlightenment.[20]

Dorothea's loss of everything in her life is measured by the loss of her lover. She brings to the home town depths of human experience unknown to any of the other characters. The fire which destroyed the town twenty years before was a cause of loss and suffering, but not on the tragic level of the death of the first fiancé, nor on the existential level of the Dorothea's refugee experiences (the attempted rape and the killing of her attackers):

'Also sprach er; und nie erschien der Edle mir wieder.
Alles verlor ich indes, und tausendmal dacht' ich der Warnung.
Nun auch denk' ich des Wortes, da schön mir die Liebe das Glück hier
Neu bereitet und mir die herrlichsten Hoffnungen aufschließt.
O verzeih, mein trefflicher Freund, daß ich, selbst an dem Arm dich
Haltend, bebe! So scheint dem endlich gelandeten Schiffer
Auch der sicherste Grund des festesten Bodens zu schwanken.'
(IX, 290-96)[21]

The image of the "one who has long been at sea," with which Dorothea excuses herself, continues the theme of the disjunctiveness of perception, introduced in the images of the wandering man dazzled by the sinking sun in canto seven, and the "schwebendes Bild" ("hovering image," IX, 281) of the first fiancé in canto nine. Where Hermann was confused by illusion and reality at the beginning of canto seven, Dorothea here in articulating her confusion, controls it. She is able to overcome her terrible past in order to find a new home with Hermann. But at the same time she has learned the lesson of the first fiancé and does not simply identify with the home town. Her image of the sailor, sea and land is unlike that of the despairing Tasso:

Berstend reißt
Der Boden unter meinen Füssen auf!
Ich fasse dich mit beiden Armen an!

---

[20] Gerd Müller makes a similar point in relation to the Mainz Jacobin, Georg Forster, whose revolutionary activism was aimed at "the realization of the ideals of reason." Müller points out the similarity between Forster's and Robespierre's moralistic idealism, *Literatur und Revolution: Untersuchungen zur Frage des literarischen Engagements in Zeiten des politischen Umbruchs*, Studia Germanistica Upsaliensia 14 (Uppsala: n.p., 1974), 43, 135.

[21] "'Those were my noble friend's words, and that was the last time I saw him. / I have lost everything since, and a thousand times thought of his warning, / And I remember his words once again now that love with such sweetness / Gives me new happiness here and such splendid hopes for the future. / Oh forgive me, dearest of friends, if even as I hold you, / Even in your arms, I tremble; as one who has long been at sea feels / Still unsafe on the firmest of ground, where at last he has landed.'"

So klammert sich der Schiffer endlich noch
Am Felsen fest, an dem er scheitern sollte.[22]

She does not cling, barely surviving, to the rocks on which she might have perished. She has landed safely. Her confusion is not existential. It is the result of the change from an unstable to a stable environment, a change which will not alter her consciousness or sense of identity. At question in the work is not her stability and intelligence, but rather the environment into which she is saved. Whether it turns out to be as solid underfoot as she hopes, or whether her sprained ankle in canto eight is symbolic of future difficulties in her new home is as yet unclear.

## The Nation as *Gemeinschaft*

When Dorothea has finished speaking and the second ring has been placed on her finger, Hermann for the first time in the work speaks out of his own accord. He takes up from where Dorothea left off. However he has misunderstood Dorothea's feelings of insecurity in the metaphor of the "endlich gelandeten Schiffer":

Also sprach sie und steckte die Ringe nebeneinander.
Aber der Bräutigam sprach mit edler, männlicher Rührung:
'Desto fester sei bei der allgemeinen Erschütterung,
Dorothea, der Bund! Wir wollen halten und dauern,
Fest uns halten und fest der schönen Güter Besitztum.
Denn der Mensch, der zur schwankenden Zeit auch schwankend gesinnt ist,
Der vermehret das Übel und breitet es weiter und weiter;
Aber wer fest auf dem Sinne beharrt, der bildet die Welt sich.'
(IX, 297-304)[23]

Directly following the words of the first fiancé, Hermann's response comes as something of a shock. Not only has he not spoken out like this before in the poem, but he supports the opposite values to those of the fiancé without appearing to

---

[22] Goethe, *Torquato Tasso*, ll. 3449-53, H.A. 6:167. "The boards beneath me split / Wide open, leave me with no foothold, none, / With both my arms I clutch at you, Antonio. / So in the end will a poor boatman cling / To the same rock on which he was to founder." Johann Wolfgang von Goethe, *Verse Plays and Epic*, ed. Cyrus Hamlin and Frank Ryder, trans. Michael Hamburger, Hunter Hannum and David Luke, vol. 8 of *Goethe's Collected Works* (New York: Suhrkamp, 1987), 139. Cf. Lukács, *Goethe*, 47.

[23] "Thus she spoke, and put on the new ring, and wore them together. / But her bridegroom now said, with noble and manly emotion: / 'Then let our bond, Dorothea, be so much the firmer in all this / General chaos; let us endure and continue and hold fast / To each other, and fast to the fine possessions we have here. / For in an unstable time, if a man himself is unstable / He will increase the unrest and spread it further and further; / But he who firmly holds to his purpose gives shape to his whole world.'"

notice the discrepancy. No direct or indirect narrative commentary surrounds his speech. It stands alone as the culmination of the work. This is an ironic reminder to the enlightened intelligentsia, of who will speak on behalf of Germany if they do not.

Hermann's talk with his mother in canto four was analysed in terms of the beginnings of a process of individuation and self-identification as a "German" in which a pietistic world-view and an internalized, transfigured patriotism are fused together. In his *Pietismus und Patriotismus im literarischen Deutschland*, Gerhard Kaiser studies the process of secularization of pietistic thought and feeling into a spiritualized, transfigured patriotism during the second half of the eighteenth century. Kaiser refers to the religious, emotional, cultural and social complex of this mystical patriotism as "the inner fatherland." Where political thinkers of the Enlightenment aimed at foreshadowing programs of practical activity, the pietistic patriot wanted to transfigure, rather than alter reality. Zeal and enthusiasm took the place of systematic thinking and reason.[24] The enlightened ideal of the nation *for* the individual is replaced with the religious-patriotic sense of the nation *in* the individual. The imagination replaces that which is lacking in reality. However while the "inner fatherland" was a spiritual possession, unassailable in reality, it also by definition existed in a state of tension with reality.[25] In place of the enlightened program of improvement of the real world, the religious patriot developed an eschatological consciousness, the roots of which lay in pietism.[26] However it is the structures rather than the contents of religion which are adopted:

> A patriotism results, which, even when it cannot be classed as Christian in essence, nevertheless is Christian in structure. ... it is not primarily ethical categories which are subsumed, but rather value-free structural categories ("wertindifferente Gestaltvorstellungen") such as the models of community, (national) awakening etc.[27]

Kaiser's thesis, that religious structures underlie the development of patriotic values in Germany during this period, can be applied to Hermann as he expresses himself in cantos four and nine. The vocabulary of pietism, patriotic emotions and sexually laden expressions transfigure the image of the local landscape (IV, 76-80) on the one hand, and the imagery of revolution and war are imagined in apocalyptic and superhuman terms (IV, 81-88) on the other. For the religious patriot the real enemy of the nation and the unseen enemy of the isolated soul are united. The undefined national consciousness in the face of the advancing enemy is buttressed by the consciousness of being one of God's chosen. Likewise the

---

[24] Kaiser, *Pietismus und Patriotismus*, 46.

[25] Kaiser, *Pietismus und Patriotismus*, 47-49.

[26] Kaiser, *Pietismus und Patriotismus*, 49-50.

[27] Kaiser, *Pietismus und Patriotismus*, 45.

spiritual and psychological loneliness which pietism reinforced finds vicarious resolution through the sense of belonging to the patriotic community, the invisible fatherland.[28]

In canto four Hermann expresses in a naive, undogmatic form what Kaiser refers to as the "fundamental categories of religious patriotism — spiritualization ('Vergeistigung'), emotionalization and subjectivization."[29] In his final speech these subjective and individual perceptions are consolidated into a hard conservatism, which contrasts with Dorothea's flexibility and resilience of character and ignores her indirect plea to at least remember, if not retain, the ideals of cosmopolitanism and political enlightenment of her first fiancé. Hermann's emotional and patriotic values in canto four have become the basis of a *Deutschtum* expressed in terms of a *kleinbürgerlich* ethos of ownership (in contrast to his earlier rejection of such materialism, IV, 181f.). The platitude, "wer fest auf dem Sinne beharrt, der bildet die Welt sich" ("he who firmly holds to his purpose gives shape to his whole world," IX, 304) shows the depths to which the "non-political" idealist philosophies of the 1790s could sink in a politically reactionary environment.[30] German "identity" is defined by the collective refusal to become involved in revolutionary or any other form of political change:

'Nicht dem Deutschen geziemt es, die fürchterliche Bewegung
Fortzuleiten und auch zu wanken hierhin und dorthin.
"Dies ist unser!" so laβ uns sagen und so es behaupten!'

(IX, 305-7)[31]

The traditional cultural identity of the Germans as "non-political," already well established by the end of the eighteenth century, is linked to a geographical identity with at least one clear border in the west (the Rhine).[32] Hermann (like many patriots of the period) seems willing to concede the left bank territories for the sake of his new Germany, with at least this well-defined *national* border.

---

[28] Kaiser uses the term "patriotische Gemeinde," *Pietismus und Patriotismus*, 70-84; cf. also Fromm, *Fear of Freedom*, 57f.

[29] Kaiser, *Pietismus und Patriotismus*, 57.

[30] Cf. Müller on Kant, *Literatur und Revolution*, 38-41; and Borchmeyer, *Höfische Gesellschaft*, 279.

[31] "'Let not us Germans continue this terrible present upheaval, / Swaying uncertainly hither and thither: it does not befit us. / Let us say rather: This is ours, and so let us maintain it.'"

[32] On the question of the Rhine as 'natural' boundary, see Biro, 1:1-6, 415-43, 2:501-5.

'Denn es werden noch stets die entschlossenen Völker gepriesen,
Die für Gott und Gesetz, für Eltern, Weiber und Kinder
Stritten und gegen den Feind zusammenstehend erlagen.'

(IX, 308-10)[33]

Rousseau's *volonté générale*, the slogan of liberation from feudalism before the Revolution, has been harnessed to the force of German conservatism, not as a democratic political category but as a spiritualized form of patriotism. Hermann envisages an anti-revolutionary *levée en masse*.[34] However the only character who has been in an existential situation, and who has killed rather than be killed (i.e. who is a "hero") is Dorothea. Hermann's personal experiences pale in comparison to hers, and he has little conception, and no experience of the things he is talking about. He has amalgamated personal feelings of persecution with pietist and biblical models in his spontaneous identification of *Deutschtum*.

Forced suddenly to confront the question of self-defense against the French in the later 1790s, the non-political German *Kleinbürger* drew heavily on the socio-religious reservoir of words, feelings and images of pietistic patriotism. The "resolute people" of Germany were not united in 1796, although there was a sense of a shared external threat, and the nature of response followed a common pattern of pietistic patriotism, as Kaiser demonstrates. In terms of political structure there was of course no common identity, although Herder had prepared for an ideology of the nation in terms of language, culture and ethnicity. In the absence of a coherent socio-political ideology, Hermann reverts to a primitive image of group identity:

'Du bist mein; und nun ist das Meine meiner als jemals.
Nicht mit Kummer will ich's bewahren und sorgend genießen,
Sondern mit Mut und Kraft. Und drohen diesmal die Feinde
Oder künftig, so rüste mich selbst und reiche die Waffen.'

(IX, 311-14)[35]

---

[33] "'They are forever still praised, those peoples who with resolution / Fought for their God and their laws, for their parents, their wives and their children, / And at the hands of their enemies perished, still standing together.'"

[34] Karl Eibl draws attention to Hermann's use of the word "erlagen" in his final speech, "Anamnesis des 'Augenblicks': Goethes poetischer Gesellschaftsentwurf in *Hermann und Dorothea*," *DVjs* 58 (1984): 138; and T.M. Holmes argues that Hermann's idyll is undermined from within by early capitalist materialism (111).

[35] "'Now you are mine: and that makes what I have more mine now than ever. / I shall not own it in sorrow, an anxiously guarded possession, / But defend it with courage and strength; and if enemies threaten / Now or in future, then arm me yourself and hand me my weapons!'"

Despite his insistence on "Gott und Gesetz," his values are naively materialistic.[36] His substantive use of the possessive pronoun ("das Meine") and the false comparative form of "meiner" sound puerile after the sophistication of expression of the first fiancé.[37] Hermann may turn out to have courage and strength, but these qualities are not sufficient to cope with the "new epoch of world history." His final image of traditional life-styles and sex-roles, of himself as national hero and leader of men and of Dorothea as wife and mother conflicts with his characterization throughout the work:

'Weiß ich durch dich nur versorgt das Haus und die liebenden Eltern,
O, so stellt sich die Brust dem Feinde sicher entgegen.
Und gedächte jeder wie ich, so stünde die Macht auf
Gegen die Macht, und wir erfreuen uns alle des Friedens.'

(IX, 315-18)[38]

The revolutionary armies of France brought an ambivalent message of political liberation and national oppression to the Rhineland. They signified the beginning of a new era of French hegemony in the German states. Yet the German patriotism that grew in opposition to French supremacy from the Revolution until the Vienna Congress (1815), incipient here in the figure of Hermann, is not presented as an ideal. Hermann's final stance is characterized by aggressive patriotism and advocacy of fundamentalist models of individual and social behavior. His outlook for the future is a reaction to the threat of foreign aggression in his homeland. The issue here is not that his response (i.e. self-defense) is justifiable, but that it is false to maintain the pretense of the provincial idyll in this situation. His aggressive stance and the perversity of invoking war in the name of peace end the poem on a harsh note.

The loss of innocence in Hermann's final speech can be demonstrated by comparison with Goethe's naive political outlook in the review of Sonnenfels's *Über die Liebe des Vaterlandes* discussed above.[39] Goethe's rejection of statehood was still possible in the political and intellectual context of 1772, as a result of the fragmented social and political history of Germany, and of the lack of participation of the intelligentsia in political processes. Hermann's credo on the other hand is neither a rejection of nationhood, nor simply an idealization of the family and small-town community (i.e. idyll). He uses the traditional ideas of the *Gemeinschaft* to support an argument for German "nationhood." His final image of armed and

---

[36] Kaiser, *Pietismus und Patriotismus*, 45.

[37] Cf. Seidlin, 110.

[38] "'For if I know you are here to look after our home and our parents, / Why, then with confidence I shall go out and confront our attackers. / And if our countrymen all felt as I do, we'd all of us rise up: / Might against might would stand, and for all of us wars would be over.'"

[39] Ch. 1, fn. 13.

aggressive neighboring lands is not promising for the future, and is certainly not "idyllic."

Scansion of Hermann's speech reveals some interesting contrasts to his earlier lines. In the meeting with Dorothea in canto seven his speech revealed many metrical irregularities. Enjambment, irregular caesurae, hesitations, breaks in logic and coherence, and disjunction between emotional stress and lexical or metrical units characterized the lines. Here at the end of canto nine the lines are unusually uniform in that they all have six stresses. However as hexameters they are irregular, in that the division of stressed and unstressed words in the lines is often disrupted by the predominance of the sense-stresses over the metrical flow.[40] This results in the breaking of the poetic rhythm in favor of the spoken stress units:

```
   x - x - x  - -  x - x - -   x - -
'Desto fester sei bei der allgemeinen Erschütterung,

   x - x -(-) - x     - x - x - -   x -
Dorothea, der Bund! Wir wollen halten und dauern,

   x -  x - -  x  -  x -  x - - x -
Fest uns halten und fest der schönen Güter Besitztum.'
```

The irregularity of the first two lines culminates on "Dorothea, der Bund." Thereafter the division of stresses becomes more regular:

```
   x  - / x -   - /x (-) - /x - (-)/ x - -  / x -
'Die für Gott und Gesetz, für Eltern, Weiber und Kinder

   x -   - / x  (-) -  /x  - /x -  - /x - - / x -
Gegen die Macht, und wir erfreuten uns alle des Friedens.'
```

However this is not the regular, if often artificial, verse of Goethe's predecessors, Voss and Klopstock. It is closer to speech rhythms and it plays off speech rhythms (prose) against metrical expectation (verse hexameters). The hexameters of Klopstock, Voss and their imitators at times forced the rhythms of German to imitate ancient Greek with its organic relationship between metrical and sense stress in the hexameter. The artificiality of hexameters in German as the classical, and therefore desirable, form for a "national" literature is questioned throughout *Hermann und Dorothea*. At the end of this work, the prose of modern life begins to emerge from the poetic language created by Klopstock.

---

[40] Cf. Ryder and Bennett, 438-40.

## Excursus: Revolutionary Enlightenment, the German Jacobins, and Dorothea's First Fiancé

The German writer and "Mainz Jacobin," Georg Forster has been linked to the fiction of *Hermann und Dorothea* at least since the mid nineteenth century, and probably from the time of publication. Viktor Hehn suggested Mainz as the town from which Dorothea fled.[41] Georg Gottfried Gervinus notes in his essay on Georg Forster that "the Germans in Paris were convinced, that a violent death threatened him, had he lived longer," thus linking his potential fate with the fictive fate of the first fiancé, and Hermann Hettner suggests Forster as the model for the hero of Klinger's novel, *Geschichte eines Teutschen der neuesten Zeit* (1798).[42]

Leslie Bodi documents an early exchange between Karl Klein and Dr. Schaunberg in Herrig's *Archiv* of 1865 on the question whether Forster was, or was not, the model for the first fiancé.[43] In 1925 Paul Zincke again suggested that Forster had been an important influence.[44] In his post-war analysis, "La Révolution française dans *Hermann et Dorothée*," Robert Leroux mentions Forster, and of more recent historians, Leslie Bodi, Richard H. Samuel, Helmut J. Schneider and Detlev Rasmussen consider Forster a significant influence, with Bodi and Rasmussen in particular supplying strong documentary and analytical evidence to support their arguments.[45]

Richard Friedenthal, Dieter Borchmeyer, and August Gassner on the other hand suggest Adam Lux, Forster's co-delegate from Mainz to the Paris National

---

[41] Hehn, 94.

[42] Georg Gottfried Gervinus, "Johann Georg Forster," *Deutsche Literaturkritik*, ed. Hans Mayer, 4 vols. (Frankfurt am Main: Fischer, 1978), 2:311; Hermann Hettner, *Geschichte der deutschen Literatur im achzehnten Jahrhundert*, 2 vols. (1856-70; Berlin: Aufbau, 1979), 2:604.

[43] Leslie Bodi, "Goethe und Forster," Lecture to the Goethe-Society, Victorian Branch, Melbourne, December 1, 1961, ms. p. 15. I am indebted to Leslie Bodi for much of the material regarding Forster in this chapter.

[44] Paul Zincke, *Georg Forsters Bildnis im Wandel der Zeiten: Ein Beitrag zur Geschichte des öffentlichen Geistes in Deutschland* (Reichenberg i.B., 1925; repr. Hildesheim: Gerstenberg, 1974), xix-xx.

[45] Leroux, 185; Bodi, "Goethe and Forster," 14; Richard Samuel, "Goethe's *Hermann und Dorothea*," *Selected Writings*, ed. D.R. Coverlid, et al. (Melbourne: University of Melbourne, Dept. of Germanic Studies, 1965), 37-38; and Helmut J. Schneider, "Idylle und bürgerliches Epos," *Zwischen Revolution und Restauration: Klassik, Romantik, 1786-1815*, vol. 5 of *Deutsche Literatur: Eine Sozialgeschichte*, ed. H.A. Glaser (Reinbek bei Hamburg: Rowohlt, 1980), 136; Detlef Rasmussen, "Georg Forster und Goethes *Hermann und Dorothea*: Ein Versuch über gegenständliche Dichtung," *Goethe und Forster: Studien zum gegenständlichen Dichten*, ed. Detlef Rasmussen (Bonn: Bouvier, 1985), 54-79.

Convention, as the main influence for Dorothea's first fiancé.[46] Adam Lux was executed for defending Charlotte Corday in mid 1793, and this is the basis for most of the arguments linking him to Dorothea's fiancé, who "Selbst hinging nach Paris und bald den schrecklichen Tod fand" ("Went to Paris himself, and soon suffered a terrible death there;" VI, 187-189). Most recently, Thomas P. Saine has reopened this question, in disagreeing with an earlier article of my own in which the similarities between Forster and the fiancé were mentioned.[47] Normally an issue such as this would deserve no more than a footnote in literary histories. In this case however the arguments have important consequences for the work as a whole.

Literary historians have investigated and detailed Goethe's knowledge of the events of the 1790s, and there is no reason to dispute that the execution of Adam Lux in Paris may have contributed to the literary fate of the first fiancé. In this discussion, literary and historical modes of discourse should not be confused. The first fiancé is a fictional "stereotype," not a historical recreation. He is most probably an amalgam of the stories of Forster, Lux and others known to Goethe and consciously or unconsciously included in the fiction of the "German Jacobin."[48] At the same time, however, the contextuality of these historical figures cannot be ignored. The background history of Forster, which was known to the German educated public of the time, offers a great many interpretative insights into the figure of the Jacobin in *Hermann und Dorothea*. The figure of Adam Lux offers nothing of significance to the story of the first fiancé other than his dramatic death. Forster's story, heightened into the figure of the fiancé, gives resonance to the central themes of the work: the crisis of enlightenment and the reformulation of German identity in the wake of the Coalition Wars.

When he became involved in revolutionary politics in 1792, Georg Forster had a reputation in Germany as a naturalist, essayist and travel writer. While still an adolescent he accompanied his father, the botanist Johann Reinhold Forster, on Cook's second South Sea voyage of 1772-1775, and, bilingual in English and

---

[46] Richard Friedenthal, *Goethe: Sein Leben und seine Werke*, 2 vols. (Munich: DTV, 1967), 2:417; Borchmeyer, *Höfische Gesellschaft*, 284, and "Weimar im Zeitalter der Revolution," 10; Gassner, 136f.

[47] Thomas P. Saine, *Black Bread — White Bread: German Intellectuals and the French Revolution* (Columbia, SC: Camden House, 1988), 380-91; repr. of "Charlotte Corday, Adam Lux, and *Hermann und Dorothea*," in *Exile and Enlightenment: Studies in German and Comparative Literature in Honor of Guy Stern*, ed. Uwe Faulhaber, Jerry Glenn, Edward P. Harris and Hans-Georg Richert (Detroit: Wayne State University Press, 1987), 87-96; Peter Morgan, "The Polarization of Utopian Idealism and Practical Politics in the Idyll: The Role of the First 'Bräutigam' in Goethe's *Hermann und Dorothea*," *German Quarterly* 57 (1984): 532-45.

[48] Goethe's biographer, Albert Bielschowsky, for example, suggests von Türkheim, the husband of Goethe's first fiancée, Lili Schönemann, *Goethe: Sein Leben und seine Werke*, 2 vols. (Munich: C.H. Beck, 1917), 1:189, 213.

German, wrote the account of the journey, the *Voyage around the World*, in 1778.[49] After returning to Germany he contributed to the German Enlightenment in areas such as anthropology and sociology. He was in touch with the leading thinkers, including Goethe. He engaged in a polemic with Immanuel Kant over racism and intellectual narrowness in "Über Proselytenmacherei" ("On Proselytizing") and "Noch etwas über die Menschenrassen" ("On the Human Races: Another Contribution") and participated in the "Enlightenment debate" in the *Berlinische Monatsschrift*.[50] Goethe was indebted to him for the translation (from the English) of the Sanskrit classic, *Sakuntala* by Kalidasa, which inspired the "Prologue in the Theatre" in *Faust*. Goethe and Forster also corresponded on areas of scientific interest. After the Mainz affair and the death of Forster in Paris, Goethe maintained contact with Forster's close friend Sömmering, who held academic posts in Mainz, and later, Frankfurt am Main. Later in the 1790s, Goethe and Schiller discussed plans for an epic poem, "Der Weltumsegler" ("The Circumnavigator") which would have been influenced by Forster's experiences.[51] Forster was a close friend of Alexander von Humboldt, and was known and admired by the circle of intellectuals who were later to become the formative figures of German romanticism, especially Friedrich Schlegel. His wife, Therese Huber, was a friend of Caroline Michaelis, and after Forster's death married the journalist and writer Ludwig Ferdinand Huber, who had been a friend of Schiller. With Huber Therese co-edited the journal, *Friedens-Präliminarien* (1794-96), in which the broad political significance of the Revolution was affirmed, while its excesses were condemned. Goethe experienced the Siege of Mainz and the French Campaign, and was in touch both personally and through correspondence with people who had been close to Forster and the other Mainz revolutionaries. Caroline Michaelis (Schlegel-Schelling), who had remained in Mainz during the siege, was the recipient of some of his last letters. Shortly after Forster's death in January 1794, and most probably in reference to him, she wrote to Amalie Reichard:

> Der Mann, den wir beyde einst innig bedauerten, sagt in einem Brief, den er mir wenig Wochen vor seinem Tode schrieb: 'ich kann mir die Lieblosigkeit der Menschen gegen Sie denken; auf eine andre Art, und doch nicht anders hab ich sie an mir erfahren. Die Unmöglichkeit zu irren ist bey den meisten derer, die so gern richten und verdammen, nur eine Folge ihres Egoismus. Daß das daraus entspringende Unglück Verirrungen schonungswerth machen kann, daß es uns mit dem Fehlenden aussöhnen muß, wenn

---

[49] Michael E. Hoare, *The Tactless Philosopher: Johann Reinhold Forster, 1729-98* (Melbourne: Hawthorne Press, 1976), 77-204.

[50] Müller, *Literatur und Revolution*, 38ff.

[51] Among the Jena circle, the term "Weltumsegler" was synonymous with Forster, see Rasmussen, 58.

wir auch unzufrieden mit ihm gewesen waren, davon haben diese Leute keinen Begriff.'⁵²

Forster, the idealistic intellectual, frustrated by the narrowness of petty-absolutist society after the experiences of his early years in England and on the South Sea voyage of Cook, saw the potential for enlightened political change and the need for revolutionary action. At the beginning of the Revolution he was not alone in this. It was a vision which had appealed to a generation of intellectuals up until 1792/3, and it expressed both their generally felt need for change since the *Sturm und Drang* of the 1770s, and their lack of political and social alternatives in the context of the Holy Roman Empire.

Forster's activity and the image of the German Jacobin which arose from it, became the symbol of the relationship between political ideals and praxis for an intelligentsia, whose thinking had moved in the vanguard of the European late Enlightenment, but whose existence was still determined by its dependence on petty-absolutist socio-economic structures. As Marx pointed out:

> Yet, even if Germany has only kept company with the development of the modern nations through the abstract activity of thought, without taking an active part in the real struggles of this development, it has nevertheless shared in the *sufferings* of this development without sharing in its pleasures and its partial satisfaction.⁵³

As the well-known representative of a liberal, enlightened humanism, Forster shocked his peers by refusing to leave Mainz and supporting the annexation of the town to the French republic. Forster involved himself in the revolutionary politics of mid-1792 in the belief that the people of Mainz wanted political change and needed leadership. He was under no illusions about the political situation in the rest of Germany, and even wrote that he considered the German territories to be unready for revolution. He was acting true to his nature as a practical philosopher,

---

⁵² "The man whom we both once deeply felt for, says in a letter which he wrote to me a few weeks before his death: 'I can imagine the unkindness of people towards you; I have experienced the same thing myself, in a different form. For most of those people who love to judge and condemn, the impossibility of making mistakes is merely the result of their egotism. These people cannot understand that the misfortune which comes of mistakes can lead to sympathy, and that this misfortune must reconcile us with an erring individual, even if we had been disappointed in him.'" *Caroline: Briefe aus der Frühromantik*, ed. Erich Schmidt, rev. ed., 2 vols. (Leipzig: Insel, 1913), 1:322. I am grateful to Prof. Leslie Bodi for drawing my attention to this letter.

⁵³ Karl Marx, "A Contribution to the Critique of Hegel's Philosophy of Right: Introduction," *Early Writings*, trans. Rodney Livingstone and Gregor Benton (Harmondsworth: Penguin, 1975), 253.

willing to predicate action on conviction. In this, as Georg Lukács observes, he differed from most of the German intellectuals of the 1790s.[54]

Several attempts were made to clear Forster of the opprobrium which was heaped on him after the retaking of Mainz. In his essay of 1797 Friedrich Schlegel tried to rehabilitate Forster as the "German classical writer," the representative of a unifying consciousness, through which all that is "national" can be expressed in the absence of a "nation." Schlegel avoids the question of the translation of *Geist* ("spirit") into *Tat* ("deed"), which made Forster the most important of the German Jacobins. Hannelore Schlaffer writes that Schlegel ignores Forster's development from literary enlightenment to Jacobin politics. Forster is represented by Schlegel not as a revolutionary, but rather as one who *writes* about revolution.[55] A less subtle form of censorship of Forster the revolutionary is to be found in Ludwig Huber's introduction to Forster's "Draft Petition of the General Administration (of Mainz) to the Commissioners of the National Convention":

> ... was he (Forster) led astray by his love of freedom, when he saw in Custine's invasion an opportunity for his adoptive fatherland to join the French Revolution? As long as these questions alone are asked, then there is no jury which could acquit him ... But the present piece of writing drafted by him demonstrates his honour from a different, much more important angle. It shows him as a public official, working courageously and honestly for the welfare of his fellow citizens.[56]

Huber tries to rehabilitate Forster on the basis that he was fulfilling his official duty (as a "Beamter" or civil official), neither overstepping authority, nor shirking unpleasant aspects. Schlegel's separation of the revolutionary from the classical prose-writer, and Huber's separation of the revolutionary from the official both indicate the importance of Forster in the self-understanding of the German intellectuals after 1792. After the critical events of 1793, political discussion died down due to censorship and the danger of publishing revolutionary or seditious material. This silence on political topics was also the result of the intellectual disorientation created by the divergence of enlightenment theory and revolutionary praxis after 1792. The dichotomy of *Geist* and *Tat* which Forster overcame in Mainz, even if he ultimately doubted his cause, was reinforced in the German

---

[54] "The translation of theory into practice was a very rare exception (Georg Forster)." Lukács, *Goethe*, 71-72.

[55] Hannelore Schlaffer, "Friedrich Schlegel über Georg Forster: Zur gesellschaftlichen Problematik des Schriftstellers im nachrevolutionären Bürgertum," *Literatursoziologie*, ed. Joachim Bark, 2 vols. (Stuttgart: Kohlhammer, 1974), 2:124.

[56] [Ludwig Ferdinand Huber], "Vorerinnerung des Herausgebers," to Georg Forster, "Entwurf des Schreibens der allgemeinen Administration (von Mainz) an die Kommissarien des National-convents," *Friedens-Präliminarien*, ed. von dem Verfasser des heimlichen Gerichts [Ludwig Ferdinand Huber] (Berlin: Voss) 7 (1795), nos. 25-6, pp. 43-44.

intellectual tradition after the failure of radical politics in Mainz. As an "enlightened Jacobin," Forster was a reminder of the past ideals — and the present compromises — of a generation of intellectuals who had supported the Revolution, but who had been intellectually and politically alienated after 1792. As the central figure in the Mainz events he came to personify the shift in consciousness among the German intelligentsia from the dangerous area of politics toward the non-political areas of literature, culture and the sciences after 1792. The Terror, the formation of a nationalist-expansionist ideology, which displaced the ideology of enlightened cosmopolitanism, and the "freeze" in political relations in the absolutist states during the Coalition Wars compromised and restrained the German intelligentsia. The rationalizations of Forster's position by Huber and Schlegel, along with the callous comments of ex-radicals such as Schiller, Heinse and Friedrich v. Stolberg, indicate the extent to which Forster's memory was a provocation after 1792.[57] Forster's doubts and disappointments in Paris, exacerbated by sickness and loneliness, as Gervinus points out, were seized upon by his opponents to discredit the long-term political results of the Revolution and of democratic political activity in Germany.[58] The literary historian, Hettner, for example selectively uses Forster's letters to suggest that he completely despaired of the Revolution as a progressive political force.[59]

Huber published the "Entwurf des Schreibens ..." and selections from Forster's letters from Mainz and Paris in the *Friedens-Präliminarien* in 1794 and 1795. Schlegel wrote his Forster essay at the same time as Goethe was writing *Hermann und Dorothea*, in late 1796 and early 1797. Schlegel created for Forster the niche in literary history which he has occupied ever since. In the figure of the first fiancé

---

[57] The authorship of individual distichs by Goethe and Schiller is not known for sure. However it is not unlikely that Schiller was the author of those aimed at Forster, such as "Phlegyasque miserrimus omnes admonet: O ich Thor! Ich rasender Thor! Und rasend ein jeder, / Der auf des Weibes Rath horchend, den Freiheitsbaum pflanzt!" and "Die dreifarbige Kokarde: Wer ist der Wüthende da, der durch die Hölle so brüllt, / Und mit grimmiger Faust sich die Kokarde zerzaus't?" W.A. I, 5, 255. On the relationship between Schiller, Goethe and Forster, see Rödel, 104-14. Heinse to Gleim: "Mainz, den 28 Merz, 1794. ... Forster, der Weltumsegler, hat sich wieder nach Stürmen gesehnt, und ist von der Revoluzion verschlungen worden; sein Staatsschiff war kein Englisches Kriegsschiff: sondern eine in der Eil elend zusammen geflickte Barke; und sein Cüstine kein Cook." Wilhelm Heinse, *Sämtliche Werke*, ed. C. Schüddekopf (Leipzig: Insel, 1910; repr. Munich: Omnia 1977), 10:268. Friedrich Stolberg to Fr. H. Jacobi: "Königsbruck, den 13ten Jan. 1793. ... laß dem Mainzer Forster Deinen Schutz nicht ferner angedeihen! Laß sein Andenken, zugleich mit Kotzebue's Büste, in irgend einer Rumpelkammer vergessen seyn! Es bedarf in diesem Augenblicke einer tüchtigen Wurfschaufel, um den Waizen zu sichten und heulenden Winden die Spreu zu überlassen." Friedrich Leopold Graf zu Stolberg, *Briefe*, ed. Jürgen Behrens (Neumünster: Karl Wachholtz, 1966), 297, cf. also 546-47.

[58] Gervinus, "Georg Forster," 311f.

[59] Hettner, *Geschichte der deutschen Literatur*, 589.

in *Hermann und Dorothea* however, Goethe created a fuller and more truthful image of the enlightened revolutionary in the critical years after 1792.[60]

The themes of enlightenment, revolution and despair associated with Forster, and suppressed and repressed in post-revolutionary German society, resurface in literary form in the figure of Dorothea's fiancé. Forster's decision to support the Revolution, to leave his wife and children and go to Paris amidst the uncertainties of the war is paralleled by the story of Dorothea's fiancé, who sacrifices his lover for his belief that a new, enlightened world order will come of the Revolution. When the Revolution turned out to be a struggle for power among the interest groups of the new society, rather than the "emergence of mankind from its self-incurred minority," Forster, like the fiancé, experienced annihilating defeat. His disappointment expressed itself in apocalyptic imagery:

> Oh, seit ich weiß, daß keine Tugend in der Revolution ist, ekelt es mich an. Ich konnte, fern von allen idealischen Träumereien, mit unvollkommenen Menschen zum Ziel gehen, unterwegs fallen und wieder aufstehen und weitergehen; aber mit Teufeln und herzlosen Teufeln, wie sie hier sind?[61]

He maintained until the end his belief that the negative aspects of Jacobinism would ultimately be transcended. He did not try to exculpate himself as a revolutionary by arguing that Jacobinism represented an aberration and lapse from revolutionary ideals, as Klopstock and many other ex-radicals did.[62] He unwillingly accepted the Jacobin phase as part of a historical dialectic, a cathartic process which would clear the way for post-revolutionary humanity. But at the same time he never came to terms with the brutality of revolutionary politics. The following passages from Forster's letters to Voss illustrate the similarity between Forster's and the fiancé's apocalyptic response to the failure of the Revolution to live up to their ideals. From Mainz on 10 November 1792, Forster wrote to Voss:

> Wir leben in einem seltsamen Zeitpunkt, wo man die Menschen kaum mehr richtig beurteilen kann, wenn man sie nur nach ihren äußeren Verhältnissen richtet; wo die Maßstäbe, womit wir sonst einander zu

---

[60] Cf. Georg Lukács who contrasts the figures of Goethe and Georg Forster to illustrate the "misère" of socio-political relationships in the 1790s in Germany: "Goethe ... fled into the world of pure contemplation. Against this, as its opposite pole is the Mainz activity of the German Jacobin, Georg Forster and his lonely death in Parisian exile," *Skizze einer Geschichte der neueren deutschen Literatur* (Darmstadt: Luchterhand, 1975), 32-33.

[61] "Oh, now that I know that there is no virtue in the Revolution, it disgusts me. Without any idealistic dreams I could march onward with imperfect human beings, fall down, struggle up and continue on; but with devils — and heartless devils like these?" Georg Forster to Therese Forster, Paris, 16 April 1793, Georg Forster, *Werke*, ed. Gerhard Steiner, 4 vols. (Frankfurt am Main: Insel, 1969), 4:847.

[62] Cf. Saine, *Black Bread — White Bread*, 323, 367-68.

messen pflegten fast möchte ich sagen, zerbrochen werden müssen und nur der eine, der Humanität allein, übrig bleibt ... [63]

and two weeks later:

Allein ums Himmels willen! daß man doch nur einsehen möge, wie die Stimmung unserer Zeiten ist, ... wie es platterdings unmöglich ist, daß die morschen Dämme halten können, die man der Freiheitsüberschwemmung entgegensetzt! Es ist eine der entscheidenden Weltepochen, in welcher wir leben.[64]

Two months after Mainz had been re-occupied by the Coalition forces, when he was in exile (on a political mission), he wrote:

Wenn es die Ereignisse dieser Zeit mit sich bringen, daß man eigentlich nur von einer Stunde zur andern leben muß, um des Lebens froh zu werden, so liegt es auch wieder in ebendieser unentwickelbaren Verwirrung, die uns in die Zukunft wie in ein dunkles Gewittergewölk blicken läßt, daß, sobald Sturm, Blitz und Donner sich entladen haben, alles eine so ganz unerwartet frische, neue Gestalt annehmen muß, wobei es sich ganz behaglich wird leben lassen ...[65]

On 28 December 1793, when he was on his death-bed, he wrote:

Die Revolution ist ein Orkan, wer kann ihn hemmen? Ein Mensch, durch sie in Tätigkeit gesetzt, kann Dinge tun, die man in der Nachwelt vor Entsetzlichkeit nicht begreift. Aber der Gesichtspunkt der Gerechtigkeit ist für Sterbliche zu hoch. Was geschieht, *muß* geschehen. Ist der Sturm vorbei,

---

[63] "We are living in strange times, when one can hardly judge men rightly any more, if one does so on the basis of the externalities of behavior; when the criteria with which we are accustomed to judge each other have to be destroyed, and one alone — that of humanity — remains standing ..." Georg Forster to Voss, Mainz, 10 November 1792, Forster, 4:782. Published in *Friedens-Präliminarien*, vol. 9 (1795), nos. 35-36, p. 182.

[64] "For Heaven's sake! If only one could gain some understanding of what the mood of our times is, ... how it is absolutely impossible for the rotten floodgates to hold up against the floods of freedom! We are living in one of the decisive epochs of the world." Georg Forster to Voss, Mainz, 21 November 1792, Forster, 4:794. *Friedens-Präliminarien*, vol. 9 (1795), nos. 35-36, p. 242.

[65] "If the events of this era force us to live from one hour to the next, in order to find any happiness in life, then this too is a result of this same inextricable confusion, which allows us to see into the future as if into a dark storm-cloud — to see that, as soon as the storm, thunder and lightning have vented themselves, everything must take on such a totally unexpected fresh, new form, that we will again be able to live secure and happy ..." Georg Forster to Therese Forster, Arras, 25 September 1793, Forster, 4:910-11. *Friedens-Präliminarien*, vol. 4 (1794), nos. 15-16, p. 260.

so mögen sich die Überbleibenden erholen und der Stille freuen, die darauf folgt.[66]

His final work, the *Parisische Umrisse*, which strongly defends the Revolution even as it had developed up until the beginning of 1794, is written from the viewpoint of a revolutionary *citoyen*, a narrative stance which allows Forster a certain detachment from his own past and his misgivings about the developments under the Jacobins. However the political optimism of this fictive persona contrasts with the strain and despair of his private correspondence to his friend and publisher Voss, and his wife, Therese.

The above selections from Forster's letters, published in the *Friedens-Präliminarien*, emphasize the self-questioning, the regret and the pathos of the German idealist-revolutionary in Paris. To this extent they offered a reconciliatory image of Forster as a repentant revolutionary, and they were influential in forming a less negative public image of Forster than, for example, the image of the traitor and fanatic portrayed by the conservative and reactionary press.[67] However neither this image, nor that of the unrepentant traitor truly represented the significance of Forster at this time, for his character and fate had become symbolic of the wider crisis of the German Enlightenment in the revolutionary period.

The language of the first fiancé echoes that of Forster in the letters from Paris in late 1793 and early 1794. Both use the imagery of natural cataclysm to describe the overwhelming effect of the Revolution on the individual. Forster uses the image of the avalanche in his letters to express his sense, after arriving in Paris, that the Revolution does not allow itself to be understood merely through reason. Forster's tone in his private correspondence contrasts with the analytical sobriety of the *Darstellung der Revolution in Mainz* and the *Parisische Umrisse*:

> Die öffentliche Meinung ist also bei uns in Absicht auf die Natur der Revolution jetzt so weit im klaren, daß man es für Wahnsinn halten würde, ihr Einhalt tun oder Grenzpfähle stecken zu wollen. Eine Naturerscheinung, die zu selten ist, daß wir ihre eigentümlichen Gesetze kennen

---

[66] "The Revolution is a hurricane, who can stop it? A human being, driven into action by it, is able to do things, which those afterwards will not be able to comprehend for horror. But the point of perspective is too high for mortals. What is happening must happen. I hope, when the storm passes, that the survivors might recover and rejoice in the peace which will follow." Georg Forster to Therese Forster, Paris, 28 December 1793, Forster, 4:959. This letter was not published in the *Friedens-Präliminarien*. However letters were commonly passed around among circles of friends-especially when they concerned people of interest such as Forster. Cf. Leo Balet and E. Gerhard, *Die Verbürgerlichung der deutschen Kunst, Literatur und Musik im 18. Jahrhundert*, ed. G. Mattenklott (Frankfurt am Main: Ullstein, 1972), 182-87.

[67] Cf. quotation from Hoffmann's *Wiener Zeitschrift* (1793) in Saine, *Black Bread — White Bread*, 252f.

sollten, läßt sich nicht nach Vernunftregeln einschränken und bestimmen, sondern muß ihren freien Lauf behalten.[68]

Saine writes that Forster occasioned great disillusionment among his admirers because of his having become "a fanatic and intolerant proselytizer for the 'republic' in Mainz," and that he is singled out in many contemporary discussions of the Mainz Revolution as one of the "more distasteful revolutionaries."[69] However Saine takes little notice of the socio-political context in which these judgements were made. After the Prussians retook Mainz, the Jacobins were social and political pariahs. It was politically dangerous to condone or even try to understand them. Forster's name was anathema to those who had never supported the Revolution. But more importantly, repudiation of Forster belonged to the general recantation of those intellectuals who had supported the Revolution for as long as it appeared to be an exercise in enlightened reform. Forster had been outlawed (i.e. the "Reichsacht" had been declared against him), and Lichtenberg, for example, declined to write an obituary for his admired colleague, on the basis that he had a family to provide for.[70]

It is hardly likely that Goethe's objections to Forster's political activity in Mainz should have led to outright rejection of the man whom he admired as a scientist and thinker.[71] And it is by no means unthinkable that Goethe was moved by the tragic self-questioning of Forster's letters.[72] And even if Goethe did co-author the distichs attacking Forster, he also expressed admiration and sorrow in the letter he wrote to Sömmering shortly after Forster's death:

So hat der arme Forster denn doch auch seine Irrthümer mit dem Leben büßen müssen! wenn er schon einem gewaltsamen Tode entging! Ich habe ihn herzlich bedauert.[73]

---

[68] "And so public opinion here is agreed regarding the Revolution, that it would be madness to try to stop or to put limits to it. A natural occurrence, which is too rare for us to know its particular laws, does not let itself be reduced or defined according to principles of reason. It must be left to run its course." Forster, *Parisische Umrisse, Werke*, 3:731.

[69] Saine, *Black Bread — White Bread*, 388. Saine also refers to the Mainz Jacobins, including Forster, as the "Quislings of 1792" (247).

[70] In a letter to Sömmering (5 June 1795), Rödel, 88. On Schlegel's bravery in defending Forster in 1797, see Rödel, 97-98.

[71] Goethe's description of the evenings spent with Forster and others in Mainz in late summer 1792 expresses cosmopolitan and intellectual tolerance rather than partisan resentment. H.A. 10:189.

[72] Cf. Saine, *Black Bread — White Bread*, 388.

[73] "So poor Forster has had to pay for his mistakes with his life after all! At least he escaped a violent death! I feel terribly sorry for him," 17 February 1794, W.A. IV, 10, 142.

Saine ignores this letter, which along with the distich, "Elpenor," shows that the possibility of Forster being executed in Paris for his beliefs had occurred to Goethe, and hence can be used to support the thesis that Forster influenced the fiction of the first fiancé.[74]

Equally important to this question is Goethe's attitude to Adam Lux. Charlotte Corday's assassination of Marat in July 1793 was an act of martyrdom which aroused great controversy in Germany. It became a symbolic event, the turning-point for early supporters of the Revolution (such as Klopstock) to recant their radical beliefs. They saw in Marat the extremism of the post-1792 developments, and in Corday a heroic gesture aimed at reasserting the republican sentiments of the early phase of the Revolution. Others were more critical. Wieland could not approve of the murder of Marat on political grounds, and those who had been critical of the Revolution from the beginning saw Corday's act as a sign of further degeneration into political anarchy.[75] Rebmann and others at the time considered her a "Schwärmerin" ("enthusiast"). Lux's defense too was an act of "Schwärmerei," the result of sexual infatuation and desire for martyrdom. Lux had earlier intended to commit suicide in front of the National Convention by shooting his brains out — an act he saw as a form of protest at revolutionary developments for which he held Marat responsible.[76] While Lux himself may have perceived his act as a supreme sacrifice, it was certainly judged by many in Germany to be an act of foolish, youthful enthusiasm. Lux's behavior in defending Charlotte Corday cannot be equated with the idealism of the first fiancé in battling against guile and injustice. And it was hardly the type of political statement calculated to arouse the admiration of the author of *Werther*.

The tragedy of the first fiancé signifies the end of enlightenment as an ideology of progress. The first fiancé like Forster, having acted to bring history into line with enlightenment, dies in despair. In the aftermath of the Revolutionary Wars — in the plight of the refugees, the bitterness of the judge, and Dorothea's experiences — revolutionary democracy with its important third component, the enlightenment ideal of *fraternité* among free nations, is seen to have degenerated into national oppression. Here too a thematic relationship exists with the fate of Georg Forster. It was not revolutionary ideals per se which provoked the popular resentment of Forster and the Mainz Jacobins, but the willingness to sacrifice national feelings for these ideals. Forster's behavior was associated with betrayal

---

[74] "Muß ich dich hier schon treffen, Elpenor? Du bist mir gewaltig / Vorgelaufen! Und wie? Gar mit gebrochenem Genick?" ("Are you here already, Elpenor? You must have raced at break-neck Speed! And how? You really did break your neck?") W.A. I, 5, 255.

[75] Schulz, 145-49.

[76] Gassner, 136.

of his country until well into the nineteenth century.⁷⁷ Hermann implies this in his accusation of the first fiancé:

'Nicht dem Deutschen geziemt es, die fürchterliche Bewegung
Fortzuleiten und auch zu wanken hierhin und dorthin.'

(IX, 305-6)⁷⁸

Hermann himself, by contrast, becomes the spokesman of a new Germany, on the basis of a statement of strong national feeling and a nascent national identity. Where the first fiancé dies, the representative of the demise of German democratic enlightenment, Hermann is born as the representative of an unenlightened nationalism, which does not bode well for the future.

Saine notes that the spirit of the "idealistic third person ... Adam Lux, speaks for the transformation of Hermann, the German, into Hermann, the German citizen of the world."⁷⁹ However the memory of the first fiancé is Dorothea's. Hermann takes little notice of what she has said. The ending of the poem does not represent a reconciliation in Germany of the spirit of past and present, pre- and post-revolutionary eras, in the spontaneous transformation of Hermann the patriotic German into Hermann the post-revolutionary cosmopolitan. The mock-epic parody finds its resolution in the false harmony of the ending. The idealism of the first fiancé has come to a tragic end, and a provincial and inexperienced youth becomes the spokesman for an armed and aggressive future Germany. The end of an enlightenment ideal — the revolutionary transfiguration of cosmopolitanism into liberty, equality and fraternity — is followed by the beginning of modern nationalism.

The first fiancé, the most often quoted example in German literature of the German Jacobin, is a German revolutionary idealist who was willing to act as well as think, and whose reasons for supporting the Revolution are expressed in terms of radical democratic enlightenment. He is not an enthusiast or "Schwärmer." The common memory of Georg Forster, who embodied the link between enlightenment and revolutionary activity, belongs to this image. In the figure of Adam Lux this commitment to the culture and thought of the Enlightenment is missing.

---

⁷⁷ Even Karl Marx mentions it (presumably ironically) in a letter to Friedrich Engels, London, 16 April 1856, *Werke* 29:47. On this issue, see Rödel, 145; Gordon Craig, "Engagement and Neutrality in Germany: The Case of Georg Forster, 1754-1794," *Journal of Modern History* 41 (1969): 2, 5; Gerhard Voigt, "Forster, Lichtenberg und die Revolution," *Vom Faustus bis Valentin: Der Bürger in Geschichte und Literatur*, ed. Fritz Haug, *Das Argument*, Sonderband AS 3 (1969): 162, 171 (note 1a); Joachim Streisand, "Revolution und Evolution im Geschichtsbild der deutschen Klassik," *Goethe Jahrbuch*, n.s. 16 (1979): 135; Müller, 36; Heinrich Scheel, *Deutscher Jakobinismus und Deutsche Nation* (Berlin: Akademie, 1966), 7.

⁷⁸ "'Let not us Germans continue this terrible present upheaval, / Swaying uncertainly hither and thither.'"

⁷⁹ Saine, *Black Bread — White Bread*, 391.

The thesis of continuity between the first fiancé and Hermann obscures the ironic indicators of crisis, rupture, and false continuity in the text. Adam Lux in an enthusiastic frenzy attempted to vindicate Charlotte Corday and the Girondins against the radical Jacobins. Georg Forster, the cosmopolitan humanist, accepted the historical dialectic of the Revolution, but was mortified and disillusioned by its everyday brutality. For Lux, the political gesture demanded by the Revolution was the pathetic and utopian one of suicide.

Forster, in his personal disillusionment, did not opt for a martyr's death, or for idyllic false consciousness, or repudiation of the Revolution and transfiguration of petty absolutism. He accepted the complexity and difficulty of the political decisions that he had made. The figure of the first fiancé brings this theme into German literature in all its breadth and depth. His words alone in German high literature of the period could be quoted in support of revolutionary democratic ideals. Not least for this reason, have they been discredited through the blackening of Forster's name (i.e. as traitor), or, most subtly, by aligning them with the historical model of empty enthusiasm (Lux) rather than revolutionary enlightenment (Forster). After the death of the first fiancé, the future belongs to Hermann, the patriotic German who is willing to fight for God, law and the family (IX, 309), if not for political freedom.

Up until 1792 the Revolution could be seen as the culmination of the critical political philosophy of the French Enlightenment. The new aspect of modern nationalism, expressed in the *levée en masse* and formulated by Goethe in the 1820s as "a new epoch in world history," could hardly be comprehended in the early 1790s.[80] The alliance of enlightenment thought and revolution was broken after 1792. In its place and in response to the Revolution, a form of German nationalism began to develop, which soon found expression in works such as Schiller's "Das Lied von der Glocke" ("Song of the Bell") and "Deutsche Größe" ("German Greatness," 1801), and which reached a peak after the Battle of Jena (1806) in the works of Fichte and Kleist.[81]

*Hermann und Dorothea* is the earliest text in which the German response to the post-1792 situation is represented. Hermann's patriotism, a sign of the coming German national awakening appears juxtaposed against the obsolete cosmopolitan enlightenment of Georg Forster and the first fiancé. Many interpreters of *Hermann und Dorothea* from the nineteenth century until the present have seen the juxtaposition of the small-town patriot and the "German Jacobin" in terms of evolution versus revolution.[82] Hermann, the non-political *Bürger* in his provincial

---

[80] Cf. Borchmeyer, *Höfische Gesellschaft*, 296-97.

[81] "Das Lied von der Glocke" was published in 1800, although Schiller had worked on it since 1791. He uses images of cannibalism and bestiality common in the counter-revolutionary literature of the 1790s. See Joseph Hansen, *Quellen zur Geschichte des Rheinlandes im Zeitalter der französischen Revolution*, 4 vols. (Bonn: P. Hahnstein, 1931-38), 2:317-18; on "Deutsche Größe" see Meinecke, *Weltbürgertum und Nationalstaat*, 54-57.

[82] Most recently (1987) in Lützeler, 123-24.

German home town, is seen against the revolutionary *citoyen* in Paris, and "bürgerliche Privatautonomie" ("private, middle class autonomy") is pitted against revolutionary society.[83] However, as we have seen, Forster's initial sympathy for the revolutionary cause was typical for the *German* enlightened intellectual. The happenings west of the Rhine represented enlightened progress to him. Questions of national identity play no part in his socio-political vision, and he had little experience of practical politics.[84] His story, heightened into the motif of the first fiancé in the literary work, is the story of the tragic conflict between political ideals and praxis, and between individual freedom and national identity.

---

[83] Borchmeyer, *Höfische Gesellschaft*, 331; Schneider, "Idylle und bürgerliches Epos," 140.

[84] Günter Jäckel, "'Land zweier Lieder': Goethes und Forsters Begegnung mit Frankreich 1792/4," *Sinn und Form* 34 (1982): 892.

# Conclusion:
# Paradox in the Idyll

INTERPRETATIONS OF HERMANN, SUCH as those of Scherer and Hehn in the nineteenth century, emphasized his function as a "national" figure and spokesman for traditional German values. After the discrediting of the German nationalist tradition in the twentieth century, the themes of traditional values and national identity in the work have been avoided. Yet the early interpreters were right in identifying Hermann as an archetypical "German." Goethe's choice of the name "Hermann" clearly identifies his character in this way.[1] The name is derived from the Old High German *hariman* (= *Heerman*) meaning "warrior," and was used as the German form of the Latin *Arminius*.[2] The figure of Hermann/Arminius had become popular after Ulrich von Hutten's *Arminius* (1529) as a symbol of old German virtue, national grandeur and heroic-patriotic feelings, and this popularity continued in works such as Lohenstein's *Grossmüthiger Feldherr Arminius ...* (1689/90) and Klopstock's *Hermann* trilogy (1769-87).[3]

While earlier critics saw the portrayal of German identity in Hermann in terms of traditional values and the national priority of "Abwehr gegen die Fremden," they did not see the irony of Goethe's attitude to Hermann and the values he embodies.[4] Hermann's incipient nationalism is symptomatic of a collective response to the history of internal fragmentation and foreign intervention in Germany since the end of the Middle Ages. Hermann's fantasies of altruism and self-sacrifice, his feeling for the sensuous beauty of the landscape, and his aggression, channelled outward against an enemy of whom he knows nothing and can only imagine the worst, are understandable in the context of the revolutionary period.

To be against the concept of a German nation-state meant implicitly accepting a future of wars, partition and lack of socio-political and cultural identity. In view

---

[1] Helmerking, 91-94. Goethe's use of the name "Hermann" is discussed in the proceedings following Rolf Christian Zimmermann's "Die kritische Replik der deutschen Spätaufklärung und Klassik auf Arminius-Enthusiasmus und Germanen-Utopie der Epoche," in *Verantwortung und Utopie: Zur Literatur der Goethezeit*, ed. Wolfgang Wittkowski (Tübingen: Niemeyer, 1988), 131-33. See Appendix for the nineteenth-century reception of Hermann.

[2] Schmidt, *Erläuterungen*, 5.

[3] Elisabeth Frenzel, *Stoffe der Weltliteratur*, 2nd rev. ed. (Stuttgart: Kröner, 1963), 54.

[4] "defense against foreigners," Scherer, 572; and see Hehn, 90-91.

of this, Goethe's belief, expressed in 1772, that patriotism and national identity were of no importance to human existence was naive. In "Literarischer Sanskulottismus" (1795) he saw little likelihood for a united Germany in the near future, but he did not thereby reject the importance of a German identity:

> Denn die Bildung der höheren Klassen durch fremde Sitten und ausländische Literatur, so viel Vorteil sie uns auch gebracht hat, hinderte doch den Deutschen, als Deutschen sich früher zu entwickeln.[5]

However Goethe was suspicious of claims for a united Germany, and distanced himself from the chauvinist movements of the later Napoleonic period. Hermann's response to the French is not presented uncritically. The ideal of *Weltbürgertum* (cosmopolitanism) of a united free Europe, the dream of the first fiancé and Georg Forster, had already been recognized to be a fairy-tale of enlightenment, a story realizable only in the form of the political utopia of "Das Märchen." For Goethe in 1797, it was not possible to resolve the problematic relationships of national identity and European civilization through mimetic or realistic modes.

Hermann and the first fiancé are not portrayed as antithetical, positive and negative characters. They each represent polarized responses to the same historical situation. Goethe rejected the Revolution from the beginning, but his admiration of Georg Forster extended beyond the events of Mainz and Paris. The tragedy of the first fiancé illustrates the consequences of the failure of enlightened absolutism to allow participation in the political processes by the middle-class intelligentsia. The first fiancé transfigures his political despair into the hope for a new world to be created from the ruins of the old. Hermann draws on contrasting aspects of German language, culture and experience, and finds refuge in an image of idyllic traditionalism. No longer the impressionable and sensitive youth of the morning, he presents himself as the spokesman for a new Germany at the end of the work. His "provincial idyll" has become politicized — and has lost the essential quality of idyll, its innocence.

Hermann's outlook prefigures the nationalism of the following decades, and it was most popular in the second half of the nineteenth century. The nationalistic interpretations of Hehn (1851) and Scherer (1883) show how Hermann's patriotism could be turned into a political and cultural force in its own right during the nineteenth century. The poet and cultural critic, Heinrich Heine wrote in the early 1830s:

> Der Patriotismus des Franzosen besteht darin, daß sein Herz erwärmt wird, durch diese Wärme sich ausdehnt, sich erweitert, daß es nicht mehr bloß die nächsten Angehörigen, sondern ganz Frankreich, das ganze Land der Zivilisation, mit seiner Liebe umfaßt; der Patriotismus des Deutschen

---

[5] H.A. 12:242. "To be sure, the education of the higher classes through foreign customs and literature was quite beneficial, but it also prevented the Germans from developing sooner as Germans." Goethe, *Essays on Art and Literature*, 191.

hingegen besteht darin, daß sein Herz enger wird, daß es sich zusammenzieht wie Leder in der Kälte, daß er das Fremdländische haßt, daß er nicht mehr Weltbürger, nicht mehr Europäer, sondern nur ein enger Deutscher sein will.[6]

Neither the revolutionary idealism of the first fiancé nor the nascent nationalism of Hermann can stand on its own as a viable answer to the political crisis of 1792. Literature mediates reality through the thinking and creative subject. It does not reflect reality in any objective sense. Through irony and parody as "modes of ambivalence," it can both offer a critique of the existing situation and aim at aesthetic resolution, without at the same time being utopian or complacent. Friedrich Schlegel's ideas on romantic irony and paradox, rather than Schiller's *Briefe über die ästhetische Erziehung des Menschen* (*Letters on the Aesthetic Education of Mankind*) provide the theoretical basis for an understanding of *Hermann und Dorothea*. The contradictory images of the revolutionary intellectual and the patriotic *Bürger* are presented as a paradox, an irresolvable contradiction in reality, which can be resolved only through irony in the work of literature. The responses of Hermann and the first fiancé are diametrically opposed, yet closely related in that they arise from, and are paradigmatic for the German situation in the 1790s.

In his *Geschichte der Religion und Philosophie in Deutschland* (1835), Heine described a youthful German traditionalist for his French readership:

Einst, im Bierkeller zu Göttingen, äußerte ein junger Altdeutscher, daß man Rache an den Franzosen nehmen müsse für Konradin von Staufen, den sie zu Neapel geköpft. Ihr habt das gewiß längst vergessen. Wir aber vergessen nichts. Ihr seht, wenn wir mal Lust bekommen, mit Euch anzubinden, so wird es uns nicht an triftigen Gründen fehlen.[7]

The stereotyped German nationalist, which finds expression in Hermann's contemporaries in the following decades, is still only latent in him. Hermann is not

---

[6] Heinrich Heine, *Sämtliche Schriften*, 12 vols., ed. Klaus Briegleb (Frankfurt am Main: Ullstein, 1981), 5:379. "A Frenchman's patriotism means that his heart is warmed, and with this warmth it stretches and expands so that his love no longer embraces merely his closest relative, but all of France, the whole of the civilized world. A German's patriotism means that his heart contracts and shrinks like leather in the cold, and a German then hates everything foreign, no longer wants to become a citizen of the world, a European, but only a provincial German." Heinrich Heine, *The Romantic School and Other Essays*, ed. Jost Hermand and Robert Holub, vol. 33 of *The German Library* (New York: Continuum, 1985), 21.

[7] Heine, *Sämtliche Schriften*, 5:640-41. "Once in a beer parlor in Göttingen a young German chauvinist remarked that we ought to take revenge on the French for Konradin von Staufen whom they beheaded in Naples. You have probably forgotten that long since. But we forget nothing. So you see that if some day we take a notion to pick a quarrel with you, we won't lack for valid reasons." "History of Religion and Philosophy in Germany," Heine, *Romantic School and Other Essays*, 244.

yet a *Burschenschaftler*. But the beginnings of the developments which discredited German national strivings are evident. His final speech stands alone at the end of the work. The absence of contextual commentary or perspective is striking.

The representatives of humane, flexible and realistic attitudes are both women: Dorothea and the mother. Dorothea's understated experience contrasts with Hermann's bombastic innocence. Perhaps Goethe's hope for the future lies with her. Alongside Iphigenie she is the most positive female figure in his oeuvre. Where Iphigenie's cold enlightenment lacks humanity, Dorothea is the embodiment of feminine warmth. Yet even she, for all her integrity and strength of character, is only a single woman in a patriarchal society in a state of change.

Despite its appearance of closed classical form, the work is in fact open-ended and paradoxical. The irony and parody signal the discrepancies between Hermann's statement of German identity and the context in which he is represented, suggesting Goethe's belief that Germany cannot opt for provincial traditionalism as the way into the future. The idyllic innocence of the home town is gone. It had been damaged at the time of the fire, and it is lost irredeemably with the passing by of the refugees and the dawning realization of what has happened in neighboring France. The ideologies of absolutist and revolutionary enlightenment had become obsolete after the early 1790s, and literature could no longer pretend to operate within absolute, or closed systems, whether linguistic, formal, metrical or ideological. In *Hermann und Dorothea*, far from reverting to an epigonal literary form and provincial-idyllic lifestyles, Goethe contributes to the beginnings of modern post-revolutionary German literature.

# Appendix: "Das erste Volksgedicht ..." The Critical Reception of *Hermann und Dorothea*

HERMANN UND DOROTHEA RECEIVED popular and critical acclaim when it was published in October 1797. While Goethe's lyric works had maintained his standing as Germany's leading poet in the mid 1790s, he had the reputation of not having lived up to his former greatness (i.e. after *Werther*). His opposition to the Revolution alienated him from many of his peers, and with the publication of *Die Unterhaltungen deutscher Ausgewanderten*, he was seen as having reached an all-time low, with a string of second-rate and unfinished works behind him.[1] Charlotte von Stein wrote to Charlotte Schiller: "Dem Goethe scheint's gar nicht mehr ernst ums Schreiben zu sein."[2] And Böttiger reported in his diary Wieland's comment: "Goethe's Unglück sei, nichts vollenden zu können."[3]

The production in close succession of *Wilhelm Meisters Lehrjahre* (published in full in late 1796) and especially *Hermann und Dorothea* (1797) changed this situation. Vieweg published *Hermann und Dorothea* in mid October 1797 as the "Taschenbuch für das Jahr 1798" in a variety of formats, from an expensive bound edition with etchings to a cheap unadorned edition.[4] For Goethe it was a welcome success, as he wrote to Schiller:

> In *Hermann und Dorothea* habe ich, was das Material betrifft, den Deutschen einmal ihren Willen getan, und nun sind sie äußerst zufrieden.[5]

---

[1] Mayer, *Goethe*, 23, 30, 53.

[2] 19 February 1795, Bode 2:30.

[3] 28-30 December 1797, Bode, 2:122.

[4] Maria Gräfin Lanckoranskaja and Arthur Rümann, *Geschichte der deutschen Taschenbücher und Almanache aus der klassisch-romantischen Zeit* (Munich: Ernst Heimeran Verlag 1954), 49; Ludwig Geiger, "Die erste Ausgabe von Goethes *Hermann und Dorothea* und ihr Verleger," *Zeitschrift für Bücherfreunde* 1 (1897): 143-49; and Heinz Helmerking, "*Hermann und Dorothea*": *Entstehung, Ruhm und Wesen* (Zurich: Artemis, 1948), 27-30.

[5] Goethe to Schiller, 3 January 1798, W.A. IV, 13, 5.

He received the handsome sum of 1000 thalers from Vieweg for the publishing rights, but more importantly perhaps, he rescued his reputation as a popular writer. None of Goethe's acquaintances, who had seen parts of the work before its publication, were surprised at its popularity. Perceptive readers, however, noted some ambivalence about the text. Körner, for example, wrote to Schiller:

> Das ganze Produkt gehört unstreitig unter Goethe's Werke vom ersten Range. Aber fast ist es von zu hohem ästhetischen Werte, um nach Verdienst aufgenommen zu werden. Der größte Teil des Publikums klebt immer am Stoffe, und hier sind die herrschenden politischen Parteien einigermaßen interessiert. Daher erwarte ich die seltsamsten Urteile im Lob und Tadel.[6]

Goethe's stature as poet and statesman, and the realization that statements about the work could be interpreted politically in the post-revolutionary situation, led critics to be careful in their choice of words. Friedrich Schlegel wrote to his brother August Wilhelm:

> Was dem Goetheschen Gedicht noch sehr merkwürdig und sehr schön ist, ist die liberale Ansicht der Zeitbegebenheiten. Kein Franzose wäre deren so fähig, und das ist doch ein Trost gegen die politische Nullität.[7]

At the same time, Böttiger's comments to Göschen in December 1796 are indicative of the patriotic feelings which the work aroused: "Es muß das erste Volksgedicht werden, das eine neuere Nation aufzuweisen hat."[8] The speed with which *Hermann und Dorothea* was included in the canon of "classical" German literature after 1797 made it difficult to criticize. Yet Goethe himself in "Literarischer Sanskulottismus" (1795) had rejected both the possibility of writing "classical" works in the absence of a "nation," and the desirability of the political upheavals which could prepare the national basis for a classical literature in Germany.

*Ordnung, Sittlichkeit* and the Beginnings of a German Classical Canon (1798-1814)

August Wilhelm Schlegel reviewed the work for the *Allgemeine Literatur-Zeitung* and Wilhelm von Humboldt used it as the basis for his influential essay on aesthetics.[9] For Schlegel and Humboldt *Hermann und Dorothea* was the work

---

[6] Wilhelm Bode, ed., *Goethe in vertraulichen Briefen seiner Zeitgenossen*, 3 vols., rev. ed., ed. Regine Otto and Paul-Gerhard Wenzlaff (Berlin: Aufbau, 1979), 2:114.

[7] Bode, 2:111.

[8] Bode, 2:95.

[9] Wilhelm von Humboldt, "Über Göthes 'Hermann und Dorothea,'" *Werke*, 5 vols., ed. Andreas Flitner and Klaus Giel (Stuttgart: Cotta, 1961), 2:125-356. Humboldt had

which both created a German identity in literature, and revived classical models in order to transcend the divisions in German society after the French Revolution.

Kantian concepts of perception and genius, and Schiller's idea of "aesthetic education" formed the basis for Humboldt's classicist theory. Using the central concepts of "Ordnung," "Zusammenhang," and "Totalität," he aimed to describe a "durchaus übereinstimmende, durchaus organisirte Natur" (241), in which *Bildung* forms the link between the individual and the nation. The aesthetic characteristics of great German art are identified as "Seele," "Innigkeit," "Wärme," and "Harmonie," against the "Leidenschaft," "Heftigkeit" and "Feuer" of other national literatures (240). These qualities are exemplified in *Hermann und Dorothea* as the "reinen und ursprünglichen Naturformen" (135). The realms of art and reality stand in opposition to each other (139), and the role of the artist is to transform elements of reality into the higher sphere of art, by subjecting the poetic imagination to productive creative laws (138, 310ff.): "Sobald man das Wesen der Kunst in den Gesetzen der Phantasie, durch die sie allein wirksam ist, aufsucht, gelangt man nothwendig auf den Begriff des Idealischen." (143)

Humboldt wrote his analysis in Paris in 1798, when the German intellectual trend away from politics toward literature and philosophy was well under way. Indeed his metaphor for the realm of art is reminiscent of Schiller's programmatic preface to *Die Horen*:

> Wohin der Mensch nur immer seine Blicke richten mag, da sucht er den Begriff eines gegenseitigen Zusammenhanges, einer innern Organisation geltend zu machen. Ueberall den Zufall zu verbannen ... ist das Streben der Vernunft. Dadurch allein schon bewährt er, daß er sich mit Recht einer höhern Abkunft rühmt, als die übrigen Geschöpfe, daß er in ein besseres Land, als das der Wirklichkeit, daß er in das Land der Ideen gehört. (139-40)

The ideological component of his metaphor of the alternative fatherland, the "Land der Ideen," is clear in the context of post-revolutionary Germany. From this metaphor he develops an idea of national ideals and identity as the product of art and culture, or *Bildung* (155-56).

Humboldt sees *Hermann und Dorothea* as the characteristic German national work, in which the abstracted elements of reality are represented with "Wahrheit," "Innigkeit," "Einfachheit" and "Stärke der Wirkung" (240-42). Goethe brings these categories to the theme of German relations in the Rhineland during the Revolution, thereby creating a characteristic, "German" work. The work of literature becomes paradigmatic for the (ideal) nation. Humboldt's ideal nation

---

originally planned to base his essay on Voss's *Luise*, cf. Georg Gottfried Gervinus, *Geschichte der deutschen Dichtung*, 4th ed., 5 vols. (Leipzig: Wilhelm Engelmann, 1853), 5:430; Karl Rosenkranz, *Göthe und seine Werke* (Königsberg: Bornträger, 1856), 256; Paul R. Sweet, *Wilhelm von Humboldt: A Biography*, 2 vols. (Columbus: Ohio State University Press, 1978-80), 1:207.

however is a far cry from the type of German identity which finds expression in the figure of Hermann. Later interpreters would see the "Germanness" of the work more literally in Hermann's vision of national awakening.

Humboldt's criticism of Dorothea's self-defense is indicative of the difference between the ironic and multivalent work of literature and the idealistic philosophical system, which obviates chance ("Zufall") from the sphere of art. He objects to the break in tone caused by the narration of the violent episode, to the disruption of aesthetic balance, and to the introduction of an aspect of necessity ("Noth") into the ideal illusion:

> Dorothea kann einen Mord, selbst den eines übermuthigen Feindes, nie im mindesten aus freiem Entschluß, immer nur durch die äußerste Noth getrieben, begehen, und dieß springt zu klar und auffallend in die Augen. Handlungen aber, die nur die Noth bewirkt, in denen mehr der Drang der Umstände, als die Energie des Charakters das thätige Motiv ist, sind sehr wenig zu einer poetischen Behandlung tauglich. (204)

Dorothea's first fiancé is seen as the "unglücklicher Beschützer der Freiheit" who confuses the realm of the ideal with that of the real in his parting words to Dorothea (IX, 262ff.):

> Welche natürliche und rührende Betrachtung! die aber freilich nur dem geläufig seyn kann, der mehr in Ideen, als in der Wirklichkeit lebt, ... Wer wird läugnen, daß dieß eine schöne und erhabene Gesinnung ist? aber wer auch erkennt nicht, daß eben diese jene fürchterliche Bewegung theils mit hervorgebracht, theils unterhalten und fortgeleitet hat? (226)

Against this, Hermann makes a natural choice for stability:

> ... wie rein läßt er alles daran fahren, was seiner kraftvollen Natur nicht gemäß ist, und hält sich allein an das Eine fest, wodurch der Mensch sich dicht an die Wirklichkeit anschliessen, seine Forderungen mit den Fügungen des Schicksals vereinigen kann! (226)

Hermann thus combines nature with order, against the fiancé, who is alienated from the natural German order by adopting the inappropriate ideals of the French Revolution.

Goethe's irritation at Humboldt's critical views can be deduced from his polite but detached praise of the work, as well as his later comment to Eckermann.[10] In his essay Humboldt stressed the ideality and autonomy of art just at the time when Goethe was in the process of formulating a new, modern paradigm of

---

[10] "Ja, mein Guter, man hat von seinen Freunden zu leiden gehabt!" Johann Peter Eckermann, *Gespräche mit Goethe in den letzten Jahren seines Lebens*, 3 vols. in one (Stuttgart: Cotta, n.d.), 2:55.

literature as ironic, multivalent and open-ended. In *Hermann und Dorothea* (as in *Wilhelm Meisters Lehrjahre* and *Faust*) Goethe refused to acquiesce to demands for this type of classicist and systematic *Ordnung* in art. He had made this clear in "Literarischer Sanskulottismus."

August Wilhelm Schlegel also devoted a long essay to *Hermann und Dorothea* in 1798. Like Humboldt, he hoped to demonstrate that it could be considered a classical work comparable to the classics of other nations, by drawing attention to its Homeric and national qualities.[11] Epic narratives are judged according to a scale ranging from narratives with epic qualities to the "Epos" proper, and *Hermann und Dorothea* meets many of the criteria:

> Ein Dichter, dem es nicht darum zu tun ist, ein Studium nach der Antike zu verfertigen, sondern mit ursprünglicher Kraft, national und volksmäßig, zu wirken, wie es einem epischen Sänger geziemt, wird seinen Stoff nicht im klassischen Altertume suchen, noch weniger aus der Luft greifen dürfen. Damit die lebendige Wahrheit nicht vermißt werde, muß seine Dichtung festen Boden der Wirklichkeit unter sich haben ..." (130)[12]

But he concludes that the work is not epic proper since it does not go beyond the "stillen Kreis des häuslichen Lebens" and deals with love and trust rather than epic passions (134), although the background of the Revolution lifts it from the level of the mundane, and links it with wider themes of human history (136). Humboldt's term "bürgerliche Epopee" (300) fits Schlegel's generic description of both *Luise* and *Hermann und Dorothea* as belonging to "einer anmutigen gemischten Gattung" (134).

Schlegel does not discuss the characters in detail, and mentions the first fiancé only once, as "den ersten Geliebten, dessen herrliches Dasein ein hoher Gedanke der Aufopferung verzehrt hat" (138). Like Humboldt however, he rates "Sittlichkeit" and "Selbstbeherrschen" above "Leidenschaft" — thereby implicitly rating Hermann above the first fiancé, and German *Gemeinschaft* above French *Gesellschaft* (147):

> *Hermann und Dorothea* ist ein vollendetes Kunstwerk im großen Stil und zugleich faßlich, herzlich, vaterländisch, volksmäßig; ein Buch voll goldner Lehren der Weisheit und Tugend. (147)

Reviews of *Hermann und Dorothea* in 1797 and 1798 emphasized its classicism alongside the Homeric epics and its *Deutschheit* in terms of genre, character and

---

[11] August Wilhelm Schlegel, "Goethes *Hermann und Dorothea*," in *Über Literatur, Kunst und Geist des Zeitalters: Eine Auswahl aus den kritischen Schriften*, ed. F. Finke (Stuttgart: Reclam, 1979), 114-47.

[12] Humboldt also argues this: 248, 278f., 300f.

milieu.¹³ The reviewer of Bitaubé's French translation in the *Neue allgemeine Deutsche Bibliothek* (1803), for example, felt that the "darin überall herrschenden Deutschheit" made translation virtually impossible (Braun, 3:69).

### National Identity and Political Liberty (1814-1848)

When *Hermann und Dorothea* was republished by Cotta in 1814, it again drew enthusiastic responses, although no longer as the paradigm of German classicism (Humboldt) or idyllic epic of the German *Bürgertum* (Schlegel). Karl Ludwig von Woltmann reviewed it in the influential *Jenaische Allgemeine Literatur-Zeitung* as a heroic national epic.¹⁴ The veiled references to German identity in Humboldt and Schlegel have become explicitly political. Woltmann emphasizes themes of national identity (e.g. the Rhine), and urges revenge on the French:

> Seine [i.e. Hermann's] Worte am Ende des Gedichts sind fast sprichwörtlich in Deutschland geworden, und Tausende jener Heldenjünglinge, die gegen den Feind Germaniens erlagen und kämpfen, tragen sie glühend in ihrer Brust. (Fambach, 201)

Hermann's words are prized as a "Katechismus für den deutschen Mann" (Fambach, 201) and Dorothea is seen as a prototype "Thusnelda" for her "Frauenmuth." *Hermann und Dorothea*, that is, provides a cultural pedigree to the emerging German nationalism of the period of the Wars of Liberation. Goethe did not approve of this type of nationalism, and his response to Woltmann's review was cool: "Man hat *Hermann und Dorothea* dem Zeitgeist auch als ein Opfer darbringen wollen" (Fambach, 202). The ideal nationalism, the "Sittlichkeit" and "Bürgerlichkeit," on which earlier reviewers focused, had merged imperceptibly into *Deutschheit* over the years from 1798 to 1814.

This attention to the national aspects of the work continued, and became embedded in the discussion of literary issues such as form, genre, and style. In his *Vorlesungen über die Ästhetik* (1820) Georg Wilhelm Friedrich Hegel drew on Humboldt's and Schlegel's analyses in his categorization of both *Luise* and *Hermann und Dorothea* as belonging to the particularly German sub-genre of the romantic epic.¹⁵ Hegel compared Goethe's "Rheinwein" and "Römer" to Voss's use of coffee in *Luise*, as an example of Goethe's greater "Deutschheit" (13:339-41).

The liberal literary historian, Georg Gottfried Gervinus, influenced by

---

¹³ Julius W. Braun, *Goethe im Urtheile seiner Zeitgenossen*, 3 vols. (1883; repr. Hildesheim: Olms, 1969), 2:266, 278, 281, 283.

¹⁴ Jena and Leipzig, No. 45, March 1814; Oscar Fambach, *Goethe und seine Kritiker* (Düsseldorf: L. Ehlermann, 1955), 199-202.

¹⁵ Georg Wilhelm Friedrich Hegel, *Vorlesungen über die Ästhetik*, Werke, ed. Eva Moldenhauer and Karl Markus Michel, 20 vols. (Frankfurt am Main: Suhrkamp, 1970), 13:330-41; 15:414-45.

Humboldt, discussed *Hermann und Dorothea* in his *Geschichte der deutschen Dichtung* (1842) in the light of Goethe's and Schiller's discussions of epic form, and in terms of literary *Formgeschichte*.[16] He does not mention the political aspects of the work — neither Hermann's militant stance, nor the first fiancé, nor the reception as a national political manifesto. This is surprising in view of his involvement in libertarian issues and interest in Forster. (Together with Forster's daughter, Therese, he had edited Forster's works in 1828.) The reasons for this may lie in the political relations in Germany at the time when Gervinus was writing the last volume of his work, or in his own disappointment with German liberalism, which came to a head after 1848. Karl Rosenkranz, writing in the early 1850s, saw in *Hermann und Dorothea* Goethe's first acceptance of the positive aspects of the Revolution (268), and tackled political and thematic issues which Gervinus ignored.[17] The philistinism of the town inhabitants is put into perspective by the refugees' plight:

> Durch diesen Contrast werden wir aus der fleischlichen Sicherheit, in welche sonst der Pfahlbürger leicht zu versinken droht, in die Weite und Schwere des allgemeinen Weltgeschickes hinausgewiesen. (273)

Interestingly, the characteristics of the home town are seen to originate from the French Revolution:

> Wir finden nämlich alle Personen von den Ideen der Französischen Revolution bewegt. Die verschiedensten Meinungen sprechen sich darüber aus, alle jedoch mit der Anerkennung des Strebens nach Freiheit. ... In Hermann und Dorothea sehen wir eine solche humane Gleichheit, einen so freien Verkehr der Stände. ... alle begegnen sich als einander wesentlich gleiche ... (276-77)

Rosenkranz, like Humboldt and Schlegel, sees the *Deutschheit* of the work in its "Innerlichkeit" (278), but at the same time he admires Hermann's patriotism in contrast to the abstract idealism of Dorothea's first fiancé:

> Von der lieblichen Enge des häuslichen Glücks wirft er sich in die Weltweite, aber nicht in eine abstract kosmopolitische, sondern in eine patriotische und, seinem kräftigen Jünglingsalter entsprechend, in eine kriegerische (279).

Rosenkranz's contradictory views on this subject, like Gervinus's silence, perhaps reflects the dilemma of the liberal intellectual of the *Vormärz* period on issues of political freedom and national unity. Rosenkranz raises the question of literary

---

[16] Gervinus, *Geschichte der deutschen Dichtung*, 5:429-34.

[17] Karl Rosenkranz, *Göthe und seine Werke*, 268-88.

"nationality" by referring to Hegel's criticism of the coffee theme in *Luise* (cf. also Hehn, 138). The inclusion of Rhine wine instead of coffee is an example of Goethe's increased national awareness:

> Hegel ... hat schon darauf aufmerksam gemacht, wie in diesem Betracht Göthe's Gedicht eine viel stärkere deutsche Localfarbe habe, als Vossen's Luise. In dieser z. B. werde viel Kaffee getrunken. Gut. Der Kaffee aber sammt dem Zucker gelangen zu uns weit her, ... Sie sind nichts eigenthümlich Deutsches. ... Ganz anders in unserem Epos ... (280)

### The *Bildung* of the Nation (1848-1918)

After his involvement in the events of 1848, when he was in exile in Tula, Viktor Hehn wrote a monograph on *Hermann und Dorothea* (1851), which was not published until after his death in 1893.[18] For Hehn, Goethe's classicism indicates a departure from the modern spirit of Shakespeare in favor of the classical spirit of Homer (28). This is seen as the choice of "innere Freiheit" as the national characteristic, in opposition to the superficial political freedom of the French, or the economic progress and colonial exploitation of the English (29ff.). Politics is foreign to the German *Bürger* in his "stillen Privatexistenz" (43), and the French Revolution was "etwas Fremdes, von dem deutschen Gefühl nicht Geteiltes" (45). The estate ("Stand") representing the extension of the family as the basic social unit (*Gemeinschaft*), is the appropriate socio-political form for Germany, corresponding to the *Gesellschaft* of other nations. *Hermann und Dorothea* is the epic of the German *Bürger*, "das Epos von der Familie und dem Privatbesitz, dieser Substanz des deutschen Geistes" (45). It is seen as explicitly "anti-politisch" (46), the artistic expression of the Germans' decision to follow their own national path (46). Hermann represents "die deutsche Natur, die deutsche nationale Eigenheit in einem meisterhaften Individualbilde" (88). Middle-class *Innerlichkeit*, and Schlegel's and Humboldt's concepts of *Sittlichkeit*, are given political significance as national identity-markers:

> Am Schlusse des Gedichts spricht er eine standhafte patriotische Gesinnung aus, ... es ist der Mut des Bürgerwehrmannes, des Nationalgardisten, der für den Bestand des Besitzes auch sterben kann und, wenn die Gefahr vorüber ist, rasch zu seiner Sphäre des Privaterwerbes zurückkehrt. ... So haben wir in Hermanns Liebe nur den Zug der Sittlichkeit, die Gestalt gewinnen will, das stille Anknüpfen eines bürgerlichen Ehebundes, ... (90-91)

Hermann and the home town milieu are characterized politically by the rejection of the Revolution and everything associated with it: the modern nation-state, the

---

[18] Viktor Hehn, *Ueber Goethes "Hermann und Dorothea,"* ed. Albert Leitzmann and Theodor Schiemann (Stuttgart: Cotta, 1893).

city, and the nascent economic system, politics and class configuration of industrial capitalism. Against these are posited traditional family values, (Protestant) *Deutschtum* and *Bürgerlichkeit*:

> Goethe (griff) nach derjenigen Schicht der Gesellschaft, die der Einfalt der Natur in Worten und Werken noch nahe stand, ... Es ist eine Bürgerfamilie, die zugleich das schöne uralte heilige patriarchalische Geschäft des Ackerbaues treibt. (104)

The view of the work as archetypically "German" is quite strong in the *Vormärz* period. Rosenkranz (280), Gervinus (5: 430), Julian Schmidt and Hermann Hettner admire Hermann as a patriot.[19] However after the failure of German liberalism in 1848, a shrill tone is audible, reminiscent of the 1814 review by Woltmann. Jingoistic nationalism and hatred of the French is pronounced in the interpretations of Hehn and Scherer.[20] Hehn, for example, suggests that the ideal humanity of *Hermann und Dorothea* is the result of the racial and cultural purity of the home town (42).[21] In his influential literary history of 1883, Wilhelm Scherer saw the work as politically tendentious and Goethe himself as loyal to dynastic petty absolutism:

> Den religiösen Gegensatz verwandelt er in einen politischen; und den Zeitereignissen gegenüber stellt er sich hier auf einen vorzugsweise nationalen Standpunkt. Die Französische Revolution war ihm wie seinem Herzog zuwider. (569)

The national theme is linked to the biblical paradigm of the national mission of the Jews, and Hermann represents "die ungebrochene Volkskraft der Deutschen: das nationale Pathos, der Instinkt der Abwehr gegen die Fremden beseelt ihn" (572). During the *Gründerjahre* many annotated school editions were produced with the aim of consolidating the national consciousness.[22] In Gude's *Erläuterungen deutscher Dichtung ... Ein Hülfsbuch beim Unterricht in der Literatur* (1866), the French are described as "Kriegslustig," and the wars against France are "heiligen

---

[19] Julian Schmidt, *Geschichte der deutschen Literatur seit Lessing's Tod*, 4th rev. enl. ed., 5 vols. (Leipzig: Friedrich Ludwig Herbig, 1858), 1:251; Hermann Hettner, *Geschichte der deutschen Literatur im 18. Jahrhundert*, 2 vols. (1856-70; Berlin: Aufbau, 1979), 2:487.

[20] Wilhelm Scherer, *Geschichte der deutschen Literatur*, 5th ed. (Berlin: Weidmannsche Buchhandlung, 1889), 568-76.

[21] Hehn's essay is partially reprinted — with the most extreme sections deleted — in Jost Schillemeit's *Interpretationen 4: Deutsche Erzählungen von Wieland bis Kafka* (Frankfurt am Main: Fischer, 1966), 23-53. This collection of critical essays was designed for use by German secondary school students, and had sold one hundred thousand copies by 1974.

[22] See Paul Michael Lützeler, "Johann Wolfgang Goethe: *Hermann und Dorothea*," *Geschichte in der Literatur: Studien zu Werken von Lessing bis Hebbel* (Munich: Piper, 1987), 88-89.

Schlachten" (64, 109).[23] Heinrich Düntzer's influential *Erläuterungen* too was reprinted many times after its publication in 1855. Where in earlier reviews the first fiancé was at least recognized as an idealist, in this period he is seen most negatively in contrast to Hermann, the heroic youth and spokesman for traditional German values. The revolutionary idealism of the fiancé is condemned as "Schwärmerei" and "Enthusiasmus" (Scherer, 573), and "die phantastische Ueberspannung einer poetischen Jugendleidenschaft" (Hehn, 91). It is seen at best as a mistaken analysis of the popular support for revolution in Germany, and at worst as "Vaterlandsverrat."[24] Even the socialist, Franz Mehring, in 1899 praised the work for its Homeric simplicity and national character:

> Mitten hinein in die kleinbürgerlichen Kreise, die nun doch einmal seit Jahrhunderten den Schwerpunkt des deutschen Lebens bildeten, schritt der Dichter, und was er aus ihnen schöpfte, war die schlichte, die unversiegliche Kraft, die in aller Not und allem Wirrsal den deutschen Namen für eine große Zukunft gerettet hatte.[25]

The tensions between German nationalism and socialist ideology had not yet reached the point where the work had to be rejected. These tensions surfaced later, in the 1920s and 30s, when the continued appropriation of the work by nationalistic literary historians led to rejection by left-wing interpreters.

### Europe and the *Volk* (The Nazi Period)

Hermann August Korff, writing at the end of the Weimar Republic and influenced strongly by Dilthey and Meinecke, was preoccupied with identifying the bases of social order and harmony in German culture and tradition, as a model for the present.[26] Drawing on Humboldt's and Schlegel's ideas of *Sittlichkeit* and family-values in *Geist der Goethezeit* (vol. 2, 1930) he considered *Hermann und Dorothea* to be the ideal of German *Bürgerlichkeit*:

> Es genügt, daran zu erinnern, daß der Grund dieser Ordnung die Idee der Familie und im Menschen selbst der Familiensinn ist, aus dem die

---

[23] C. Gude, *Erläuterungen deutscher Dichtungen nebst Themen zu schriftlichen Aufsätzen ...* (Leipzig: Friedrich Brandstetter, 1866), 60-122.

[24] Albert Bielschowsky sees him as a victim of his idealism and of German political relations, *Goethe: Sein Leben und seine Werke*, 32nd ed., 2 vols. (1895; Munich: Beck, 1917), 2:215.

[25] Franz Mehring, *Aufsätze zur deutschen Literatur von Klopstock bis Weerth*, vol. 10 of *Gesammelte Schriften*, 3rd ed. (Berlin: Dietz, 1977), 60.

[26] Hermann August Korff, *Geist der Goethezeit: Versuch einer ideellen Entwicklung der klassisch-romantischen Literaturgeschichte*, repr. 7th and 8th eds. (= 10th ed.), 5 vols. (Berlin: Koehler & Amelang, 1979), 2:362-74.

einzelnen Lebensformen und Normen entspringen. Ihr innerstes Zentrum: die Ehe, daraus hervorgehend der Kreis der Kinder, das Leben gegründet auf Erhaltung und Vermehrung des Familienbesitzes sowie auf die Verbindung vieler Familien zum größeren Ganzen einer kleinen ländlich-städtischen Gemeinde, die ihrerseits usw. — Das Entscheidende dabei ist, daß der Mensch hier wesentlich als Familienglied erscheint und sich selbst als solches empfindet. (2:344)

Korff obliquely refers to the first fiancé and the problematic of the German revolutionary, but overtly suppresses politics from his discussion of German classical literature in the context of the crisis of Weimar Germany. He thereby continues the avoidance of libertarian, democratic and revolutionary themes, which had begun with Humboldt:

Zwar fehlt es auch in *Hermann und Dorothea* nicht an Stellen, in denen die neuen Ideen zum wenigsten in ihrer Verführungskraft geschildert werden, aber es kann das die Grundüberzeugung Goethes nicht erschüttern, daß jede Revolution in erster Linie Auflösung, Zerstörung, Bedrohung der Ordnung und auch des Ordnungsgeistes bedeutet. ... Denn auch die besten Ideen vorausgesetzt, hat noch jede Revolution den Beweis geliefert, daß die Ideen sehr bald die Herrschaft über die von ihnen entfesselten Leidenschaften verlieren und daß nicht neue Ordnung, sondern Anarchie das erste sichere Resultat gewaltsamen Umsturzes ist. (2:350)

Korff's preoccupation with the twin symbols of "Blut" and "Ordnung" (2:346) at a time when these concepts were being used in the ideology of Nazism, puts his analysis in a questionable light, although he himself was neither a Nazi or a Nazi sympathizer. In the Nazified literary histories of Josef Nadler and Adolf Bartels the work was praised as the beginning of an ideology of the rebuilding of the German Reich:

Den Umwälzungen der Zeit war etwas Geistiges und Dauerndes entgegengesetzt. Da fehlten alle großen Worte. Da war kein Schweifen ins Ferne ... Da wurde einfach groß verkündet: baut das neue Reich von dort auf, wo alle Staaten gebaut wurden, vom Herd des Hauses, und packt das Nahe und nüchtern Tatsächliche unverzagt an.[27]

Nadler here also introduces an anti-intellectual note which is new to the reception of the work. Adolf Bartels prefaces his quotation of Hermann's final speech with:

---

[27] Josef Nadler, *Literaturgeschichte des deutschen Volkes: Dichtung und Schrifttum der deutschen Stämme und Landschaften*, 4th fully rev. ed., 4 vols. (Berlin: Propyläen, 1939), 2:301.

"Wir wollen aus ihr doch die Stelle anführen, die Goethes, den man in neuester Zeit zum Pazifisten hat machen wollen, gesunden vaterländischen Sinn zeigt."[28]

In 1935 Robert Petsch published a proto-fascist interpretation, in which the term "heldische Idylle" (131) is used as a generic description.[29] Petsch approvingly quotes the aggressively anti-French review by Woltmann (1814), and uses *völkisch* terminology (201) to describe the German tradition. Hermann is seen as a modern Parzifal (202), and Goethe as the epic bard of a resurgent national Germany:

> Der Dichter beabsichtigt auch nichts weniger, als seinen Deutschen aus der kleinen Stadt in der Nähe der Grenze irgendwelchen kriegerisch-heldischen Anstrich zu geben und ihnen den Stempel des Ausnahmemenschentums aufzudrücken. (130)

Idealistic and Nazi-oriented studies such as those of Korff and Petsch respectively were accepted within Germany during the late 1920s and 30s. The Hungarian Marxist Georg Lukács mentioned the work only briefly in his discussion of Goethe's and Schiller's correspondence in *Goethe und seine Zeit*, but made clear his view of it in non-classicist terms as a reflection of the revolutionary period:

> *Hermann und Dorothea* [ist] dem Wesen nach viel weniger klassizistisch, als Goethe und Schiller in dieser ihrer Formbegeisterung vermeinten. ... Er [Goethe] war viel zu sehr modern-realistischer Künstler, um den gegenwärtigen Lebensstoff jemals wirklich vergessen oder beiseite schieben zu können. *Hermann und Dorothea* verdankt seine Existenz und seine Form ebenso der Französischen Revolution wie das bewußt in klassizistischer Richtung gestaltete Drama *Die natürliche Tochter*.[30]

Thomas Mann at the same time, increasingly isolated by National Socialism, used his essay, "Goethes Laufbahn als Schriftsteller" (1934) to distinguish the honest, critical and distanced "national" author from the "grölenden Selbst- und Volksbestätigung der Hurrapatrioten" (341).[31] In this essay he devotes over a page to the discussion of *Hermann und Dorothea* in terms which reflect on contemporary Germany:

---

[28] Adolf Bartels, *Goethe der Deutsche* (Frankfurt am Main: Diesterweg, 1932), 93.

[29] Robert Petsch, "'Hermann und Dorothea': Ein Epos vom deutschen Bürgertum," *Deutsche Grenzlande* 14 (1935): 128-34; cont. *Deutsche Monatsblätter für Volk und Heimat* 14 (1935): 200-7.

[30] Georg Lukács, *Deutsche Literatur in zwei Jahrhunderten*, vol. 7 of *Gesammelte Werke* (Neuwied: Luchterhand, 1964), 110-11.

[31] Thomas Mann, "Goethes Laufbahn als Schriftsteller," *Werke*, 13 vols. (Frankfurt am Main: Fischer, 1974), 9:333-62; and "Goethe als Repräsentant des bürgerlichen Zeitalters," 9:297-332.

> ... seine [i.e. Goethes] bewußte Tendenz, sein volkserzieherischer Wille richtet sich gegen das Nichts-als-Volkhafte, ... und [er] betrachtet das Ethnisch-Barbarische als einen Exotismus, der Neugier errege, aber im tiefsten nicht zu befriedigen vermöge. (352)

*Hermann und Dorothea* does not glorify *Deutschtum*, but rather expresses the unity of German and European humanism: "das Deutsche und das Mediterran-Klassische, das Volkhafte und das Europäische." In Mann's analysis, the provincial, potentially philistine *Bürger* of the home town turn out to be capable of accepting the "foreigner," Dorothea. The German home town milieu thereby gives evidence of its roots in the European humanistic tradition ("Goethes Laufbahn," 352; "Goethe als Repräsentant," 301). Mann's interpretation has been extremely influential for later critics such as Seidlin, Lützeler and Eibl (discussed below).

During the Second World War period one American-German analysis of *Hermann und Dorothea* stands out in importance. Melitta Gerhard's "Chaos und Kosmos in Goethes *Hermann und Dorothea*" was delivered as a lecture to the Modern Language Association in 1941.[32] Like Thomas Mann, Gerhard tried to "rescue" Goethe's work from the association with Nazism. She does so however by lifting the work out of the historical-political context: "ist es ein anderer, überzeitlicher Gehalt, den Goethe im Bilde dieser scheinbaren Bürgerwelt verkörpert hat?" (53) Gerhard concludes:

> ... die Darstellung der einfach ländlichen Gebräuche in *Hermann und Dorothea* [ist] nicht Selbstzweck wie in der *Luise*, sondern Symbol und Beispiel eines von innerem Gesetz geleiteten Lebens angesichts einer gesetzlos gewordenen Welt. (60)

The tradition of *Innerlichkeit* and renunciation of politics (the problems of which are thematized in the figure of the first fiancé) was thereby transplanted into American post-war criticism, out of the sense of shame that Goethe could be associated with the culture which produced Nazism.

## In the Shadow of Nazism (1949-1968)

Interpretation of *Hermann und Dorothea* since the 1850s and especially during the Nazi period had glorified the representation of German national characteristics by Germany's greatest poet. Nazism and the discrediting of German nationalism after 1933/1945 led to the exclusion of the poem from the canon of Goethe's greatest works after the war.

---

[32] Melitta Gerhard, "Chaos und Kosmos in Goethes *Hermann und Dorothea*," *Leben im Gesetz* (Bern: Francke, 1966), 52-63.

Heinz Helmerking's *Hermann und Dorothea: Entstehung, Ruhm und Wesen*, published in Zurich in 1948 focuses on the way Goethe reforms Göcking's historical subject to create a work "mit urewigem Gehalte in ... dauernd klassischen Form gestaltet."[33] Helmerking is clearly in a difficult position when trying to discuss Hermann's *Deutschtum* at this point in history, and it is typical of the attempts to "rescue" the work after the war, that its "classicism" is stressed but not defined. He does not discuss the nationalist appropriation of the work, but he does point out that the Hermann legend signified for the German *Bürger* of the eighteenth century "dasselbe, was für die damaligen Schweizer der eben erstandene Wilhelm Tell war" (91-92). The disparities in characterization between the Teutonic chieftain and Goethe's Hermann, however, are ignored. In 1949 Karl Viëtor responded to what he saw as the misuse of "classicism" as a critical term in such interpretations by completely rejecting *Hermann und Dorothea*.[34] Viëtor considered it a faded attempt to reinvigorate classical Homeric forms in a period for which they were no longer appropriate (155). Emil Staiger's long analysis in his three-volume study of Goethe (1956) is, if anything, the opposite of Viëtor's.[35] Combining biographical criticism with English and American practical criticism techniques, he reduces the work to a bland summary which avoids all problematic or controversial areas.

An early objective historical analysis after the war came from a French source: Robert Leroux's "La Révolution française dans *Hermann et Dorothée*."[36] Leroux identifies Goethe's political preferences in Hermann's final speech, but stresses throughout Goethe's impartiality in the presentation of opposing attitudes to the Revolution (175). Taking a less biographically and historically determined approach to the work, Oskar Seidlin, drawing on Thomas Mann, identifies the central theme as the confrontation with, and acceptance of foreignness by the inhabitants of the home town.[37] Seidlin rejects the view that the work uncritically glorifies the German *Bürgertum* (108), seeing this rather in Voss's *Luise* (108). The "fordernde und messende Selbstbegegnung" (108) which Seidlin sees in the work introduces questions of individual and collective identity (110-11) which are resolved artistically (115ff.). The theme of the acceptance of the "foreigner," Dorothea, is reflected in the literary form, in the artist's coming to terms with the "foreign" classical tradition. This interpretation provides an interesting counter-argument to the nineteenth-century interpretation (derived from Humboldt and

---

[33] Helmerking, 108.

[34] Karl Viëtor, *Goethe: Dichtung, Wissenschaft, Weltbild* (Bern: Francke, 1949), 151-58.

[35] Emil Staiger, *Goethe*, 3 vols. (Zurich: Atlantis, 1962), 2:220-66.

[36] Robert Leroux, "La Révolution française dans *Hermann et Dorothée*," *Etudes Germaniques* 4 (1949): 174-86.

[37] Oskar Seidlin, "Über Goethes *Hermann und Dorothea*: Ein Vortrag," in *Lebendige Form: Interpretationen zur deutschen Literatur, Festschrift für Heinrich E.K. Henel*, ed. Jeffrey Sammons and Ernst Schürer (Munich: Fink, 1970), 101-21.

Schlegel), that Goethe perfected the provincial, small literary form as a national genre (cf. Hettner, 487). For Seidlin, Goethe's hexameters signify acceptance of differences in language and poetic rhythm and meter between modern German and classical Greek, not glorification of provinciality, or slavish imitation of classicism as in Voss:

> ... die ehrfürchtig liebevolle Bemühung um das andere, das Ferne und Polare, dessen Fremdheit sich keineswegs unter dem selbstsicher anmaßlichen Griff auflöst, aber das, gerade als das Fremde angeschaut, das wahrhaft Eigene in den erkennenden Blick treten läßt, in der Hoffnung, daß an solchem Maße das Eigene sich steigere und erhöhe. (110)

For the Italian critic, Giuliano Baioni, the provincial idyll of *Hermann und Dorothea* is an alternative to the utopianism of *Wilhelm Meisters Lehrjahre* as a literary resolution of the problems of the economically underdeveloped German middle classes:

> So also kann sich die bürgerliche Welt in eine neo-klassische Idylle verwandeln, und so preist das kleine Epos das politische Abseitsstehen des deutschen Bürgertums, das durch sein fast totales Versagen in der Geschichte eine der politisch unterentwickelten Klassen des damaligen Europa war, als eine ewige und archetypische Situation des Menschen. (120)[38]

The Homeric form imparts to the German *Bürgertum* classical or even humanistic qualities which it, as a class, could not generate for itself:

> Gewiß verdiente das tüchtige, arbeitsame und gehorsame deutsche Bürgertum angesichts eines vom Chaos der Revolution erschütterten Europa gefeiert zu werden, und Goethe zögert nicht, seine Klasse durchaus begeistert zu feiern, denn in der patriarchalischen Unbewegtheit ihrer Bräuche erschien sie ihm tatsächlich als eine ewige und paradigmatische Form, die die 'Klassizität' der homerischen Form rechtfertigte oder gar gebot. (121)

The absence of intellectuals in the poem is seen in Hegel's terms as the exclusion of foreign or disruptive elements (121). However both the vicar and the judge are intellectuals in the sense that they reflect on and articulate the state of their respective societies. And the first fiancé is the German enlightened intellectual *par excellence* in literature of the 1790s. The suggestion that critical questioning is excluded from the world of the poem is not tenable, considering the presence of

---

[38] Giuliano Baioni, "'Märchen,' *Wilhelm Meisters Lehrjahre*, *Hermann und Dorothea*: Zur Gesellschaftsidee der deutschen Klassik," *Goethe Jahrbuch* n.s. 92 (1975): 73-127; also *Classicismo e Rivoluzione: Goethe e la Rivoluzione Francese* (Naples: Guida Editori, 1969).

these characters. Focusing his analysis on line 304 of Hermann's final speech ("Aber wer fest auf dem Sinne beharrt, der bildet die Welt sich"), Baioni (like Seidlin, 102) views the first fiancé negatively as an idealist who abandoned Dorothea in his utopian wish to remake history:

> Seine Schuld besteht für Goethe nun nicht darin, ein Revolutionär gewesen zu sein, sondern zum Anwachsen der zentrifugalen Bewegung der Geschichte beigetragen zu haben, in einem Wort, nicht neben Dorothea geblieben zu sein und die aufgelösten Bande der Welt nicht wieder angeknüpft zu haben, wie es Hermann mit der Heirat tun wird. (126)

Hermann by contrast represents the positive aspect of the German *Bürgertum* as a force of social and political consolidation:

> Ein aufgeklärter, bewahrender, häuslicher und bürgerlicher, idealistischer und gemäßigter Humanismus also, auf den sich zu berufen die Weimarer Republik zwischen dem Zusammensturz des Wilhelminischen Reiches und dem Machtantritt des Faschismus umsonst versuchen wird. (127)

Baioni is presumably referring here to Korff's emphasis on *Bürgerlichkeit* and *Ordnung* — but Nadler's and Bartels's use of Hermann's speech in support of Nazism shows how this appeal could be misused. While Baioni sees celebration, rather than parody, in the use of Homeric and classical conventions, he concludes (surprisingly) that *Hermann und Dorothea* is the "höchsten und sublimsten Kitsch der gesamten europäischen Literatur" (122).

### "A Sleeping Hercules" — Re-Evaluations of German Identity (1970-1989)

As a result of the traumatic national legacy of Nazism, discussion of issues of German identity in *Hermann und Dorothea* was repressed or avoided by many German critics until the late 1970s and 80s. While progress has certainly been made in opening up these areas, there is still some reluctance in approaching them directly and in detail. National characteristics have not been thoroughly analyzed by those critics who see Hermann in a positive light. Lützeler writes that the qualities and nuances of the poem had been misrepresented by nationalist and Nazi interpretations, to the point where it is as good as forgotten.[39] I would rather suggest that *Hermann und Dorothea* has led a curious existence in literary history since the war. While excluded from the canon of great works, it was by no means forgotten, and discussion of it has been characterized by uneasiness in those defending it, and shrill overreaction in those who condemn it.

---

[39] Lützeler, 96.

Many recent critics sense a tension between idyllic form and ironic-parodic tone, and a weakness in the character of Hermann himself as the spokesman for a resurgent Germany. Dieter Borchmeyer writes that first fiancé and Hermann represent two opposed attitudes of the German *Bürgertum* towards the Revolution.[40] The former exhibits the spontaneous enthusiasm with which the early stages of the Revolution were viewed in Germany, but which turned out to be a tragic illusion. Hermann on the other hand manifests:

> eine zunächst im privaten Kreis des Hauses und der Familie sich vollendende Bürgerlichkeit, die dann freilich die Schwelle des Hauses überschreitet und, durch Sicherheit und Glück der Privatsphäre gestärkt, mit der notwendigen Freiheit ausgestattet, in den Dienst des Gemeinwesens tritt. (331)

The ending is defended against charges of philistinism through the "positive Beziehung des häuslich-familiären Bereichs zum öffentlichen, zum Leben des Gemeinwesens" (331-32). (Borchmeyer is here referring to Hermann's patriotic fervor on behalf of wife and family, rather than the father's civic consciousness.) In his contribution to Viktor Zmegac's literary history, Borchmeyer views Hermann less conditionally, as the representative of "eine im privaten Kreis des Hauses und der Familie sich vollendende Bürgerlichkeit, die sich freilich bewußt in den Dienst des Gemeinwesens stellt ..."[41]

Gerhard Kaiser also views Hermann positively as a force of the future:

> Der gegenüber dem scheinbar aufgeschlossenen Wirt und Vater scheinbar ganz altväterliche Hermann, der Konservative ist es, der sich als der wahre Erneuerer bewährt.[42]

Hermann at the end repudiates the politics of the first fiancé and recreates the destroyed idyll. However Kaiser views Goethe's recreation of the genre as conditional upon the reduction of the idyll to the idyllic character, whose perspective in the narration is relative to the perspectives of others. As a result of this, the ending does not constitute a closed idyllic program:

---

[40] Dieter Borchmeyer, *Höfische Gesellschaft und französische Revolution bei Goethe: Adliges und bürgerliches Wertsystem im Urteil der Weimarer Klassik* (Kronberg/Ts.: Athenäum, 1977).

[41] Dieter Borchmeyer, "Weimar im Zeitalter der Revolution und der Napoleonischen Kriege: Aspekte bürgerlicher Klassik," *Geschichte der deutschen Literatur vom 18. Jahrhundert bis zur Gegenwart*, ed. Viktor Zmegac, 3 vols. (Königstein/Ts.: Athenäum, 1979-84), 1/2:10.

[42] Gerhard Kaiser, *Wanderer und Idylle: Goethe und die Phänomenologie der Natur in der deutschen Dichtung von Gessner bis Gottfried Keller* (Göttingen: Vandenhoeck & Ruprecht, 1977), 49.

Hermanns Schlußworte sind schon deshalb nicht das letzte Wort des Epos, weil die von Dorothea berichteten Gesinnungen des toten Bräutigams, die von dem Richter erzählten Erfahrungen aus der hoffnungsvollen Anfangsphase der Revolution in seinem Denken wenig Widerhall finden. (50)

In a more recent article, Karl Eibl offers a different reading of the relationship between idyll and reality in the work.[43] Where Kaiser sees the idyll made relative through the reduction to an individual point of view, Eibl argues that the idyll is deconstructed through the irony of form. Eibl's argument builds on the interpretations of Mann and Seidlin. Just as the town is the model of a flexible order capable of integrating the foreign (111), so too the form is a flexible order capable of integrating reality. Irony is used not as creative playfulness or as a means of distancing the subject, but rather in order to subordinate form to truth, to hinder the impression that an "ideal" is being represented:

Indem er Leben 'nah' der Natur,' auf einem fiktiven 'griechischen' oder, wie hier 'bürgerlichen' Schauplatz geformt darstellt, will er beitragen zur gesellschaftlichen *Anamnesis*, damit das Chaos gebändigt, die Ordnung transparent gehalten werde für die Augenblicks-Erfahrung der Wahrheit (137).

Where Kaiser accepts unresolved tension, Helmut J. Schneider suggests transfiguration.[44] Goethe's modern idyll is the result of the "bloodless revolution" of the German *Bürgertum*, in which "Kampf und politische Vermittlung" were unnecessary (134). Consequently Hermann's final speech represents the postrevolutionary consciousness of the German middle classes, finding its image in the house and the family:

... der geschlossene Bund erscheint als Garant politischen 'Beharrens,' als eine Art heroischer Vorwärtsverteidigung und Friedensbewahrung gegen die 'allgemeine Erschütterung,' ... Die Gediegenheit des Interieurs, für das zu Beginn die mächtigen Füße des Tisches stehen, ist zur symbolischen Festung gesteigert, die familiäre 'Autarkie' zum Bild bürgerlicher Autonomie. (135)

Hermann is seen positively as "ein schlafender Herkules, Symbol des unterdrückten Volks" (135), who proclaims:

---

[43] Karl Eibl, "Anamnesis des 'Augenblicks': Goethes poetischer Gesellschaftsentwurf in *Hermann und Dorothea*," DVjs 58 (1984): 111-38.

[44] Helmut J. Schneider, "Idylle und bürgerliches Epos," in *Zwischen Revolution und Restauration: Klassik, Romantik 1786-1815*, vol. 5 of *Deutsche Literatur: Eine Sozialgeschichte*, ed. Horst Albert Glaser (Reinbek bei Hamburg: Rowohlt, 1980), 130-43.

> ... die Bewahrung eines Alten, ... das sich als das Ur-Anfängliche erwiesen hat. Die Entscheidung gegen eine Umwälzung auf deutschem Boden ist das letzte Wort, die homerisch-allgemein menschliche Typik wird zur tagespolitischen Botschaft (136).

The positive interpretations of the ending — especially by Borchmeyer and Schneider — ignore not only the characterization of Hermann throughout the text, but also the contextual questions which must arise from their implied readings of German history. How, for example, can the German *Bürgertum* of the revolutionary period be seen in positive political terms, or as a politically liberated class in terms of German petty absolutism? And how can Hermann's stance be seen as a positive statement of national identity, when it so clearly fails to address the questions of individual and social liberty for which Dorothea's fiancé was the spokesman? In view of the appropriation of Hermann as a spokesman for the *deutscher Sonderweg* in the nineteenth century, and for National Socialism in the twentieth, these questions must be answered in full. Friedrich Sengle proves to be more direct than the younger critics in approaching such issues.[45] In an article devoted to the relationships between Voss and Goethe he accepts that the ending of *Hermann und Dorothea* is not without problems, "denn in der Aufforderung zur wie immer berechtigten nationalen Notwehr liegt eine Einschränkung des von Voss so leidenschaftlich vertretenen kosmopolitischen Humanismus." However these questions are left unanswered: "das nationale kriegerische Handeln [ist] in Goethes Augen nur Forderung des geschichtlichen Moments ... und das kosmopolitische Fundament der Aufklärung noch nicht ernstlich bedroht." (220) In a recent contribution by Thomas P. Saine, the memory of the first fiancé in canto nine "speaks for the transformation of Hermann the German, into Hermann, the German citizen of the world." However Saine's article is based on a few selections from the text, and does not address either the tensions apparent in the work as a whole, or the discussion of these issues in the broader critical literature on *Hermann und Dorothea*.[46]

Werner Krauss and Frank Ryder and Benjamin Bennett are among the few modern critics who condemn Hermann's final speech as narrow and philistine. Krauss sees this in terms of epic realism:

---

[45] Friedrich Sengle, "'Luise' von Voss und Goethes 'Hermann und Dorothea': Didaktisch-epische Form und Funktion des Homerisierens," in *Europäische Lehrdichtung: Festschrift für Walter Naumann zum 70. Geburtstag*, ed. Hans Gerd Rötzer and Herbert Walz (Darmstadt: Wissenschaftliche Buchgesellschaft, 1981), 209-23. Sengle offers an interesting new perspective on Dorothea's act of self-defense as "eine symbolische Vorausdeutung auf den so sorgfältig bedachten wehrhaften Schluß" (217).

[46] See the Excursus, "Revolutionary Enlightenment, the German Jacobins and Dorothea's First Fiancé," in chapter eight for a fuller analysis of Saine's arguments.

Vielleicht konnte das große Epos kein anderes Ende nehmen als in der Verherrlichung der Spießermoral objektivere Verhältnisse darzustellen.(89)[47]

Ryder and Bennett took an important new approach in analyzing formal and metrical inconsistencies as textual irony.[48] Goethe comes "dangerously close to making Hermann ridiculous" (437). However while the mock-epic aspects of the text are fully analyzed for the first time, little significance is given to the irony beyond the rather general interpretation that it expresses the historical need for bourgeois stability. Ryder and Bennett provide excellent linguistic and metrical analysis to support their view that the verse "suddenly becomes more inspired, more elevated and powerful" (441) when Dorothea reports the words of her first fiancé, but this analytical work does not lead to a detailed description of the function of the first fiancé in the work as a whole.

In an indignant response to those critics who "trivialize" the text (Ryder and Bennett?), Jane K. Brown stresses the seriousness of the irony of *Hermann und Dorothea*.[49] Supporting the critical line of Borchmeyer, Schneider and Kaiser, and drawing on Schiller's theoretical writings, Brown identifies mock-heroic and ironic-parodic aspects in the subsidiary characters (207), but not in Hermann. He reaches epic grandeur as a spokesman for the principles of conservatism, who at the same time accepts the transitoriness of history, symbolized in the figure of the first fiancé (209-12). Goethe's "Ernsthaftigkeit" (214) is thereby saved from frivolous attacks. Brown, like Korff (2:344), Gerhard (63), Staiger (2:254, 262) and Ilse Graham[50] sees the literary form as bringing about a transcendent resolution of human conflicts:

Der Triumph von *Hermann und Dorothea* ist also eine Versöhnung über die soziale Versöhnung hinaus, jenseits der Versöhnung von Epik und Idylle, jenseits der von Antike und Moderne. Er stellt eine Versöhnung zwischen dem Abstrakten und dem Konkreten dar. (213-14)

The official *Geschichte der deutschen Literatur* of the German Democratic Republic stresses the unity of artistic form and idyllic reality: "Diese idyllisch-harmonische Grundkonzeption hat Goethe durch die mit höchster Meisterschaft

---

[47] Werner Krauss, "Goethe und die französische Revolution," *Neohelicon* 1 (1973): 89.

[48] Frank G. Ryder, and Benjamin Bennett, "The Irony of Goethe's *Hermann und Dorothea*: Its Form and Function," *PMLA* 90 (1975): 433-46.

[49] Jane K. Brown, "Schiller und die Ironie von *Hermann und Dorothea*,"in *Goethezeit: Studien zur Erkenntnis und Rezeption Goethes und seiner Zeitgenossen, Festschrift für Stuart Atkins*, ed. Gerhart Hoffmeister (Bern: Francke, 1981), 203-16.

[50] Ilse Graham, "A Delicate Balance: *Hermann und Dorothea*," *Goethe: A Portrait of the Artist* (Berlin: de Gruyter, 1977), 311.

gehandhabte künstlerische Form unterstützt."[51] Such a critical perspective is surprising in view of the way this text had been used in the past by the nationalist and Nazi movements. The resolution of the tensions between revolutionary idealism and provincial idyll is simply seen as the reflection of Goethe's own political outlook:

> Das Zurückwerfen der 'großen Bewegungen und Veränderungen des Welttheaters' findet seine Begrenzung nicht darin, daß die Welt, die als Spiegel dient, klein, sondern darin, daß sie in statischer Ruhe und harmonischem Gleichgewicht bleibt und daß der Dichter seiner Sympathie dafür durch die epische Ausgewogenheit und durch das dadurch geförderte Hinausheben in das 'reine Menschliche' deutlichen Ausdruck gibt. (179)

The later *Kurze Geschichte der deutschen Literatur* pays less attention to the idyllic form, and more to political issues.[52] Hermann is viewed positively as shy, modest, and above all, unwilling to become a "Geldbürger" (298), and Goethe is seen to support a provincial, non-political Germany:

> Sein Rat an seine Landsleute war, sich aus den Kämpfen der Zeit herauszuhalten. Er wurde genährt von der Illusion, Deutschland könne sich als Stätte ruhiger Bildung und sozialen Friedens vervollkommnen. (299)

In the most recent volume of the Newald-de Boor *Geschichte der deutschen Literatur*, Gerhard Schulz notes the irony and the tensions in *Hermann und Dorothea*, but considers the comic resolution of these as evidence of "die lebendige Kraft dieser deutschen Bürger, ihre Bereitschaft zur Katharsis und zum Neuen, das aus dem Alten hervorwächst" (326).[53] The history of diverse interpretations is noted as a symptom of weakness in the text, which could allow "so viele Leseweisen ... allerdings nur, wenn man es von den Umständen und Bedingungen seiner Entstehungszeit entfernt" (326). K.O. Conrady is also at best ambivalent towards the sentiments expressed in Hermann's final speech.[54] The contradiction between Hermann's inexperience and his ethos of idyllic traditionalism is noted:

---

[51] Hans-Dietrich Dahnke, Thomas Höhle, and Hans-Georg Werner, eds., *Geschichte der deutschen Literatur von den Anfängen bis zur Gegenwart*, vol. 7, *1779 bis 1830* (Berlin: Volk und Wissen, 1978), 178.

[52] K. Böttcher and Hans Jurgen Geerts, eds., *Kurze Geschichte der deutschen Literatur* (Berlin: Volk und Wissen, 1981), 298-99.

[53] Gerhard Schulz, *Die deutsche Literatur zwischen Französischer Revolution und Restauration: 1789-1806*, vol. 7/1 of *Geschichte der deutschen Literatur von den Anfängen bis zur Gegenwart*, ed. Helmut de Boor and Richard Newald (Munich: Beck, 1983).

[54] Karl Otto Conrady, *Goethe: Leben und Werk*, 2 vols. (Königstein/Ts.: Athenäum, 1985), 2:163-76.

Was Hermann dann in seinem Schlußwort geradezu programmatisch verkündet, nachdem die Fremde aufgenommen und jeder sich der Basis seines künftigen Lebens versichert hat, gerät allerdings zu Weisheiten, die nicht mehr zu erkennen geben, welcher Anstrengungen es bedürfte, bis der Bund geschlossen werden konnte, und welche Perspektiven des Weltbürgerlichen die 'bürgerliche Idylle' auch eröffnete. (2:174)

However Conrady avoids coming to terms with this, pointing out merely that Hermann's words could later be adopted by a "saturiertes, selbstzufriedenes Bürgertum," and that "die Verse mußten dazu nicht einmal entstellt werden" (175), a point also made without further commentary by Schneider: "Kein Wunder freilich, daß spätere Generationen ihre Gipsvitrine damit schmückten" (136). These critics presumably also believe that the text itself is to blame for the use to which it has been put.

Christa Bürger attacks the work as "eine Schnulze" in terms of its status and function in bourgeois society (486).[55] The use of interpretative concepts such as irony is condemned for avoiding the question of Goethe's status in the canon of national classics:

Die Distanz zwischen dem normativen Gehalt des Werks und den gesellschaftlichen Vorstellungen gegenwärtiger Interpreten ist so unübersehbar, daß sie eine Reflexion erzwingen müßte mit dem Ergebnis einer Kanon-revision. Genau dieser Konsequenz aber weicht man mit der Ironie-These aus, mit deren Hilfe sich der störende Gehalt weginterpretieren läßt. (496)

These comments are aimed at a particular literary and cultural history, rather than the literary text. Bürger ignores both Dorothea and the first fiancé (neither of whom can be dismissed as traditional elements of the *bürgerlich* patriarchal idyll), and rejects the work as middle-class kitsch:

*Hermann und Dorothea* [ist] eben nicht nur ein reines Kunstwerk, sondern auch 'vaterländisches Gedicht.' (487) ... Projiziert in einen zeitlosen Raum patriarchalischer Ordnung erkennt in Goethes *Hermann und Dorothea* das deutsche Bürgertum des 19. Jahrhunderts sein eigenes verklärtes Bild. (503-4)

Finally, T.M. Holmes argues that Hermann's stance at the end is a defensive and insecure reaction to internal developments in the German town itself. Like Baioni, Holmes compares the idyll of *Hermann und Dorothea* to the utopianism of

---

[55] Christa Bürger, "Hermann und Dorothea oder: Die Wirklichkeit als Ideal," in *Unser Commercium: Goethes und Schillers Literaturpolitik*, ed. W. Barner, E. Lämmert, and N. Oellers (Stuttgart: Cotta, 1984), 485-505.

*Wilhelm Meisters Lehrjahre*. The idyll is condemned to destruction not from the external upheavals of the Revolution, but from its own conservative ethos of property rights and the "momentum of private accumulation" (118).[56] Holmes refers to Eibl's article, in which Hermann's use of the word "erlagen" (IX, 310) is seen as an elegiac intimation of the approaching destruction of the patriotic idyll (Eibl, 138; Holmes, 111).

Most recent critics recognise that Hermann is presented to some degree as a national stereotype, and that there is a degree of ambivalence in this representation. However critical opinion is still split over Hermann's final stance and the issues of German identity that it raises. Those who view it positively (Schneider, Borchmeyer) have not analyzed in detail the questions of literary form and national identity which arise from their interpretations. And those who see it as jingoism or *bürgerlich* sentimentality tend to reject the work as a whole, because of the perceived authorial sympathy with Hermann's patriotic message (Bürger, Krauss). Where the first fiancé was seen negatively as an over-enthusiastic idealist in earlier criticism, post-war critics have tended to see him as a tragic revolutionary idealist (except for Seidlin and Baioni, who are more critical of his actions). While some cast doubt on the quality of the text (Viëtor, Schulz, Conrady, Bürger), the amount of critical interest and controversy that it has generated since the war, suggests that it is still felt to be a complex and significant work of literature.

Paul Michael Lützeler probably best sums up the contemporary critical consensus, in stressing the conservative and conciliatory aspect: "Auch hier ist letztlich eine deutsche Alternative von Evolution und Kontinuität gegenüber der Revolution und Diskontinuität im Spiel," while noting that the ending is not presented in unproblematic or utopian terms: "Zur Versinnbildlichung der soziopolitischen Synthese führt Goethe ein Ehebändnis vor, auf dessen zukünftige Konflikte er im Text ironisch bereits hingewiesen hatte."[57]

*Hermann und Dorothea* touches on central questions of German identity, national self-perception and the role of literature in German culture. From its first appearance, its reception has been determined by spoken or unspoken attitudes to these questions. In 1989 changes have occurred in East-West relations, and particularly in relationships between the Federal Republic of Germany and the German Democratic Republic, which will have important and far-reaching consequences for the cultural as well as political and social self-perception of the German people. It is not unlikely, given the history of *Hermann und Dorothea* as an indicator of national self-perceptions, that its place in German literature and culture will be substantially re-evaluated over the coming years.

---

[56] T.M.Holmes, "Goethe's *Hermann und Dorothea*: The Dissolution of the Embattled Idyll," *Modern Language Review* 82 (1987): 109-18.

[57] Lützeler, 123-24.

Helbig, Louis F. "Goethe's *Hermann und Dorothea* as Refugee Epic." *Goethe in the Twentieth Century.* Ed. Alexej Ugrinsky. New York: Greenwood Press, 1987. 139-46.
Helmerking, Heinz. *"Hermann und Dorothea": Entstehung, Ruhm und Wesen.* Zurich: Artemis, 1948.
Hettner, Hermann. "Geschichtliche Vorerinnerungen." *Aesthetische Versuche über Goethes "Hermann und Dorothea."* By Wilhelm von Humboldt. 3rd ed. Brunswick: Vieweg, 1861. v-xviii.
—. *Geschichte der deutschen Literatur im 18. Jahrhundert.* 2 vols. 1856-70. Repr. Berlin: Aufbau, 1979. 2:486-91.
Hewett, Waterman Thomas: "A Study of Goethe's Printed Text: *Hermann und Dorothea.*" *PMLA* (1899): 108-36.
Holmes, T.M. "Goethe's *Hermann und Dorothea*: The Dissolution of the Embattled Idyll." *Modern Language Review* 82 (1987): 109-18.
Humboldt, Wilhelm von. *Aesthetische Versuche: Über Goethes "Hermann und Dorothea." Werke.* 5 vols. Ed. Andreas Flitner and Klaus Giel. Stuttgart: Cotta, 1961. 2:125-356.
Jöns, Dietrich Walter. "Dichtungen Goethes im Urteil von Hegels Ästhetik." *Studien zur Goethezeit: Erich Trunz zum 75. Geburtstag.* Ed. Hans-Joachim Mähl and Eberhard Mannack. *Euphorion* Beiheft, 18. Heidelberg: Carl Winter, 1981. 121-52.
Kaiser, Gerhard. *Wanderer und Idylle: Goethe und die Phänomenologie der Natur in der deutschen Dichtung von Gessner bis Gottfried Keller.* Göttingen: Vandenhoeck & Ruprecht, 1977. 47-52, 92-95.
Koberstein, August. *Grundriß der Geschichte der deutschen Nationalliteratur.* 5th rev. ed. Ed. Karl Bartsch. Leipzig: F.C.W. Vogel, 1873. 4:456-64.
Korff, Hermann August. *Geist der Goethezeit: Versuch einer ideellen Entwicklung der klassisch-romantischen Literaturgeschichte.* Repr. 7th and 8th eds. (= 10th ed.). 5 vols. Berlin: Koehler & Amelang, 1979. 2:362-74.
Krauss, Werner. "Goethe und die französische Revolution." *Neohelicon* 1 (1973): 77-90.
Kullmer, Charles Julius. *Pössnek und "Hermann und Dorothea."* Heidelberg: Carl Winter, 1910.
Lanckoranskaja, Maria Gräfin and Arthur Rümann. *Geschichte der deutschen Taschenbücher und Almanache aus der klassisch-romantischen Zeit.* Munich: Ernst Heimeran Verlag 1954. 48-58.
Lange, Victor. *The Classical Age of German Literature 1740- 1815.* London: Edward Arnold, 1982. 144-52.
Leroux, Robert. "La Révolution française dans *Hermann et Dorothée.*" *Etudes Germaniques* 4 (1949): 174-86.
Ludwig, Emil. *Goethe, History of a Man.* London: G.P. Putnam's Sons, 1928.
Lützeler, Paul Michael. "Johann Wolfgang Goethe: *Hermann und Dorothea.*" *Geschichte in der Literatur: Studien zu Werken von Lessing bis Hebbel.* Munich: Piper, 1987. 86-130. Also published in *Goethes Erzählwerk: Interpretationen.* Ed. Paul Michael Lützeler and James E. McLeod. Stuttgart: Reclam, 1985. 216-67.

Lypp, Maria. "Bürger und Weltbürger in Goethes *Hermann und Dorothea.*" *Goethe: Neue Folge des Jahrbuchs der Goethe-Gesellschaft* 31 (1969): 129-42.
Mann, Thomas. "Goethe als Repräsentant des bürgerlichen Zeitalters." *Werke.* 13 vols. Frankfurt am Main: Fischer, 1974. 9:297-332.
—. "Goethes Laufbahn als Schriftsteller." *Werke.* 9:333-62.
Martens, Wolfgang. "Halten und Dauern? — Gedanken zu Goethes *Hermann und Dorothea.*" *Verlorene Klassik? Ein Symposium.* Ed. Wolfgang Wittkowski. Tübingen: Niemeyer, 1986. 79-93.
Mehring, Franz. *Aufsätze zur deutschen Literatur von Klopstock bis Weerth. Gesammelte Schriften,* vol. 10. 3rd ed. Berlin: Dietz, 1977. 60-1.
Mommsen, Momme. *Die Entstehung von Goethes Werken.* 2 vols. to date. Berlin: Akademie, 1958-.
Morgan, Peter. "The Polarization of Utopian Idealism and Practical Politics in the Idyll: The Role of the First 'Bräutigam' in Goethe's *Hermann und Dorothea.*" *German Quarterly* 57 (1984): 532-45.
—. "Parody and Middle-Class Identity: The Function of the Idyll in Voss and Goethe." *Comic Relations: Studies in the Comic, Satire, and Parody.* Ed. Pavel Petr, David Roberts, and Philip Thomson. Frankfurt am Main: Lang, 1985. 219-26.
Nadler, Josef. *Literaturgeschichte des deutschen Volkes: Dichtung und Schrifttum der deutschen Stämme und Landschaften.* 4th fully rev. ed. 4 vols. Berlin: Propyläen, 1939. 2:301-2.
Neudecker, Georg. *Die innere Komposition in Goethes epischer Dichtung 'Hermann und Dorothea': Zur ersten Zentenarfeier ihrer Entstehung.* Programm Würzburg 1896.
Oellers, Norbert. "Goethes und Schillers Balladen vom Juni 1797 — auch Nebenwerke zu *Hermann und Dorothea* und *Wallenstein.*" Barner, 507-28.
Petsch, Robert. "'Hermann und Dorothea': Ein Epos vom deutschen Bürgertum." *Deutsche Grenzlande* 14 (1935): 128-34; cont. *Deutsche Monatsblätter für Volk und Heimat* 14 (1935): 200-7.
Rasmussen, Detlef. "Georg Forster und Goethes *Hermann und Dorothea*: Ein Versuch über gegenständliche Dichtung." *Goethe und Forster: Studien zum gegenständlichen Dichten.* Bonn: Bouvier, 1985. 54-79.
Reimann, Paul. *Hauptströmungen der deutschen Literatur, 1750-1848: Beiträge zu ihrer Geschichte und Kritik.* 2nd. rev. ed. Berlin: Dietz, 1963. 358-59.
Robertson, J.G. *The Life and Works of Goethe 1749-1832.* London: Routledge, 1932. 197-202.
Rosenkranz, Karl. *Göthe und seine Werke.* Königsberg: Bornträger, 1856. 268-88.
Ryder, Frank G. and Benjamin Bennett. "The Irony of Goethe's *Hermann und Dorothea*: Its Form and Function." *PMLA* 90 (1975): 433-46.
Saine, Thomas P. "Charlotte Corday, Adam Lux and *Hermann und Dorothea.*" *Exile and Enlightenment: Studies in German and Comparative Literature in Honor of Guy Stern.* Ed. Uwe Faulhaber, Jenny Glenn, Edward P. Harris, and Hans Georg Rickert. Detroit: Wayne State University Press, 1987. (Repr. in Saine: *Black Bread — White Bread,* 380-91.)

—. *Black Bread — White Bread: German Intellectuals and the French Revolution.* Columbia, S.C.: Camden House, 1988.
Samuel, Richard. "Goethe's *Hermann und Dorothea.*" *Selected Writings.* Ed. D.R. Coverlid, J. Smit, H. Wiemann, and C. Kooznetzoff. Melbourne: University of Melbourne, Dept. of Germanic Studies, 1965. 24-43.
Schadewaldt, Wolfgang. *Goethestudien: Natur und Altertum.* Stuttgart: Artemis, 1963. 148-52.
Scheibe, Siegfried. "Neue Zeugnisse zur Druckgeschichte von Goethes *Hermann und Dorothea.*" *Goethe: Neue Folge des Jahrbuchs der Goethe-Gesellschaft* 23 (1961): 265-98.
Scherer, Wilhelm. *Geschichte der deutschen Literatur.* 5th ed. Berlin: Weidmannsche Buchhandlung, 1889. 568-76.
Schlegel, August Wilhelm. "Goethes *Hermann und Dorothea.*" *Über Literatur, Kunst und Geist des Zeitalters: Eine Auswahl aus den kritischen Schriften.* Ed. F. Finke. Stuttgart: Reclam, 1979. 114-47.
Schmidt, Josef, ed. *Johann Wolfgang Goethe: "Hermann und Dorothea." Erläuterungen und Dokumente.* Stuttgart: Reclam, 1970.
Schmidt, Julian. *Geschichte der deutschen Literatur seit Lessing's Tod.* 4th rev. and enl. ed. 5 vols. Leipzig: Friedrich Ludwig Herbig, 1858. 1:249-53.
Schneider, Helmut J. "Idylle und bürgerliches Epos." *Zwischen Revolution und Restauration: Klassik, Romantik 1786-1815. Deutsche Literatur: Eine Sozialgeschichte,* vol. 5. Ed. Horst Albert Glaser. Reinbek bei Hamburg: Rowohlt, 1980. 130-43.
Schreyer, Hermann. "Goethes Arbeit an 'Hermann und Dorothea.'" *Goethe-Jahrbuch* 10 (1889): 196-211.
Schulz, Gerhard. *Die deutsche Literatur zwischen Französischer Revolution und Restauration: 1789-1806. Geschichte der deutschen Literatur von den Anfängen bis zur Gegenwart,* vol. 7/1. Ed. Helmut de Boor and Richard Newald. Munich: Beck, 1983.
Seidlin, Oskar. "Über Goethes *Hermann und Dorothea*: Ein Vortrag." *Lebendige Form: Interpretationen zur deutschen Literatur, Festschrift für Heinrich E.K. Henel.* Ed. Jeffrey Sammons and Ernst Schürer. Munich: Fink, 1970. 101-21.
Sengle, Friedrich. "'Luise' von Voss und Goethes 'Hermann und Dorothea': Didaktisch-epische Form und Funktion des Homerisierens." *Europäische Lehrdichtung: Festschrift für Walter Naumann zum 70. Geburtstag.* Ed. Hans Gerd Rötzer and Herbert Walz. Darmstadt: Wissenschaftliche Buchgesellschaft, 1981. 209-23.
Sintennis, F. "Zu *Hermann und Dorothea.*" *Goethe-Jahrbuch* 25 (1904): 227-32.
Staiger, Emil. *Goethe.* 3 vols. Zurich: Atlantis, 1962. 2:220-66.
Steckner, Hans. *Der epische Stil von Hermann und Dorothea.* Halle: M. Niemeyer, 1927.
Trevelyan, Humphry. *Goethe and the Greeks.* Cambridge: Cambridge University Press, 1942. 205-15.
Viëtor, Karl. *Goethe: Dichtung, Wissenschaft, Weltbild.* Bern: Francke, 1949. 151-58.
Yxem, E.F. *Über Goethes "Hermann und Dorothea."* Berlin, 1836.

## General Bibliography

Aris, Reinhold. *A History of Political Thought in Germany from 1789 to 1815*. 1936. London: Cass, 1965.

Baioni, Giuliano. *Classicismo e Rivoluzione: Goethe e la Rivoluzione Francese*. Naples: Guida Editori, 1969.

Becker, Eva. D. "'Klassiker' in der deutschen Literaturgeschichtsschreibung 1780-1860." *Zur Literatur der Restaurationsepoche 1815-48*. Ed. Jost Hermand and Manfred Windfuhr. Stuttgart: Metzler, 1970. 349-70.

Bendix, Reinhard. *Kings or People: Power and the Mandate to Rule*. Berkeley: University of California Press, 1978.

—. "Province and Metropolis: The Case of Eighteenth-Century Germany." *Culture and its Creators: Essays in Honor of Edward Shils*. Chicago: University of Chicago Press, 1977. 119-49.

Berlin, Isaiah. *Four Essays on Liberty*. London: Oxford University Press, 1969.

—. "The Bent Twig: a Note on Nationalism." *Foreign Affairs* 1 (1972): 11-30.

—. *Vico and Herder: Two Studies in the History of Ideas*. London: Hogarth, 1976.

Biedermann, Karl. *Deutschland im 18. Jahrhundert*. 4 vols. 1854. Repr. 2nd ed. Leipzig, 1880. Aalen: Scientia, 1969.

Biro, Sydney Seymour. *The German Policy of Revolutionary France: A Study in French Diplomacy during the War of the First Coalition 1792-1797*. 2 vols. Cambridge (Mass.): Harvard University Press, 1957.

Blackall, Eric. *The Emergence of German as a Literary Language 1700-1775*. 2nd ed. Ithaca: Cornell University Press, 1978.

Blanning, T.C.W. *Reform and Revolution in Mainz 1743-1803*. London: Cambridge University Press, 1974.

—. "The Enlightenment in Catholic Germany." *The Enlightenment in National Context*. Ed. Roy Porter and Mikulas Teich. Cambridge: Cambridge University Press, 1981. 118-26.

—. *The French Revolution in Germany: Occupation and Resistance in the Rhineland 1792-1802*. Oxford: Clarendon Press, 1983.

Bode, Wilhelm, ed. *Goethe in vertraulichen Briefen seiner Zeitgenossen*. 3 vols. Rev. ed. Edited by Regine Otto and Paul-Gerhard Wenzlaff. Berlin: Aufbau, 1979.

Bodi, Leslie. "Georg Forster: The 'Pacific Expert' of 18th Century Germany." *Historical Studies: Australia and New Zealand* 8 (1959): 345-363.

—. "Introduction." *Adventures on a Journey to New Holland and The Death Bed*. By Therese Huber. Trans. Rodney Livingstone. Melbourne: Lansdowne Press, 1966. 1-17.

—. *Tauwetter in Wien: Zur Prosa der österreichischen Aufklärung, 1781-1795*. Frankfurt am Main: Fischer, 1977.

Borst, Arno. "Valmy 1792 — Ein historisches Ereignis?" *Der Deutschunterricht* 26 (1974): 88-104.

Böschenstein, Renate. *Idylle*. Sammlung Metzler 63. Stuttgart: Metzler, 1967.

—. "Idylle." *Fischer-Lexikon: Literatur*. Ed. Wolf-Hartmut Friedrich and Walther Killy. 2 vols. Frankfurt am Main: Fischer, 1974. 2/1:293-304.

Bouloiseau, Marc. *The Jacobin Republic 1792-1794*. Trans. Jonathan Mandelbaum. Cambridge: Cambridge University Press, 1983.

Braun, Julius W. *Goethe im Urtheile seiner Zeitgenossen*. 3 vols. Berlin, 1883. Repr. Hildesheim: Georg Olms, 1969.

Brinkmann, Richard, Claude David, Gonthier-Louis Fink, et al. *Deutsche Literatur und Französische Revolution*. Göttingen: Vandenhoeck & Ruprecht, 1974.

Bruford, Walter Horace. "Goethe's 'Literarischer Sanskulottismus.'" *Classicism and Society: Festgabe für L.L. Hammerich*. Copenhagen: Naturmetodens Spooginstitut, 1962. 45-59.

—. *Germany in the 18th Century: The Social History of the Literary Revival*. Cambridge: Cambridge University Press, 1968.

Brunschwig, Henri. *Enlightenment and Romanticism in 18th Century Prussia*. Trans. F. Jellinek. Chicago: University of Chicago Press, 1974.

Buchner, Eberhard. *Die französische Revolution: Kulturgeschichtlich interessante Dokumente aus alten deutschen Zeitungen*. 2 vols. Munich: Langen, 1913.

Butler, Eliza Marian. *The Tyranny of Greece over Germany: A Study of the Influence Exercised by Greek Art and Poetry over the Great German Writers of the 18th, 19th and 20th Centuries*. Cambridge: Cambridge University Press, 1935.

Craig, Gordon A. "Engagement and Neutrality in Germany: The Case of Georg Forster." *Journal of Modern History* 41 (1969): 1-16.

Curtius, Ernst Robert. *Europäische Literatur und lateinisches Mittelalter*. Bern: Francke, 1948.

Dedner, Burghard. "Wege zum 'Realismus' in der aufklärerischen Darstellung des Landlebens." *Wirkendes Wort* 18 (1968): 303-19.

—. "Vom Schäferleben zur Agrarwirtschaft: Poesie und Ideologie des Landlebens in der deutschen Literatur des 18. Jahrhunderts." Garber, 347-90.

Demetz, Peter. *Goethes "Die Aufgeregten": Zur Frage der politischen Dichtung in Deutschland*. Hann-Munden: Nowack, 1952.

Deutsch, Karl. *Nationalism and Social Communication*. Cambridge, Mass.: MIT Press, 1953.

—. "The Trend of European Nationalism: The Language Aspect." *Readings in the Sociology of Language*. Ed. Joshua Fishman. The Hague: Mouton, 1968. 598-606.

Dippel, Horst. *Germany and the American Revolution 1770- 1800: A Sociohistorical Investigation of late 18th Century Political Thinking*. Trans. B.A. Uhlendorf. Wiesbaden: Fritz Steiner, 1978.

Droz, Jacques. *L'Allemagne et la Révolution française*. Paris: Presses universitaires de France, 1949.

Dülmen, Richard van. *Der Geheimbund der Illuminaten: Darstellung, Analyse, Dokumentation*. Stuttgart/Bad Cannstatt: Frommann-Holzboog, 1975.

Eade, J.C. ed. *Romantic Nationalism in Europe*. Humanities Research Centre Monograph 2. Canberra: Australian National University, Humanities Research Centre, 1983.

Enzensberger, Ulrich. *Georg Forster: Weltumsegler und Revolutionär*. Berlin: Wagenbach, 1977.
Epstein, Klaus. *The Genesis of German Conservatism*. Princeton: Princeton University Press, 1966.
Ergang, Robert Reinhold. *Herder and the Foundations of German Nationalism*. 1931. New York: Octagon Books, 1966.
Fambach, Oscar. *Goethe und seine Kritiker*. Düsseldorf: Ehlermann, 1953.
Fetscher, Iring. "Die Suche nach der nationalen Identität." *Stichworte zur 'Geistigen Situation der Zeit'*. Ed. Jürgen Habermas. 2 vols. Frankfurt am Main: Suhrkamp, 1979. 1:115-32.
Feuerlicht, Ignaz. "Vom Wesen der deutschen Idylle." *Germanic Review* 22 (1947): 202-17.
Fink, Gonthier-Louis. "Das Frankreichbild in der deutschen Literatur und Publizistik zwischen der französischen Revolution und den Befreiungskriegen." *Jahrbuch des Wiener Goethe-Vereins* 81-3, 1977-9 (1979): 59-87.
Fishman, Joshua. *Language and Nationalism: Two Integrative Essays*. Rowley, Mass.: Newbury House, 1973.
Fonagy, Ivan. "Communication in Poetry." *Word* 17 (1961): 194-218.
—. *Die Metaphern in der Poetik: Ein Beitrag zur Entwicklungsgeschichte des wissenschaftlichen Denkens*. The Hague: Mouton, 1963.
Forbes, H.D. *Nationalism, Ethnocentrism and Personality: Social Science and Critical Theory*. Chicago: University of Chicago Press, 1985.
Freund, Winfried. *Die literarische Parodie*. Sammlung Metzler 200. Stuttgart: Metzler, 1981.
Gagliardo, John. *From Pariah to Patriot: The Changing Image of the German Peasant, 1770-1840*. Lexington: University Press of Kentucky, 1969.
—. *Reich and Nation: The Holy Roman Empire as Idea and Reality, 1763-1806*. Bloomington: Indiana University Press, 1980.
Gärber, Jörn ed. *Revolutionäre Vernunft: Texte zur jakobinischen und liberalen Revolutionsrezeption in Deutschland, 1789-1810*. Kronberg/Ts.: Scriptor, 1974.
Garber, Klaus, ed. *Europäische Bukolik und Georgik*. Wege der Forschung, 355. Darmstadt: Wissenschaftliche Buchgesellschaft, 1976.
Geerdts, Hans-Jürgen. "Ironie und revolutionärer Enthusiasmus: Zu Georg Forsters 'Erinnerungen aus dem Jahr 1790.'" *Weimarer Beiträge* 1 (1955): 296-312.
Geiger, Ludwig. *Therese Huber 1764-1829: Geschichte einer deutschen Frau*. Stuttgart: Cotta, 1901.
Gellner, Ernest. *Nations and Nationalism*. Oxford: Blackwell, 1983.
Gerth, Hans. *Bürgerliche Intelligenz um 1800: Zur Soziologie des deutschen Frühliberalismus*. Göttingen: Vandenhoeck & Ruprecht, 1976.
Gooch, G.P. *Germany and the French Revolution*. London: Frank Cass, 1920.
Grab, Walter. *Eroberung oder Befreiung? Deutsche Jakobiner und die Franzosenherrschaft im Rheinland, 1792-9*. Schriften aus dem Karl Marx Haus 4. Trier: n.p., 1971. Rev. ed., *Studien zu Jakobinismus und Sozialismus*. Ed. H. Pelger Berlin: Dietz, 1974. 1-102.

—. *Leben und Werke norddeutscher Jakobiner*. Stuttgart: Metzler, 1973.

—. *Friedrich von der Trenck: Hochstapler und Freiheitsmärtyrer und andere Studien zur Revolutions- und Literaturgeschichte*. Kronberg/Ts.: Scriptor, 1977.

—. *Freiheit oder Mord und Todt: Revolutionsaufrufe deutscher Jakobiner*. Berlin: Wagenbach, 1979.

—. *Ein Volk muß seine Freiheit selbst erobern: Zur Geschichte des deutschen Jakobinismus*. Frankfurt am Main: Büchergilde Gutenberg, 1984.

Gräf, Hans Gerhard. *Goethe über seine Dichtungen: Versuch einer Sammlung aller Äusserungen des Dichters über seine poetischen Werke*. 3 pts. in 9 vols. Frankfurt am Main, 1901. Repr. Darmstadt: Wissenschaftliche Buchgesellschaft, 1968.

Grassl, Hans. *Aufbruch zur Romantik: Bayerns Beitrag zur deutschen Geistesgeschichte, 1765-85*. Munich: Beck, 1968.

Groote, Wolfgang von. *Die Entstehung des Nationalbewußtseins in Nordwestdeutschland 1790-1830*. Göttingen: Musterschmidt, 1955.

Gruner, Wolf D. *Die deutsche Frage: Ein Problem der europäischen Geschichte seit 1800*. Munich: Beck, 1985.

Günther, H.R.G. "Psychologie des deutschen Pietismus." *DVjs* 4 (1926): 144-76.

Habermas, Jürgen. *Strukturwandel der Öffentlichkeit: Untersuchungen zu einer Kategorie der bürgerlichen Gesellschaft*. Neuwied: Luchterhand, 1962.

Harprecht, Klaus. *Georg Forster oder Die Liebe zur Welt: Eine Biographie*. Reinbek bei Hamburg: Rowohlt, 1987.

Hempel, Wido. "Parodie, Travestie und Pastiche: Zur Geschichte von Wort und Sache." *Germanisch-Romanische Monatsschrift* (1965): 150-76.

Hermand, Jost. *Von deutscher Republik 1775-95: Texte radikaler Demokraten*. Frankfurt am Main: Suhrkamp, 1975.

Herminghouse, Patricia. "Trends in Literary Reception Coming to Terms with Classicism: Goethe in GDR Literature of the 1970s." *German Quarterly* 56 (1983): 273-84.

Highet, Gilbert. *The Classical Tradition: Greek and Roman Influences on Western Literature*. New York: Oxford University Press, 1957.

Hoare, Michael E. *The Tactless Philosopher: Johann Reinhold Forster 1729-98*. Melbourne: Hawthorne Press, 1976.

Hoffmeister, Johannes. "Goethe und die französische Revolution." *Viermonatsschrift der Goethe-Gesellschaft* n.s. 6 (1941): 138-68.

Horkheimer, Max and Theodor W. Adorno. *Dialektik der Aufklärung*. 1944. Amsterdam: Verlag de Munter, 1968.

Hubatsch, Walter, ed. *Absolutismus*. Wege der Forschung, 314. Darmstadt: Wissenschaftliche Buchgesellschaft, 1973.

Huber, Ernst Rudolf. *Nationalstaat und Verfassungsstaat: Studien zur Geschichte der modernen Staatsidee*. Stuttgart: Kohlhammer, 1965.

Jäckel, Günter. "'Land zweier Lieder': Goethes und Forsters Begegnung mit Frankreich." *Sinn und Form* 34 (1982): 887-93.

Jacobs, Jürgen. "Das Verstummen der Muse: Zur Geschichte der epischen Dichtungsgattungen im 18. Jahrhundert." *Arcadia* 10 (1975): 129-46.

Jäger, Georg. "Der Deutschunterricht auf Gymnasien 1780 bis 1850." *DVjs* 47 (1973): 120-47.

Jäger Hans-Wolf. *Politische Kategorien in Politik und Rhetorik der zweiten Hälfte des 18. Jahrhunderts*. Stuttgart: Metzler, 1970.

—. *Politische Metaphorik im Jakobinismus und im Vormärz*. Stuttgart: Metzler, 1971.

—. "Gegen die Revolution: Beobachtungen zur konservativen Dramatik in Deutschland um 1790." *Jahrbuch der Deutschen Schillergesellschaft* 22 (1978): 362-403.

Jakobson, Roman. "The Beginning of National Self- Determination in Europe." *Readings in the Sociology of Language*. Ed. Joshua Fishman. The Hague: Mouton, 1968. 585-97.

Jordan, Sabine Dorothea. *Ludwig Ferdinand Huber 1764-1804: His Life and Works*. Stuttgarter Arbeiten zur Germanistik, 57. Stuttgart: Akademischer Verlag Hans-Dieter Heinz, 1978.

Juttner, Siegfried. "Großstadtmythen: Paris-Bilder des 18. Jahrhunderts: Eine Skizze." *DVjs* 55 (1981): 172-203.

Kaiser, Gerhard. *Pietismus und Patriotismus im literarischen Deutschland: Ein Beitrag zum Problem der Säkularisation*. 2nd rev. ed. Frankfurt am Main: Athenäum, 1973.

—. "Über den Umgang mit Republikanern, Jakobinern und Zitaten." *DVjs* 49 Sonderheft (1975): 226-42.

Kamenka, Eugene. *Nationalism: The Nature and Evolution of an Idea*. Canberra: Australian National University Press, 1973.

Kiesel, Helmuth and Paul Münch. *Gesellschaft und Literatur im 18. Jahrhundert: Voraussetzungen und Entstehung des literarischen Marktes in Deutschland*. Munich: Beck, 1977.

Kindermann, Heinz. *Das Goethebild des 20. Jahrhunderts*. Vienna: Humboldt, 1952.

Klein, Karl. *Georg Forster in Mainz 1788-93*. Gotha, 1863.

Koberstein, August. *Geschichte der deutschen Nationalliteratur vom zweiten Viertel des 18. Jahrhunderts bis zu Goethes Tod*. 5th ed. Leipzig: Vogel, 1872.

Kohn, Hans. *The Idea of Nationalism: A Study in its Origins and Background*. New York: Macmillan, 1944.

—. *The Mind of Germany: The Education of a Nation*. London: Macmillan, 1960.

—. *Prelude to Nation-States: The French and German Experience, 1789-1815*. Princeton: D. van Nostrand, 1967.

Koopmann, Helmut. *Freiheitssonne und Revolutionsgewitter: Reflexe der Französischen Revolution im literarischen Deutschland zwischen 1789 und 1840*. Tübingen: Niemeyer, 1989.

Kopitsch, Franklin, ed. *Aufklärung, Absolutismus und Bürgertum in Deutschland*. Munich: Nymphenburg, 1976.

Koselleck, Reinhard. *Kritik und Krise: Eine Studie zur Pathogenese der bürgerlichen Welt*. 1959. Frankfurt am Main: Suhrkamp, 1973.

Krauss, Werner. *Gesammelte Aufsätze zu Literatur und Sprachwissenschaft*. Frankfurt am Main: Vittorio Klostermann, 1949.

—. *Perspektiven und Probleme: Zur französischen und deutschen Aufklärung und andere Aufsätze*. Neuwied: Luchterhand, 1965.
Krieger, Leonard. "The Intellectuals and European Society." *Political Science Quarterly* 67 (1952): 225-47.
—. *The German Idea of Freedom: History of a Political Tradition*. 1957. Chicago: University of Chicago Press, 1972.
—. *An Essay on the Theory of Enlightened Despotism*. Chicago: University of Chicago Press, 1975.
Kruse, Jens. "Flamme im Wasser, Schimmel im Kalk: Französische Revolution und Naturwissenschaft im Werk Goethes." *Goethe Yearbook: Publication of the Goethe Society of North America* 4 (1988): 209-34.
Kuhn, Axel. *Linksrheinische deutsche Jakobiner*. Stuttgart: Metzler, 1978.
Lange, Victor. "Die Sprache als Erzählform in *Werther*." *Formenwandel: Festschrift zum 65. Geburtstag von Paul Böckmann*. Ed. Walter Müller-Seidel and Wolfgang Preisendanz. Hamburg: Hoffmann und Campe, 1964. 261-72.
—. *The Classical Age of German Literature 1740-1815*. London: Edward Arnold, 1982.
Langen, August. *Der Wortschatz des deutschen Pietismus*. 2nd rev. ed. Tübingen: Niemeyer, 1968.
Lasky, Melvin J. *Utopia and Revolution: On the Origins of a Metaphor, ....* Chicago: University of Chicago Press, 1976.
Leitzmann [Leissmann], Albert. *Georg und Therese Forster und die Brüder Humboldt*. Bonn: Ludwig Rohrscheid, 1936.
Lenz, M. "Deutsches Nationalempfinden im Zeitalter unserer Klassiker." *Jahrbuch der Goethe-Gesellschaft* 2 (1915): 265-300.
Lukács, Georg. *Skizze einer Geschichte der neueren deutschen Literatur*. Darmstadt: Luchterhand, 1975.
—. *Goethe and his Age*. Trans. Robert Anchor. London: Merlin, 1968.
Lutz, Bernd, ed. *Deutsches Bürgertum und literarische Intelligenz 1750-1800*. Stuttgart: Metzler, 1974.
Mandelkow, Robert. *Goethe in Deutschland: Rezeptionsgeschichte eines Klassikers*. 2 vols. Vol. 1, *1773-1918*. Munich: Beck, 1980.
—, ed. *Goethe im Urteil seiner Kritiker: Dokumente zur Wirkungsgeschichte Goethes in Deutschland*. 4 vols. Munich: Beck, 1975-1984.
Mannheim, Karl. "Das konservative Denken: Soziologische Beiträge zum Werden des politisch-historischen Denkens in Deutschland." *Archiv für Sozialwissenschaft* 57 (1927): 470-95.
—. *Ideology and Utopia: An Introduction to the Sociology of Knowledge*. Trans. Louis Wirth and Edward Shils. London: Routledge and Kegan Paul, 1972.
Mayer, Hans. *Goethe: Ein Versuch über den Erfolg*. Frankfurt am Main: Suhrkamp, 1973.
—. *Das Unglückliche Bewußtsein: Zur deutschen Literaturgeschichte von Lessing bis Heine*. Frankfurt am Main: Suhrkamp, 1986.
Mehring, Franz. *Die Lessing Legende. Gesammelte Schriften*, vol. 9. 2nd rev. ed. Berlin: Dietz, 1975.

Meinecke, Friedrich. *Die Entstehung des Historismus. Werke*, vol. 3. Ed. Carl Hinrichs. Munich: Oldenbourg, 1959.

—. *Weltbürgertum und Nationalstaat. Werke*, vol. 5. Ed. Hans Herzfeld. Munich: Oldenbourg, 1962.

Meyer, Hermann. "Hütte und Palast in der Dichtung des 18. Jahrhunderts." *Formenwandel: Festschrift zum 65. Geburtstag von Paul Böckmann*. Ed. Walter Müller-Seidel and Wolfgang Preisendanz. Hamburg: Hoffmann und Campe, 1964. 138-55.

Minogue, K.R. *Nationalism*. London: Methuen, 1967.

Mommsen, Wilhelm. *Die politischen Anschauungen Goethes*. Stuttgart: Deutsche Verlagsanstalt, 1948.

Moskovskaja, Julija. "Georg Forster in Paris: Eine deutsch-französische Revolutionsbeziehung." *Studien über die Revolution*. Ed. Manfred Kossok. Berlin: Akademie, 1969. 120-38.

Mosse, George L. *The Crisis of German Ideology: Intellectual Origins of the Third Reich*. London: Weidenfeld and Nicolson, 1966.

—. *The Nationalization of the Masses: Political Symbolism and Mass Movements in Germany from the Napoleonic Wars through the Third Reich*. New York: Howard Fertig, 1975.

Muecke, D.C. *The Concept of Irony*. London: Methuen, 1969.

Müllensiefen, Paul. "Die französische Revolution und Napoleon in Goethes Weltanschauung." *Jahrbuch der Goethe-Gesellschaft* 16 (1930): 73-108.

Müller, Gerd. *Literatur und Revolution: Untersuchungen zur Frage des literarischen Engagements in Zeiten des politischen Umbruchs*. Studia Germanistica Upsaliensia 14. Uppsala: n.p., 1974.

Mumford, Lewis. *The City in History*. Harmondsworth: Penguin, 1979.

Nagel, Leo. "Zum Problem der Idyllendichtung." *Weimarer Beiträge* 7 (1970): 89-111.

Naumann, Manfred. "Goethes Auffassung von den Beziehungen zwischen Literatur und Nationalliteratur." *Weimarer Beiträge* 1 (1972): 156-78.

Pinson, Koppel Schub. *Pietism as a Factor in the Rise of German Nationalism*. New York: Columbia University Press, 1934.

Plat, Wolfgang. *Deutsche Träume oder der Schrecken der Freiheit: Aufbruch ins 19. Jahrhundert*. Düsseldorf: Econ, 1981.

Plessner, Helmuth. *Die verspätete Nation: Über die politische Verführbarkeit bürgerlichen Geistes*. 1959. Frankfurt am Main: Suhrkamp, 1974.

Polanyi, Karl. *The Great Transformation*. 1944. Boston: Beacon, 1968.

Pütz, Peter. *Die deutsche Aufklärung*. Erträge der Forschung, 81. Darmstadt: Wissenschaftliche Buchgesellschaft, 1978.

—. "Zwischen Klassik und Romantik: Georg Forsters 'Ansichten vom Niederrhein.'" *Zeitschrift für deutsche Philologie* 97 Sonderheft (1978): 4-24.

Rasmussen, Detlef, ed. *Der Weltumsegler und seine Freunde: Georg Forster als gesellschaftlicher Schriftsteller der Goethezeit*. Tübingen: Narr, 1988.

Reinalter, Helmut. *Jakobiner in Mitteleuropa*. Innsbruck: Inn, 1977.

Reiss, Hans. *The Political Thought of the German Romantics 1793-1815.* Oxford: Oxford University Press, 1955.

Riha, Karl. *Die Beschreibung der 'Großen Stadt': Zur Entstehung des Großstadtmotivs in der deutschen Literatur, c. 1750-1850.* Bad Homburg v.d.H.: Gehlen, 1970.

Ritter, Gerhard. *Das deutsche Problem: Grundfragen deutschen Staatslebens gestern und heute.* Munich: Oldenbourg, 1962.

Rödel, Wolfgang. *Forster und Lichtenberg: Ein Beitrag zum Problem deutsche Intelligenz und französische Revolution.* Berlin: Rütten und Loening, 1960.

Rose, Margaret. *Parody/Metafiction: An Analysis of Parody as a Critical Mirror to the Writing and Reception of Fiction.* London: Croom Helm, 1979.

Rudolph, Ekkehart. "'... Über alles in der Welt': Anfänge und Weg des deutschen Nationalismus im 19. Jahrhundert." *Propheten des Nationalismus.* Ed. Karl Schwedhelm. Munich: List, 1969. 7-17.

Saine, Thomas P. *Georg Forster.* TWAS 215. New York: Twayne, 1972.

Sauer, Eberhard. *Die französische Revolution von 1789 in zeitgenössischen Flugschriften und Dichtungen.* Weimar: Alexander Duncker, 1913.

Scheel, Heinrich. *Süddeutsche Jakobiner: Klassenkämpfe und republikanische Bestrebungen im deutschen Süden am Ende des 18. Jahrhunderts.* Berlin: Akademie, 1962.

—. *Deutscher Jakobinismus und deutsche Nation: Ein Beitrag zur nationalen Frage im Zeitalter der großen französischen Revolution.* Berlin: Akademie, 1966.

—. "Unbekannte Zeugnisse aus der revolutionären Tätigkeit Georg Forsters in und um Mainz 1792/3." Reinalter, 151-66.

—. "Der Revolutionär Forster und das klassische Weimar." *Impulse* 2 (1979): 3-22.

Schneider, Helmut J. "Naturerfahrung und Idylle in der deutschen Aufklärung." Putz, *Erforschung*, 289-315.

—. "Gesellschaftliche Modernität und ästhetischer Anachronismus: Zur geschichtsphilosophischen und gattungsgeschichtlichen Grundlage des idyllischen Epos." *Idylle und Modernisierung in der europäischen Literatur des 19. Jahrhunderts.* Ed. Hans Ulrich Seeber and Paul Gerhard Klussmann. Bonn: Bouvier Verlag Herbert Grundmann, 1986. 13-24.

—, ed. *Deutsche Idyllentheorien im 18. Jahrhundert.* Tübingen: Narr, 1988.

Schöffler, Herbert. *Protestantismus und Literatur.* Göttingen: Vandenhoeck & Ruprecht, 1958.

Schöne, Albrecht. *Säkularisation als sprachbildende Kraft: Studien zur Dichtung deutscher Pfarrersöhne.* Göttingen: Vandenhoeck & Ruprecht, 1958.

Schulz, Gerhard. *Die deutsche Literatur zwischen Französischer Revolution und Restauration: 1789-1806.* Vol. 7/1 of *Geschichte der deutschen Literatur von den Anfängen bis zur Gegenwart.* Ed. Helmut de Boor and Richard Newald. Munich: Beck, 1983.

Sengle, Friedrich. "Wunschbild Land und Schreckbild Stadt: Zu einem zentralen Thema der neueren deutschen Literatur." *Studium Generale* 16 (1963): 619-31. Repr. Garber, 432-60.

—. "Formen des idyllischen Menschenbildes: Ein Vortrag." *Formenwandel: Festschrift zum 65. Geburtstag von Paul Böckmann.* Ed. Walter Müller-Seidel and

Wolfgang Preisendanz. Hamburg: Hoffmann und Campe, 1964. 156-71. Repr. F.S.: *Arbeiten zur deutschen Literatur 1750-1850*. Stuttgart: Metzler, 1965. 212-31.

Smith, Anthony D. *Nationalist Movements*. New York: St. Martin's Press, 1976.

Snyder, Louis L. *The Roots of German Nationalism*. Bloomington: Indiana University Press, 1978.

Sommerfeld, Martin. "Aufklärung und Nationalgedanke." *Das literarische Echo* 17 (1915): 1353-63.

Sorel, Albert. *Europe and the French Revolution: The Political Traditions of the Old Regime*. Trans. Alfred Cobban and J.W. Hunt. 1885. London: Collins, 1969.

Sperber, Hans. "Beiträge zur Geschichte der deutschen Sprache im 18. Jahrhundert." *Zeitschrift für deutsche Philologie* 52 (1927): 331-45.

—. "Der Einfluß des Pietismus auf die deutsche Sprache." *DVjs* 8 (1930): 497-515.

Staiger, Emil. "Goethes antike Versmasse." *Die Kunst der Interpretation: Studien zur deutschen Literaturgeschichte*. Zurich: Artemis, 1955. 115-131.

Stammen, Theo. *Goethe und die Französische Revolution: Eine Interpretation der "Natürlichen Tochter."* Munich: Beck, 1966.

—. "Goethe als politischer Denker." *Die Revolution des Geistes: Politisches Denken in Deutschland 1770-1830*. Ed. Jürgen Gebhardt. Munich: List, 1968. 16-42.

—, and Friedrich Eberle, eds. *Deutschland und die Französische Revolution, 1789-1806*. Darmstadt: Wissenschaftliche Buchgesellschaft, 1988.

Steiner, Gerhard. *Georg Forster*. Sammlung Metzler 156. Stuttgart: Metzler, 1977.

Stemme, F. "Die Säkularisation des Pietismus zur Erfahrungsseelenkunde." *Zeitschrift für deutsche Philologie* 72 (1953): 144-58.

Stephan, Inge. *Literarischer Jakobinismus in Deutschland*. Sammlung Metzler 150. Stuttgart: Metzler, 1976.

Stern, Alfred. *Der Einfluß der französischen Revolution aufs deutsche Geistesleben*. Stuttgart: Cotta, 1928.

Stern, Fritz. "The Political Consequences of the Unpolitical German." *History* 3 (1960): 104-34.

Streisand, Joachim. "Revolution und Evolution im Geschichtsbild der deutschen Klassik." *Goethe Jahrbuch* n.s. 16 (1979): 130-45.

Strich, Fritz. *Goethe und die Weltliteratur*. 2nd rev. and exp. ed. Bern: Francke, 1957.

Talmon, J.L. *The Origins of Totalitarian Democracy*. London: Secker and Warburg, 1952.

Tönnies, Ferdinand. *Gemeinschaft und Gesellschaft: Grundbegriffe der reinen Soziologie*. Repr. of 8th ed., 1935. Darmstadt: Wissenschaftliche Buchgesellschaft, 1979.

Träger, Claus. *Mainz zwischen Rot und Schwarz: Die Mainzer Revolution 1792-1793 in Schriften, Reden und Briefen*. Berlin: Rütten und Loening, 1963.

Trevelyan, Humphry. *Goethe and the Greeks*. Cambridge: Cambridge University Press, 1942.

Tümmler, Hans. *Goethe als Staatsmann*. Göttingen: Musterschmidt, 1976.

—. *Das klassische Weimar und das große Zeitgeschehen*. Cologne: Böhlau, 1976.

Uhlig, Ludwig. *Georg Forster: Einheit und Mannigfaltigkeit in seiner geistigen Welt*. Tübingen: Niemeyer, 1965.

Valjavec, Fritz. *Die Entstehung der politischen Strömungen in Deutschland 1770-1815.* 1951. Kronberg/Ts.: Athenäum; Düsseldorf: Droste, 1978.

—. *Geschichte der abendländischen Aufklärung.* Vienna: Herold, 1961.

—. "Die Aufklärung." *Ausgewählte Aufsätze.* Ed. K.A. Fischer and M. Bernath. Munich: Oldenbourg, 1963. 270-93.

Vierhaus, Rudolph. "Politisches Bewußtsein in Deutschland vor 1789." *Der Staat* 6 (1967): 175-96.

—. "Deutschland im 18. Jahrhundert: Soziale Gefüge, politische Verfassung, geistige Bewegung." *Lessing und das Zeitalter der Aufklärung.* Göttingen: Vandenhoeck & Ruprecht, 1968. 12-29.

—. "Aufklärung und Freimaurerei in Deutschland." *Das Vergangene und die Geschichte: Festschrift für R. Wittram.* Ed. R. v. Thadden. Göttingen: Vandenhoeck & Ruprecht, 1973. 23-41.

Voegt, Hedwig. *Die deutsche jakobinistische Literatur und Publizistik 1789-1800.* Berlin: Rütten und Loening, 1955.

Voigt, Gerhard. "Forster, Lichtenberg und die Revolution: Eine These zum Verhalten der literarischen bürgerlichen Intelligenz in Deutschland gegenüber der Entwicklung der Französischen Revolution." *Vom Faustus bis Valentin: Der Bürger in Geschichte und Literatur.* Ed. Fritz Haug. *Das Argument.* Sonderband AS 3 (1976): 162-76.

Voss, E. Theodor. "Arkadien und Grünau: Johann Heinrich Voss und das innere System seines Idyllenwerkes." Garber, 391-431.

Walker, Mack. *German Home Towns: Community, State and General Estate 1648-1871.* Ithaca: Cornell University Press, 1971.

Wellbery, David E. "Die Grenzen des Idyllischen bei Goethe." Barner, 221-240.

Wuthenow, Ralph-Rainer. *Vernunft und Republik: Studien zu Georg Forsters Schriften.* Bad Homburg: Gehlen, 1970.

—. "Das Problem der Revolution in Forsters Schriften." *Germanisch-Romanische Monatsschrift* 25 (1973): 422-38.

Zincke, Paul. *Georg Forsters Bildnis im Wandel der Zeiten: Beitrag zur Geschichte des öffentlichen Geistes in Deutschland.* Reichenberg i. B., 1929. Repr. Hildesheim: Gerstenberg, 1974.

# THE CRITICAL IDYLL

## INDEX

Absolutism (incl. petty absolutism) 1-3, 4-9, 14, 15, 17, 18, 22, 31, 57, 58, 64, 65, 66, 68, 79, 101, 133, 137, 148, 158
Adorno, Theodor W. 5n
*Allgemeine Literaturzeitung* 141
Altenkirchen 103
Amberg 103
American Revolution 5, 105
*Ancien Régime* 2, 3, 42, 113
Aris, Reinhold 58n
Arminius (Hermann) 136, 153
Arndt, Ernst Moritz 36
Aubin, Hermann 31n
Augsburg, Peace of (1555) 101, 103

Baden 103
Baioni, Guiliano 154-55, 161, 162
Balet, Leo 129n
Barnard, M. 66n
Bartels, Adolf 150-51, 155
Basle, Peace of (1795) 42n, 102
Bavaria 6, 14, 103
Bendix, Reinhard 52n
Bennett, Benjamin 21n, 37, 48n, 97n, 109n, 114n, 121n, 158-59
Berlin, Isaiah 66n
*Berlinische Monatsschrift* 6, 123-24
Bible 88, 114
Biedermann, Karl 5n
Bielschowsky, Albert 123n, 149
Biro, Sydney Seymour 42n, 103n, 118n
Bitaubé, Paul Jeremias 145
Blackall, Eric A. 67
Blanning, T. C. W. 7n, 11n, 14n, 35n, 42n, 58n, 60n
Bodi, Lesie 5n, 6n, 11, 13, 122, 124n
Böschenstein, Renate 40, 81
Böttcher, K. 160n
Böttiger, Karl August 15n, 101, 140, 141
Borchmeyer, Dieter 23n, 27n, 42, 43, 122, 134n, 156, 158, 159, 162
Bräker, Ulrich 57

Brown, Jane K. 159
Brüggemann, Fritz 17n
Bürger, Christa 161, 162
Butler, Samuel 20

Catholicism 7, 14, 100
Charles I 8n
Cincinnatus 64
Cipolla, Carlo M. 31n
Coalition Wars 35, 36, 47, 60, 69, 70, 80, 97, 123, 126
Committee of Public Safety 7
Conrady, Karl Otto 160-61, 162
Cook, Captain James 123, 125, 127n
Corday, Charlotte 92n, 122, 131-32, 133
Cotta, Johann Friedrich 145
Craig, Gordon 132n
Curtius, Ernst Robert 82, 86-88
Custine, Adam-Philippe de (Cüstine) 127n

Dahnke, Hans-Dietrich 160n
de Boor, Helmut 160
"Declaration of Independence" 14
*Deutsche Gesellschaft* 65
*Die Horen* 142
Dilthey, Wilhelm 149
Dippel, Horst 6n
Dülmen, Richard van 6n
Düntzer, Heinrich 149
Düsseldorf 101

Eberle, Friedrich 58n
Eckermann, Johann Peter 31n, 143
Eggers, Hans 67n
Eibl, Karl 119n, 152, 157, 162
Elias, Norbert 35n
Enlightenment 1-3, 4-9, 12, 13, 14, 31, 58, 60, 69, 72, 76-80, 95-96, 104, 107, 111-16, 117, 118, 121-35, 137, 139
"Enlightenment Debate" 5-6
Epstein, Klaus 6n, 7n, 35n, 58n
Erfurt 100

Ergang, Robert 66n
Exodus (Old Testament) 72

Fambach, Oscar 145
Federal Republic of Germany 162
Fichte, Johann Gottlob 7, 134; *Reden an die deutsche Nation* 58, 60
Firmian, Archbishop of Salzburg 100-1
Fishman, Joshua 12n, 66n
Fonágy, Ivan 85n
Forster, Johann Georg Adam 5, 8, 101, 104, 111n, 115n, 121-35, 137, 146; *Darstellung der Revolution in Mainz* 130; "Draft Petition of the General Administration (of Mainz) to the Commissioners of the National Convention" 126-27; "Noch etwas über die Menschenrassen" 123; *Parisische Umrisse* 130; "Über Proselytenmacherei" 123; *Voyage around the World* 123
Forster, Johann Reinhold 123
Forster Therese (b. Heyne, later m. Huber) 124, 129n
Forster, Therese (daughter of Georg Forster) 146
Frankfurt am Main 23, 52, 101, 124
Freemasons 6
French Revolution 1-3, 6-8, 10, 12, 16, 21, 31, 32, 33, 34, 36, 46, 57, 60, 64, 66, 69, 70-76, 82, 83, 86, 88-89, 92, 95, 98, 104, 111-16, 119, 121-35, 137, 140, 142, 143, 144, 146, 147, 151, 153, 154, 156, 157, 162
Frenzel, Elisabeth 136n
Friedel, Johann 5n
*Friedens-Präliminarien* 124, 127
Friedenthal, Richard 122
Friedrich II (of Prussia) 18, 64
Fromm, Erich 113n, 118n

Gagliardo, John 58n, 66n
Gassner, August 104n, 122, 132n
Geiger, Ludwig 140n
Genesis (Old Testament) 84
Gentz, Friedrich von 7
Gerhard, E. 129n
Gerhard, Melitta 152, 159

German Democratic Republic 162
German Identity, Nationalism, and Patriotism 3, 4, 12, 19, 21, 22, 30, 35-36, 41, 55-60, 62, 63-68, 104, 117-20, 123, 133, 134, 135, 136-38, 141, 145, 146-49, 151-3, 157-58, 162
Gerth, Hans 5n
Gervinus, Georg Gottfried 122, 127, 142n, 145-46, 148
*Geschichte der deutschen Literatur von den Anfängen bis zur Gegenwart* (GDR) 160
Gessner, Salomon 15, 82, 88
Girondins 133
Glazer, Nathan 12n
Gleim, Johann Wilhelm Ludwig 38n, 64, 127n
Göcking, Gerhard Gottlieb Günther 100, 103, 104, 153; *Vollkommene Emigrationsgeschichte von denen aus dem Erzbistum Salzburg vertriebenen ... Lutheranern* 100-1
Göschen, Georg Joachim 141
Goethe, Johann Wolfgang passim; "Alttestamentliches" 94; *Campagne in Frankreich* 2, 36n, 73n, 97; "Das Deutsche Reich" 35n, 65; "Das Märchen" 2, 16, 88, 89, 97, 137; *Der Bürgergeneral* 2, 102; *Der Groß-Cophta* 2; "Der Versuch als Vermittler von Objekt und Subjekt" 17n; "Der Wanderer" 81; "Der Weltumsegler" 124; "Deutscher Nationalcharakter" 35n, 65; *Dichtung und Wahrheit* 17; *Die Aufgeregten* 2, 102; "Die dreifarbige Kokarde" 127n; *Die Leiden des jungen Werthers* 1, 8, 9, 15-19, 21, 22, 57, 67-68, 81, 132, 140; *Die Natürliche Tochter* 151; *Die Wahlverwandtschaften* 79, 94; "Elpenor" 131; *Faust* 2, 15, 124, 144; *Hermann und Dorothea* passim; "Hermann und Dorothea" (Elegy) 88; *Iphigenie auf Tauris* 1, 15, 95-96, 105, 139; "Israel in der Wüste" 84n; "Literarischer Sanskulottismus" 19-20, 22, 35, 64, 137, 141, 144;

"Materialien zur Farbenlehre" 8; "Noten und Abhandlungen zu besserem Verständnis des west-östlichen Divans" 90n, 94n; *Reineke Fuchs* 2, 101; "Philemon and Baucis" 15; "Phlegyasque miserrimus omnes admonet" 127n; scientific theory 2; "Tag- und Jahreshefte" 9, 101; *Torquato Tasso* 15, 101, 105, 115-16; "Unglückliche Eilfertigkeit" 111n; *Unterhaltungen deutscher Ausgewanderten* 2, 102n, 105, 140; *Wilhelm Meisters Lehrjahre* 1, 20, 140, 144, 154, 162; "Wilhelm Tischbeins Idyllen" 81; "Xenien" 2, 35, 111n

*Göttinger Gelehrte Anzeigen* 18
Goldsmith, William 15
Gottsched, Johann Christoph 65
Grab, Walter 7n, 8n, 58n
Graham, Ilse 159
Graßl, Hans 6n
Grimm, Jacob and Wilhelm 63
Groote, Wolfgang von 8n, 58n, 66
*Gründerjahre* 148
Gude, C. 148, 149n

Habermas, Jürgen 11
Habsburg Monarchy 6, 7, 18, 64
*Hamburger Musenalmanach* 37
Hansen, Joseph 134n
Hegel, Georg Wilhelm Friedrich 38, 145, 147, 154
Hehn, Viktor 42, 121, 122n, 136, 137, 147-48, 149
Heine, Heinrich 63, 137-38; *Geschichte der Religion und Philosophie in Deutschland* 138
Heinse, Wilhelm 126, 127n
Heller, Erich 17n
Helmerking, Heinz 20n, 103n, 136n, 140n, 153
Herbst, Wilhelm 15n
Herder, Johann Gottfried 4, 7, 58, 65-66, 93, 119
Herrig's *Archiv* 122
Hettner, Hermann 122, 127, 148, 154
Hoare, Michael E. 123n
Hoffmann, Leopold Alois 130

Holmes, T. M. 29n, 119, 161-62
Holy Roman Empire of the German Nation 10, 21, 35, 60, 64, 100-1, 103, 104, 113, 125
Homer 36, 37n 114; *Iliad* 36
Horkheimer, Max 5n
Huber, Ludwig Ferdinand 124, 126-27
Humboldt, Alexander von 124
Humboldt, Wilhelm von 37, 96, 141-44, 145, 146, 147, 149, 150, 153
Hutten, Ulrich von 136

Idyll 3, 4, 14-19, 20, 21, 22, 23, 36-40, 44, 49, 54, 56, 62, 67-68, 74, 75, 79, 81-89, 120, 136, 137-39, 154, 156-57, 159, 160, 161-2
"Illuminati" 6
Irony 3, 4, 12-13, 16, 17, 21, 22, 23, 48, 62, 86, 95, 104-5, 136, 138-39, 156, 159, 160, 161, 162
Italy 2, 103

Jacobi, Friedrich Heinrich 127n
Jacobins and Jacobinism 6, 7, 10, 82, 121-35
Jäckel, Günter 134n
Jahn, Friedrich Ludwig 36
Jean Paul (Friedrich Richter) 20
Jena, Battle of (1806) 134
*Jenaische Allgemeine Literatur-Zeitung* 145
Jenisch, Daniel 19, 21, 22; *Borussias* 19; "Über Prose und Beredsamkeit der Deutschen" 19
Joseph II 6
Joshua (Old Testament) 70, 90
Jourdan, Jean Baptiste 103
Judges (Old Testament) 90
Judith 92
Jung, Carl Gustav 87

Kaiser, Gerhard 8n, 15n, 62n, 64, 65n, 117-19 156-57, 159
Kalidasa 124; *Sakuntala* 124
Kant, Immanuel 5, 80n, 123, 142; *Kritik der reinen Vernunft* 80n
Karl August, Duke of Saxe-Weimar 101
Karl Ludwig Johann, Archduke 103

Kiesel, Helmuth 5n, 31n
Klein, Karl 122
Kleist, Ewald von 64
Kleist, Heinrich von 36, 134
Klinger, Maximilian 122; *Geschichte eines Deutschen der neuesten Zeit* 122
Klopstock, Friedrich Gottlieb 4, 7, 14, 15 65, 75, 80, 89, 93, 114, 121, 128, 132; "An La Rochefoucaulds Schatten" 75n; "Der Erobrungskrieg" 75; "Die Etats Généraux" 74-75; "Die Jakobiner" 75; *Hermann* trilogy 136; "Kennet Euch Selbst" 74-75, 96; "Mein Irrtum" 92n
Knox, Norman D. 12
Körner, S. 5n
Körner, Christian Gottfried 141
Kohn, Hans 6n, 12n, 65, 66n
Kopitsch, Franklin 5n
Korff, Hermann August 23n, 29, 30, 41, 42, 43, 54, 149-50, 151, 155, 159
Koselleck, Reinhard 5n
Krauss, Werner 14, 64n, 158-59, 162
Kuhn, Axel 8n
*Kurze Geschichte der deutschen Literatur* (GDR) 160

Lafayette, Marquis de 73
Lanckoranskaja, Maria Gräfin 140n
Lange, Victor 17n
Langen, August 67
Leopold II 6
Leroux, Robert 27n, 122, 153
Lessing, Gotthold Ephraim 6; *Die Erziehung des Menschengeschlechts* 79; *Masonic Dialogues* (*Ernst und Falk*) 6; *Minna von Barnhelm*, 8, 57; Odoardo Galotti 64n
*Levée en masse* 35, 119, 134
Lichtenberg, Georg Christoph 5, 131
Lohenstein, Daniel Casper von 136; *Grossmüthiger Feldherr Arminius* ... 136
London 30
Lützeler, Paul Michael 42, 43n, 134n, 152, 155, 162
Lukács, Georg 1, 5n, 17, 57, 116n, 125, 127n, 151
Lux, Adam 122-23, 131-35
Lypp, Maria 29n

Mainz 8, 10, 35, 101, 104, 121-22, 124-32, 137
Mann, Thomas 151-52, 153, 157
Mannheim 23, 52
Marat, Jean-Paul 131-32
Maria Theresia 18, 100
Marie Antoinette 1
Marx, Karl 125, 132n
Max, Frank Rainer 81
Mayer, Hans 2, 3n, 42n, 79n, 140n
Mehring, Franz 149
Meinecke, Friedrich 58n, 134n, 149
Merck, Johann Heinrich 64n
Meyer, Heinrich 16n, 20, 31n, 100n
Michaelis, Caroline (Schlegel-Schelling) 124
Milfull, John 94n
Minder, Robert 62n
Mirabeau, Comte de 73
Modern Language Association 152
Möser, Justus 7, 64
Moore, Barrington 42
Morgan, Peter 3n, 123n
Moses (Old Testament) 70, 84n, 90
Moynihan, Daniel P. 12n
Mozart, Wolfgang Amadeus 30; *Magic Flute* 30, 52, 54
Muecke, D. C. 12-13
Müller, Gerd 115n, 118n, 124n, 132n
Müller, Maler 88
Münch, Paul 5n, 31n
Münster 101

Nadler, Josef 150, 155
Naomi (Book of Ruth) 90
Napoleon Bonaparte 41, 80, 97, 103, 137
Napoleonic Wars 60
National Convention, Paris 122, 132
National Socialism 151, 158
Nazism 4, 149-52, 155, 160
"Necklace Affair" 1, 79n
Netherlands 31
*Neue allgemeine Deutsche Bibliothek* 145
Newald, Richard 160
Nisbet, H. B. 17n

Old Testament 70-72, 79-80, 86, 90-91, 94
Opitz, Martin 65

Paine, Thomas 14; *Rights of Man* 14
Palmer, R. R. 6n
Paradox 12-13, 136, 138-39
Paris 9-10, 23, 86, 96, 111-13, 122, 124, 127, 129, 131, 134, 137, 142
Parody 3, 4, 12-13, 21, 23, 36-40, 61, 80, 86, 89, 93, 104-5, 133, 138-39, 155, 156, 159
Parzifal 151
Peasants' Wars 101
Petsch, Robert 151
Pietism 14-15, 46, 48, 67, 117, 119
Pope, Alexander 20
Potter, G. R. 31n
"Pragmatic Sanction" 100
Protestantism 30, 101, 103
Prussia 8, 41, 64, 102
Pütz, Peter 5n

Rasmussen, Detlev 122, 124n
Rebecca (Old Testament) 84
Rebmann, Andreas Georg Friedrich 132
Reformation 31
Rehberg, August Wilhelm 7
Reichard, Amalie 124
Renaissance 4, 15, 65
Rhine 8, 21, 23, 32, 34, 35, 57, 101, 103, 118, 134, 145
Rhineland 8, 14, 30, 60, 85, 88, 103, 120, 142
Robespierre, Maximilien de 115n
Rödel, Wolfgang 5n, 111n, 127n, 131n, 132n
Rose, Margaret 13, 21
Rosenkranz, Karl 142n, 146, 148
Rousseau, Jean-Jacques 12, 65, 104, 119
Rümann, Arthur 140n
Ruth (Old Testament) 90-91
Ryder, Frank 21n, 37, 48n, 97n, 109n, 114n, 121n, 158-59

Saine, Thomas P. 103n, 122, 123n, 128n, 130-33, 158
Salzburg 100, 103
Samuel, Richard H. 122

Schaunberg, Dr. 122
Scheel, Heinrich 8n, 132n
Scherer, Wilhelm 42, 136, 137, 148, 149
Schiller, Charlotte 140
Schiller, Friedrich 7, 37, 65, 101, 126, 127n, 141, 151, 159; *Briefe über die ästhetische Erziehung des Menschen* 138, 142; "Das Lied von der Glocke" 77n, 134; "Der Weltumsegler" 124; "Deutsche Größe" 134; Karl Moor (*Die Räuber*) 8
Schlaffer, Hannelore 125, 126n
Schlegel, August Wilhelm 1, 141, 144-45, 146, 147, 149, 153
Schlegel, Friedrich 13, 37n 124, 125-27, 138, 141
Schlözer, A. L. v. 6, 64
Schmidt, Josef 37n, 48n, 113n, 136n
Schmidt, Julian 148
Schneider, Helmut J. 122, 157-58, 159, 161, 162
Schönemann, Lili 123n
Schreyer, Hermann 20n
Schubart, Christian Friedrich Daniel 64
Schulz, Gerhard 23n, 64, 65n, 132n, 160, 162
Seidlin, Oskar 27n, 120n, 152, 153-54, 155, 157, 162
Sengle, Friedrich 9-10 19, 158
Seven Years' War 14, 57, 64
Shakespeare, William 147
Sömmering, Samuel Thomas 124, 131
Sonnenfels, Joseph von 18; *Über die Liebe des Vaterlandes* 18, 64, 120
Sorel, Albert 58n, 60n
Sperber, Hans 67n
*Staats-Anzeigen* 7
Staiger, Emil 23n, 153, 159
Stammen, Theo 58n
Stein, Charlotte von 140
Stolberg, Friedrich Leopold Graf zu 126, 127n
Strasbourg 23, 52, 79, 98
Streisand, Joachim 132n
*Sturm und Drang* 4, 5, 125
Sweet, Paul R. 142n

Tamino (*Magic Flute*) 54
Taylor, A. J. P. 60n
Tell, Wilhelm 153
Terror 86, 126
*Teutscher Merkur* 37
Thirty Years' War 2, 31, 35, 103, 104
Thorlby, Anthony 17n
Thümmel, Moritz August von 20, *Wilhelmine* 21, 87
Thusnelda 145
Tönnies, Ferdinand 9; *Community and Association (Gemeinschaft und Gesellschaft)* 9-10, 11
*Topoi* 10, 86-87
Türkheim, Bernhard von 123n
Tula 147

Valjavec, Fritz 5n, 7n, 58n
Valmy, Cannonade of 2, 97, 103
Veit, Walter 87, 88n
Vergil 69, 81
Vienna 6, 32, 52, 54
Vienna Congress (1815) 120
Vierhaus, Rudolf 7n
Viëtor, Karl 153, 162
Vieweg, Hans Friedrich 140-41
Voigt, Christian Gottlob 2
Voigt, Gerhard 132n
Voltaire 71; *Candide* 71
*Vormärz* 146, 148
Voss, Christian Friedrich 128-130
Voss, Johann Heinrich 7, 15-16, 19, 20, 21, 22, 36-40, 48, 65, 74, 86, 87-89, 93, 114, 121, 158; *Luise* 15-16, 21, 36-40, 61, 98n, 142n, 144, 145, 147, 152, 153-54; "Der siebzigste Geburtstag" 15, 81; "Die Freigelassenen" 21
Voss, Johann Heinrich (son of the poet) 48

Walker, Mack 10-11
Wangermann, Ernst 6n
Wars of Liberation 4, 43, 145
Weber, Max 52
Weimar 2, 101
Weimar Classicism 65
Weimar Republic 149
Wells, George A. 17n
Westfalia, Peace of (1648) 101
Wickram, Georg 30; *Von Guten und boesen Nachbaurn* 30
Wieland, Christoph Martin 7, 8n, 22 65, 132, 140; *Oberon* 21, 22, 87
*Wiener Zeitschrift* 130
Winckelmann, Johann Joachim 65
Wolff, Christian 71, 79, 85, 107
Woltmann, Karl Ludwig von 145, 148, 151
Württemberg 103
Würzburg 103

Yxem, E. F. 100

Zachariä, Friedrich Wilhelm 20-21
Zimmermann, Rolf Christian 136n
Zincke, Paul 122
Zmegac, Viktor 156
Zorn, Wolfgang 31n